PATH OF LIGHT

and Native culture in the Glen Canyon and Bears Ears country of southern Utah. Sjogren and her wanderluster companions learn two truths. Hidden passages lead through unimaginable places. And, water and friends are the source of life in the desert."

—Stephen Trimble, editor of *Red Rock Stories* and
The Capitol Reef Reader

"Sjogren has a unique knack for transporting the reader to the stark and sensual lands she calls home so that we are on the journey beside her, whether it's a parched search for stagnant, scuzzy water in a slick rock pothole, a sun-baked trek through the bleak beauty of Red Canyon, or a perilous and lonely slog through a dark, boulder-choked canyon. With both toughness and vulnerability, Sjogren lets us in on what she sees and feels and experiences as she pursues the 'path of light,' and somehow manages to give even grizzled veterans of Slickrock country a new appreciation for the land known as Bears Ears."

—Jonathan P. Thompson, author of *River of Lost Souls*
and *Sagebrush Empire*

"*Path of Light* is as deep, complex and labyrinthine as the convoluted canyon country through which Morgan Sjogren traverses. Sjogren expertly braids multiple compelling narrative threads as she follows the footsteps of Charles Bernheimer through some of the most-rugged territory in the country. It was a joy to vicariously tag along. I could smell the campfire smoke as I did so."

—M. John Fayhee, former editor of the *Mountain Gazette*
and author of *Smoke Signals* and *Bottoms Up*

"Retracing the series of expeditions organized by Charles L. Bernheimer a century before her, Sjogren weaves the narrative of her own life and desert experiences with others, both contemporary and long dead, in this love letter to canyon country. With a raucous and wonderful cast of characters and a keen eye toward the natural history of the region as well as colonialism's ongoing attempts at conquest and Indigenous erasure, she doesn't sugarcoat the impact that white explorers and settlers had, and continue to have, on this 'desolate' place that has been a sacred home to people—human and otherwise—for millennia. The love on display in this book is infectious: love for people, for place, and for history. More than anything else, Sjogren reminds us of all the magnificent life that abounds in these red deserts: life ancient and reverberating across time, and life desperately struggling to endure."

—Chris La Tray (Little Shell Chippewa), author of
Becoming Little Shell and *One-Sentence Journal:
Short Poems and Essays From the World At Large*

"Morgan Sjogren is among the brightest emerging voices in an ongoing and increasingly urgent conversation regarding the landscape of the American Southwest. *Path of Light* is filled with passion, intensity, and longing that reflect and amplify similar qualities in the terrain itself."

—Annette Avery, Bright Side Bookshop, Flagstaff

"This book is a wealth of history and land. Its pages smell of libraries, desert, and the inside of a well lived-in vehicle. Right times, right places, right people, she's got a knack for the journey. I'm reading this thinking, cool, I'd do that."

—Craig Childs, author of *Tracing Time*, *Virga and Bone*, and *Atlas of a Lost World*

"Intrepid desert wanderer, writer and social media influencer Morgan Sjogren could not be more different than the wealthy New York business man Charles Bernheimer who embarked on an expedition across Utah's canyon country in 1929. Yet they are united through their love of adventure and slickrock. As Sjogren retraces Bernheimer's route a century later, she takes us on a courageous, soul-centered journey that ventures into the dark shadows of colonization and environmental destruction but ultimately emerges in a luminous place of hope and healing for ourselves and the Earth."

—Annette McGivney, author of *Pure Land: A True Story of Three Lives, Three Cultures, and the Search for Heaven on Earth;* winner of the National Outdoor Book Award

"Educational and thought-provoking. Author and journalist Morgan Sjogren in the 2020s retraced the 1920s Southwestern trails of eccentric, preservationist Charles Bernheimer—the 'Cliff Dweller From Manhattan.' Exploring today's Bears Ears National Monument and evaporating Lake Powell via her aching feet and a mercurial yellow Jeep, Sjogren in *Path of Light* takes a vision quest. In landscape prose that is lovingly evocative, she grapples alongside a fascinating cast of companions with her—and our—covenant with a scarred, sacred, imperiled, and still-extraordinary redrock empire."

—Nate Schweber, author of *This America of Ours: Bernard and Avis DeVoto and the Forgotten Fight to Save the Wild.*

"*Path of Light* is a true adventure of a read. What a pleasure following Morgan Sjogren as she explores the mythic landscape in and around Bears Ears. The traditional joys of the nature quest are all here—the canyons, the mountains, the morning coffee—but Sjogren also questions the macho ethos of man vs. nature and, best of all, has a deep and respectful dialogue with those who came before, both the early 20th century explorers and the Native peoples who had known the same land intimately for millennia."

—David Gessner, New York Times best-selling author of *All The Wild That Remains* and *Quiet Desperation, Savage Delight*

"Morgan Sjogren donned her backpack, and over a span of winters and summers dauntlessly trekked through remote back-country of the Colorado Plateau. She documents her journeys, both physical and spiritual in this beautifully crafted book. Morgan Sjogren is a fine writer—a true desert rat with the courage to follow the path of light no matter where it leads."

—Jack Loeffler, author of *Adventures With Ed: A Portrait of Abbey*

"Author Morgan Sjogren lives most comfortably within two walls, not four—canyon walls that reach toward the stars. She wears juniper smoke like clothing. Her visceral connection to the desert Southwest sends her on a quest to get to know other desert dwellers, and in following the trail of Charles L. Bernheimer, Morgan finds different truths in the oral stories of generations, simultaneously learning new layers of herself. Path of Light is the best kind of book: one that haunts and compels and brings tears, wonder, and reverence for the land that inspired it."

—Kathryn Wilder, Colorado Book Award Winner for *Desert Chrome: Water, a Woman, and Wild Horses in the West*

"When we read Morgan Sjogren's *Path of Light*, we are walking through a story, a seamless ramble through geography, history,

PATH OF LIGHT

A Walk Through Colliding Legacies of Glen Canyon

Morgan Sjogren

TORREY HOUSE PRESS

Salt Lake City • Torrey

Author's Note:
Select human and place names have been altered or omitted out of respect, privacy, and mystery.

Portions of this work originally appeared, in different form, in *Arizona Highways* and *The Gulch*.

First Torrey House Press Edition, April 2023
Copyright © 2023 by Morgan Sjogren

Published by Torrey House Press
Salt Lake City, Utah
www.torreyhouse.org

International Standard Book Number: 978-1-948814-73-7
E-book ISBN: 978-1-948814-74-4
Library of Congress Control Number: 2021952964

Cover photos: *Above*: Earl Morris Archive, Copyright University of Colorado Museum of Natural History. *Below*: Stephen Eginoire.
Cover design by Kathleen Metcalf
Interior design by Rachel Buck-Cockayne
Distributed to the trade by Consortium Book Sales and Distribution

Torrey House Press offices in Salt Lake City sit on the homelands of Ute, Goshute, Shoshone, and Paiute nations. Offices in Torrey are on the homelands of Southern Paiute, Ute, and Navajo nations.

For Clyde Whiskers and Phil, who joined me on the early steps of this expedition before crossing the Rainbow Bridge toward their next adventures.

In celebration of restored protections for Bears Ears National Monument. May the designation continue to honor the Hopi Tribe, Navajo Nation, Ute Indian Tribe, Ute Mountain Ute Tribe, and Pueblo of Zuni. In support of designated reservation lands for the San Juan Southern Paiute Tribe. And with faith for a once and future wild river flowing through Glen Canyon.

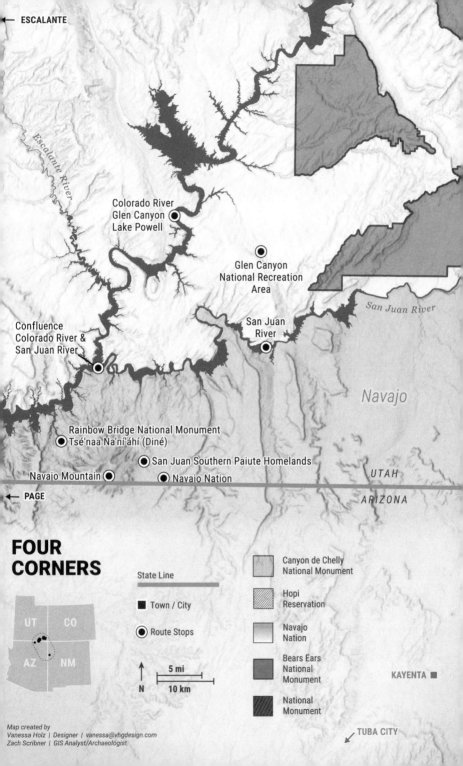

ESCALANTE

Escalante River

Colorado River
Glen Canyon
Lake Powell

Glen Canyon
National Recreation
Area

San Juan River

Confluence
Colorado River &
San Juan River

San Juan
River

Navajo

Rainbow Bridge National Monument
Tsé'naa Na'ní'áhí (Diné)

San Juan Southern Paiute Homelands

Navajo Mountain
Navajo Nation

UTAH

← PAGE

ARIZONA

FOUR
CORNERS

State Line

UT   CO

■ Town / City

◉ Route Stops

AZ   NM

5 mi

N   10 km

Canyon de Chelly
National Monument

Hopi
Reservation

Navajo
Nation

Bears Ears
National
Monument

National
Monument

KAYENTA ■

Map created by
Vanessa Holz | Designer | vanessa@vhgdesign.com
Zach Scribner | GIS Analyst/Archaeologist

↙ TUBA CITY

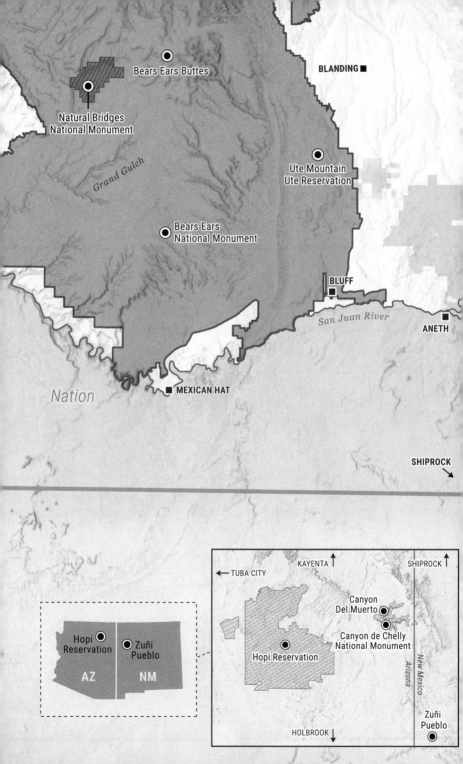

Charles L. Bernheimer

TABLE OF CONTENTS

Part 2: The 1929 Expedition

PART 1:

Early Explorations

CHAPTER ONE

Palimpsest

Man can do almost anything if he is persistent, wisely coura-
geous, and has sufficient imagination.
                                           —Charles L. Bernheimer

Discoveries either happen or are the result of planned expedi-
tions. Pilgrimages, on the other hand, are inspired not by men
but by the gods themselves.
                                           —Karl W. Luckert

She had learned that she was searching not for self-transforma-
tion (she liked herself) but for something good to do.
                                           —Edward Abbey

A t the edge of the sandstone precipice, wind gusts against my torso as I lean over Glen Canyon, now a damned reservoir known as Lake Powell. I stretch my imagination to drain the glaring blue water, letting it pass through the antiquated dam. I repaint the white bathtub ring red, and scour the sediment down to bedrock. After the cleanup, a free-flowing muddy ribbon returns, caressing the high walls of this sensuously curving canyon, its exposed walls revealing golden tributaries alive with running springs, coyote willows, wild orchids, and weeping maidenhair ferns.

Between my feet and the water, I read the rust, orange, and

cream-colored strata, a document spanning millions of years. In this palimpsest, human life is but a blip, yet it leaves the deepest scars. To orient myself requires ongoing study—the earth's creases, faults, and sinews have more to teach than lines across folded sheets of paper. I let the desert guide me because I can always get lost in the stories it tells.

Mine dwells here too.

In the winter of 2019, I was living out of my Jeep in Bears Ears National Monument, located in southeastern Utah. All my possessions were packed inside my mud-encrusted Jeep, a cliff dwelling on wheels. I slept between two stacks of books, curled up in a thrift store fur coat and a pile of down blankets. On interminable winter nights, I communed with the people walking the pages of canyon country history, whose stories were an antidote to the lonesome atmosphere of the frozen desert.

Among the books in my collection, one captivated me: *Rainbow Bridge: Circling Navajo Mountain and Explorations in the "Badlands" of Southern Utah and Northern Arizona.* It was written in 1924 by Charles L. Bernheimer, based upon his journals from a series of expeditions to Rainbow Bridge, Glen Canyon, and the Navajo Nation. These were places I had not yet traveled to, but were connected to my current location by canyon country's arterial system.

Inspired to be more than a sightseeing tourist, Bernheimer wanted, "to do in a small way what our big explorers and discoverers were permitted to do on a heroic scale." To accomplish this, he organized a series of ten expeditions between 1919 and 1930. These were funded on behalf of the American Museum of Natural History in New York City to contribute archaeological reconnaissance, data collection, and documentation in remote corners of southeastern Utah and northern Arizona. His adventures resonated. Not that I, a nomadic freelance writer, seemingly had anything in common with a wealthy businessman from New York.

As snow fell and the temperatures dropped outside the Jeep, Bernheimer's mission statement encouraged me:

> To instill a love for nature even in its bleakest and sternest mood where the conventional exhibits of beauty are not found, but where beauty, if the traveler wishes to see, exists in fullest measure, and to urge upon others to do as I have done.

Exactly one hundred years earlier, Bernheimer's first expedition had passed right by my campsite. I filled in the white page of snow and solitude with visions of old explorers and a packtrain sitting around a campfire. Bernheimer's whimsical tone directed me not only to turn the page but, in time, to also follow his path.

My unexpected connection to Bernheimer deepened when I received an email from my friend, archaeologist Bill Lipe:

> Morgan, maybe you can take on the Bernheimer Expeditions one of these days. It was a series of pack train treks across parts of the canyon country by a wealthy New York guy—Charles Bernheimer....Like other members of the elite who wanted to explore unknown lands, he depended on local Navajos, Paiutes, cowboys, and guides like John Wetherill, who lived year-round in the mysterious places and referred to them as home.

Lipe encouraged me to consider hiking Bernheimer's 1929 route, an unfathomable journey encompassing over three hundred miles of present-day Bears Ears National Monument and Glen Canyon National Recreation Area. The challenge captivated and terrified me. Physically, I knew I was capable of such an endeavor. I had spent many of my days running and backpacking long distances in the backcountry, but this would be several hundred miles farther than I had ever gone in one push.

Bernheimer's book is not a guidebook. His month long pack trips did not follow signs or defined trails, and his murky notes are hardly directions. It is unclear if this was intentional or because he had no idea where the hell he was. He alluded to both. While he initially hoped to inspire other people's adventures, by 1924 he admonished, "I do not recommend that others follow in our footsteps, excepting for scientific purposes."

The duality of his messaging made the idea more irresistible, but I filed it in the backcountry of my mind. Besides, there was still too much snow on the ground to go hiking. During long winter nights curled up in my Jeep, I read anything I could get my hands on related to Bernheimer's expeditions, Glen Canyon, and Bears Ears. I kept a pile of topo maps under the blankets and marked locations in Bernheimer's stories to begin to piece his routes together. Between his written pages and my own imagination, I had the urge to examine something deeper. Why was Bernheimer so drawn to exploring this landscape? I was still trying to understand this same question about myself. Only more time spent out on the land could expose an answer.

To enrich my research, I contacted John Wetherill's great-grandson, Harvey Leake. He has studied the Bernheimer expeditions extensively, even retracing portions of their routes on backpacking trips. Harvey responded quickly, and three days later we met up to talk and look at maps. Harvey gave me a brief overview of John Wetherill's life, as an explorer and guide in southern Utah's canyon country. He also owned and operated a trading post in Kayenta, Arizona on the Navajo Nation where he lived with his family.

Then Harvey abruptly shifted the direction of the conversation and insisted on reading something to me. He reached into his backpack and pulled out a book titled, *Wolfkiller: Wisdom from a Nineteenth-Century Navajo Shepherd*. Wolfkiller, a Diné elder, was a close friend and neighbor to the Wetherill family and influenced their philosophy about life.

Harvey turned to an earmarked passage and read aloud:

The path of light is always running beside us on either side, but we cannot see it for the darkness in our hearts. Now we have decided to have some ceremonies and pray for our minds to turn into the path of light. I should not fear the future. You must live today and keep your thoughts in the path of light. Everything will come out all right. You must always think that the next year of your life will be more happy and peaceful than the year before, and must try to make it come true.

Harvey explained that the story stemmed from the Diné cultural belief in personal choice; that the outcomes of our lives and our contributions to society are directly linked to the decisions we make. Harvey then set the book down and looked me directly in the eyes:

"When you get to a fork in the trail, will you choose the path of progress or the path of light?"

This is not what I anticipated at a meeting to discuss maps. The question prompted me to look at the terrain within, as well as the prevailing winds that pushed me to this place in my life.

I ended my marriage in 2017. The divorce settlement granted me my Jeep and what I owed in taxes. The painful circumstances warranted starting my life over. Without a dollar to my name, I drove from my beloved home in the eastern Sierra range of light to Utah's redrock canyons, where the safety of solitude and horizon of unknown possibilities felt limitless. Embraced by sagebrush and sandstone, I generously refilled potholes with tears. I sought out the desert not merely to hide out from my problems; I needed the open space to heal and to dream of what lay ahead.

I lost almost everything but won my freedom, and with it an opportunity to finally pursue writing. I quit my marketing job and became a hunter-gatherer of stories. The financial insecurity was daunting, but hunkering in the wild allowed me to save money by not spending any money in between my meager freelance-writing paychecks. I subsisted on cold bean burritos, nut butter, beef jerky, and warm beer because I did not even own a cooler. Lingering in remote places and writing about them became the divine luxury of my untethered life. If I stayed in the desert long enough, I trusted it would give me a sense of direction. One trip blurred into a season, and then three more. Even in the bone-chilling troughs of winter, or the bellows of summer heat, my instincts told me to stay.

Harvey snapped me out of my contemplative trance, asking again, "Will you choose the path of progress or the path of light?"

Eyes wide open, I replied, "I choose the path of light."

I knew deep down this was a path I needed to follow.

Harvey smiled and pulled out an old map to Rainbow Bridge. He then handed me a copy of *Wolfkiller*. This, he assured me, would be most helpful of all.

We waved goodbye and I tiptoed through the icy parking lot to the Jeep. Daggers of blinding sunlight obstructed my rear view as I pulled out of the parking lot and headed north to Bears Ears.

- - - - -

I arrived late that night. The new moon concealed White Mesa Uranium Mill located on Ute Mountain Ute land. The winter chill had deterred other campers. The desert gave me the freedom to choose a refuge where, if only for a night, both the land and my heart could conceal our wounds and truly rest.

The desert is less nature's blank slate than it is an ever-growing chronicle, collecting stories for a millennium and sharing them with those willing to listen. Collective marks left here have the potential to build upon this tradition or tear it apart. Mistakes compound in the desert. A single footprint in delicate cryptobiotic soil or a name carved into a sandstone wall alter the desert's story. No matter the intention, these once tiny marks accumulate as human visitation continues to exponentially increase. The desert documents more clearly how we behave than is evident in less dry and exposed places.

The lens of Bernheimer's journals unraveled my understanding of a region on the brink of irreversible harm. A century later, Bernheimer would not even recognize this place: Mineral extraction blighting the mesas and polluting groundwater. A uranium boom poisoning Indigenous communities. Glen Canyon Dam halting the natural flow of the Colorado River. Highways cutting through geological formations. Rampant looting of ancestral sites. Footsteps and tire tracks from millions of tourists a year across delicate soils.

The abuses inflicted on the land since Bernheimer passed this way raise an urgent question: how can we protect this landscape for the next one hundred years—and beyond?

- - - - -

My first trip to Bears Ears was during the 2016 presidential election. Tucked away in a slot canyon without cell service, the earth sheltered me from the final tally, until I emerged to the news about Donald Trump. Life in this country would never be the same. Neither would mine, as I returned from the canyon to a view of my then husband sitting on the ground drinking a beer at nine in the morning. I vowed to return to Bears Ears alone.

In December 2016, before leaving office, President Obama designated 1.35 million acres of land as Bears Ears National Monument, protecting it from future mineral extraction, oil and gas leases, and new grazing permits. To manage the land, the Bureau of Land Management (BLM) and the United States Forest Service would consult a tribal advisory committee, the Bears Ears Commision, that includes the Hopi Tribe, Navajo Nation, Ute Indian Tribe, Ute Mountain Ute Tribe, and Pueblo of Zuni for guidance.

A few months later, separated from my past and living in my Jeep, I accepted my first story assignment about the monument. Bears Ears was on the news almost every day, yet the new national monument did not even have an official sign. The complexity of the terrain made it clear to me that one trip here would hardly scratch the surface. I accepted another assignment, and then another. Instead of moving on to a story about another location, I stayed. Without a permanent abode, seeking a connection with place grounded me. More than feeling at home in the desert, I wanted to belong to it. Bears Ears inexplicably touched my heart, readying it to heal and love again.

To acquaint myself intimately with the land, I spent four seasons exploring different canyons, mesas, and mountains. At night, the coyotes and owls sang me to sleep under a dark sky bedazzled with stars. On my occasional trips to town, I chatted with locals who used to work in the uranium mines, or whose great-grandparents traveled here on the Hole-in-the-Rock expedition. Diné women taught me to make fry bread and told me stories. I hitchhiked on the back of wood-hauling trucks, holding tightly to fresh-cut juniper logs. During cold nights and harsh weather conditions, I looked to my ancient neighbors, the blackened walls of their stone shelters reminding me that if I built a warm fire, I would probably be fine. Seamless as the shift in seasons, Bears Ears started to echo a sense of home.

And that's when, in December 2017, President Trump reduced the Bears Ears monument protections by eighty five percent. At the same time, he dismantled the twenty-five-year-old Grand Staircase–Escalante National Monument, slashing it in half—the largest removal of public lands protections in United States history. These briefly protected areas were now reopened to extractive use.

The outcry was swift: the Bears Ears Inter-Tribal Coalition, conservation groups, and outdoor industry brands filed lawsuits against the Trump administration. Each lawsuit approached the proclamation from a different angle but, because of the unified goal, were combined into one case arguing that, under the Antiquities Act, a president has no legal right to undo or remove national monument protections—a power that rests only with Congress.

The tides shifted in 2021 after the election of President Joe Biden, who restored both southern Utah national monuments. However, without a legal resolution, the risk remains that monument status for Bears Ears and Grand Staircase will become a punting match if the next president disagrees with the designation. Full protections are over a century overdue. The need for effective protection of the Bears Ears area dates back to Bernheimer and even earlier.

Bernheimer fell in love with this part of the desert Southwest, which spurred him to reorient his focus from research to conservation. Before the 1929 trip, Bernheimer proposed Rainbow National Park, hoping to protect portions of the Navajo Nation, Glen Canyon, and Rainbow Bridge from development. By 1931, his vision expanded to include areas of present-day Bears Ears, and eventually it converged with the proposed 1937 Escalante National Monument. Though the national park never came to fruition, Bernheimer's dream eventually rippled toward the present Bears Ears and Grand Staircase–Escalante National Monuments.

The last century reflects the clashing values of preserving the natural world and extracting resources from it in the name of so-called progress. In 1963, a dam and Lake Powell reservoir drowned 186 miles of Glen Canyon, ninety-six tributary canyons, a riparian wildlife habitat, and a cultural landscape worthy of the same protections as Bears Ears. It's proof that the worst can happen. Bernheimer does not come across as vindictive, or the type to say, "I told you so." No doubt he would be on the front lines of restoring both southern Utah monuments today.

- - - - -

A free-range life can be daunting. As I moved through the worlds of Navajo and Cedar Mesa Sandstone, the Bernheimer expeditions gave me a sense of direction, and a light to guide me home. After my meeting with Harvey in 2019, I began following bits and pieces of Bernheimer's routes around the Four Corners, to Rainbow Bridge, and into the Glen Canyon backcountry. The hikes focused my direction in country so brimming with possibility it can swallow wanderlusters like me whole. But it took me two years to muster the courage to retrace his 1929 expedition. The outbreak of the COVID-19 pandemic and a complete Jeep breakdown halted my progress the next year. Distanced from the desert and my once wild life, I found myself in circumstantial domesticity and societal chaos. I desperately needed to release myself back into my natural habitat. On March 17, 2021, I took the first step.

For over one month I immersed myself in the heart of Glen Canyon and the farthest edges of Bears Ears. I hiked with Bernheimer's spirit, across Mancos Mesa, down Grand Gulch, and through golden waves of Navajo Sandstone, to the confluence of the San Juan and Colorado Rivers, now flooded by Lake Powell Reservoir, and up White Canyon to Natural Bridges National Monument. On this archive-induced, hallucinatory vision quest, I carried Bernheimer's journals and photos. These are an elegy to a lost world.

Deciphering Bernheimer's enigmatic notes initially provided a refuge from my personal woes, until the desert finally made me face those too. Through my efforts to protect the wild spaces, I am slowly learning to defend the backcountry of my spirit by walking away from people and places that harm my homeostasis. The clear desert light exposes new passageways and, on the horizon, hope; but it takes courage to step toward them.

To love Glen Canyon is to love a tortured soul. Perhaps it would be wise to walk away and abandon my hope that it will fully reclaim its freedom, but that is not in my nature. I like to see things through.

At the confluence, sunlight reflects off the faint river current threaded below the reservoir surface, where the drowned river flows on. In time, the river will reclaim its power by refusing to be a slave to ours. Human attempts to control the environment are failing while nature continues its course. Ninety-two years after Bernheimer's pilgrimage, I am anguished by the human impacts and optimistic for change. The future awaits between these realities. How we proceed requires our delicate attention. I walk alongside Bernheimer with hopeful steps, witnessing a landscape miracle. At nature's pace, there is time for renewal.

CHAPTER TWO

Camp Snowball

The lure of the desert is so intense that, if my own inclinations prevail, each year shall find me in the saddle with my boon companions, disturbing the past to inform the present.
—Charles L. Bernheimer

Deep snow crunches beneath my oversized tires when I turn off the icy highway onto the unpaved road. I pull over, park, and swing open the Jeep door. After a three-hour drive from my meeting with Harvey, I am eager to get out and stretch my legs. I hop out and the snow buries my boots. A flickering campfire and the scent of smoldering juniper lures me through a shoveled walkway. My friend Ralph, "R. E.," Burrillo is hunkered down beside the flames. I greet him and he hands me a slushy frozen beer.

Ralph is an archaeologist and writer devoted to documenting and protecting the cultural heritage of the Colorado Plateau. His tattoo-covered arms, bald head, pierced ears, and subtly goth style reflect his warrior spirit, almost disguising what a genuinely kind guy he is. His smile gives that away quickly.

We had met randomly at a southwest Colorado coffee shop in 2017. While I was writing, I noticed a Bears Ears sticker on his laptop and inquired about it. Ralph was contributing to a legal report on Bears Ears archaeology, in grim anticipation of Trump reducing the monument. We chatted and passed a bottle of hot sauce between us—a token of our shared enthusiasm for spicy food and land management issues. The next morning, we drove to Cedar Mesa, part of the original Bears Ears National Monument, and went hiking. Our friendship grew quickly, and now we hike together often and collaborate on conservation-minded writing projects.

I received a text message from Ralph earlier today: "So much snow! Fuck it, going to Bears Ears anyway." I told him I was already heading that way. He quickly replied, "Meet me at the spot." Our paths align frequently, and it never seems to take much effort to coordinate our plans.

Ralph is here to do fieldwork for his employer, a Salt Lake City–based environmental consulting agency. Except for the ring Ralph shoveled out around the fire, we are surrounded by three feet of snow that will make his survey work impossible. I ask him what he will do if the snow doesn't melt, and he looks at me wide-eyed, as if to turn the question back on me. He has a good point. I could go anywhere in the world right now. It is not exactly an ideal time to camp here, unless you love this place in all its moods as we do. We salute each other with our last sips of beer—this is exactly where we want to be.

- - - - -

The first glint of sunlight pries my eyes open. I watch the orange tint ascend the wall of creamy sandstone towering above our camp. This morning, its jagged golden layers are frosted with white stripes. The sandstone monocline created from a single uplifted fold in the earth's crust extends for seventy miles, from the Abajo Mountains, south across Bears Ears National Monument to Kayenta, Arizona. Its west-facing wall and the talus slope beneath rise seven hundred vertical feet over the valley floor.

I crawl out of the back of my Jeep, still fully dressed from the night before. I even slept with my boots on to keep my feet warm. Ralph is already out of his tent, scooping snow into his pot to melt and boil. "Welcome to Camp Snowball!" he announces. It sounds like one of Bernheimer's cute names for campsites, like Mushroom, King Bird, and Clematis. Ralph walks over to me through the shoveled walkway in the snow and hands me a tin cup of black coffee. The first sip defrosts me from the inside.

We sit and drink in our camp chairs under the cottonwood tree. Wet snowdrops, melting under the warm rays of sun, fall onto my face in cold bursts. Cottonwoods only live upwards of 150 years, so this massive tree was probably a sapling when Bernheimer was here.

I read while Ralph scribbles in his notebook, tinkering with a draft of the book he is writing, *Behind the Bears Ears,* about the current monument dispute and the human history layered beneath it. Ralph looks up from his page. "Have you ever thought about running his 1929 expedition? You know, the one that covered all of Grand Gulch and White Canyon?" He laughs. "Only a couple hundred miles to finally tire you out." Ralph raises his eyebrows when I tell him that Bill Lipe suggested this to me a few days ago.

Last year, it was Ralph who connected me with Lipe. I interviewed him for a story I wrote about the Glen Canyon Project (GCP), an effort in the late 1950s and early 1960s to survey the ancestral and historical sites to be affected by Glen Canyon Dam. The GCP sparked the beginning of Lipe's acclaimed career as an archaeologist, including the Cedar Mesa Project, which contributed to the study of early Indigenous people living within present-day Bears Ears National Monument. Now eighty-five, Lipe remains devoted to his work and assisting others with their research. We email each other like pen pals, trading stories about Glen Canyon and Cedar Mesa, which he describes as his "home place" in archaeology and as a human being.

At the end of Lipe's recent email he lamented, "Too bad there's so much snow out. I'd like to follow some of Bernheimer's routes too." Ralph and I are already on our way. Bernheimer passed Camp Snowball on his inaugural 1919 expedition, a backcountry horseback trip into Natural Bridges National Monument.

Bernheimer's vision for his expeditions originated an ocean apart from the desert in Ulm-on-Danube, Baden-Württemberg, Germany, where he was born in 1864. His parent's home was built upon the base of one of Charlemagne's castles, and the Roman wine cellar was their basement. Living atop a foundation of European history, Bernheimer's imagination migrated west at an early age. His favorite books to read as a child were about the Southwest and its "mystery to be penetrated only by the most hardy and brave." These stories "laid the foundation for a wish …" and "the romances and exquisite descriptions of Zane Grey contributed their share" to his dream.

He attended school in Geneva, Switzerland, until 1881, when, at age sixteen, he went to New York City to work in his uncle's dry goods business. He performed a myriad of jobs until he became President of Bear Mill Manufacturing Co. in 1907 and shifted the company's focus to cotton textiles. He married Clara S. Silberman, the daughter of a successful silk manufacturer, and they had two daughters. The family lived in a multi-story Manhattan brownstone, complete with servants and secretaries to help them handle day-to-day affairs.

Bernheimer's wealth allowed him to submit to that craving for adventure and to turn his vacations "to something more substantial." The relative proximity of New York to the Southwest, a mere train ride across the country, allowed him to realize his boyhood dream at the age of fifty-five with his first backcountry expedition in 1919:

The desire to do this as an old man…ended with a real

craving to explore and to endure the hardships that go with the penetration into unknown, uncharted regions; taking chances finding water, food for the animals, passable trails, and a way in and a way out. The charm and lure of exploring, once one yields to this craving, becomes irresistible.... The contrast between such exploits and one's daily occupation has a unique attraction.

At home he prepared for trips with extensive research:

I read many books and articles on the subject, but none influenced me more in my final determination than Prof. Herbert E. Gregory's treatise on the Navajo country, printed by the United States Geological Survey. It gave me something definite on which to plan. I believed him to be a safe pilot.

Where Bernheimer went on his expeditions was influenced by what he considered blank spaces on Gregory's topographical maps of the Southwest. This country, of course, was never blank nor unnamed; these places have been known intimately by Indigenous people since time immemorial. The manifest destiny of mapmaking in the Four Corners ignored the human history long embedded in sand and stone with shelters, rocks stories, fragments of pottery, and ancient roads.

While Indigenous people held intimate knowledge of the land for millennia, cartography of the Southwest was nascent in the 1920s. Bernheimer carried Gregory's maps on the trips, adding his team's observations. Afterward, maps were hand drawn for documentation, and Bernheimer dreamed up many of the English names used on modern United States Geological Survey (USGS) maps.

My love affair with maps stems from the layers and stories they hold, details that cannot be transmitted through sanitized

GPS coordinates. Maps do not tell you where to go, they hint at what is possible. And though humans have tried to cover every inch of the earth, there are always minor discrepancies between the lines and marks drawn and the land itself. A map is a prompt beckoning me to go into the land, see it for myself, and develop a personal geography.

Of course, a map would be of no use to Bernheimer without on-the-ground knowledge of where he was or how to prepare. So, for his 1919 expedition Bernheimer enlisted the guiding services of San Juan County local, Ezekiel, "Zeke," Johnson:

> My Mormon guide Mr. Johnson is as fine a fellow as he was on the first day. Nothing is too much for him. He is a real gentleman, though a guide. He is intelligent & knows the country as a book & his knowledge of horses is almost staggering.

Bernheimer's boyhood fantasy was the way of life that reared Johnson. Born near St. George and raised outside Kanab in southern Utah, Zeke Johnson was the twenty-fourth child in a polygamist Mormon family. Rather than going to school, he worked in the fields during his childhood. Johnson was only thirteen when his father passed away, and he started delivering mail on horseback between Kanab and St. George to support his family. During his mail courier years, he married and had two daughters.

His first marriage ended in divorce. He then remarried five more times and had seven more children. Unlike his father, he was not a polygamist—he outlived his other sweethearts. Bernheimer described Johnson as a loving and attentive dad to his "kiddies," depicting a heartwarming scene where they ran out to greet him after a monthlong trip. He built a home for his family in Bluff, Utah, which he endearingly referred to as Cozy Corner. Back in Manhattan, Bernheimer started calling his home Cozy

Corner too, which is pretty darn cute. Johnson later moved his family to Blanding, Utah, where he maintained a farm, ran a trading post in Mexican Hat, and was active in the Mormon Church.

In the early 1890s, Johnson briefly mined for gold along the San Juan River. He never struck it rich, but mining helped forge his incredible on-the-ground knowledge. He furthered that education working as a cowpuncher. Johnson's career in the cattle business was his unlikely inspiration to pursue land conservation. He first saw Natural Bridges in 1898 while rounding up his cattle and resolved that he would protect its geological and cultural wonders, especially from vandalism. In 1908, the same year it was designated a national monument, he was hired on as its custodian, a role he served for thirty-three years with an annual salary of $12—the equivalent of roughly $198 to $226 today. He was instrumental in developing twelve miles of trails within the monument and building a road from Natural Bridges on through the Bears Ears to Blanding in 1929.

Noble intentions aside, enlisting white males to stand guard over Indigenous cultural sites is characteristic of the National Park Service's (NPS) colonialist approach. After all, Indigenous people have always cared for and looked after these lands. The very designations of national park and public lands systems are anchored to the legacies of racism and colonialism. The federal government stole Indigenous homelands under the noble intent of conservation and the guise of protection. Parks were then managed to cater to and benefit tourists and wealthy concessionaires. The romantic veil of conservation shrouds the dark side of public lands to this day. As I invest in efforts to protect these places, I grapple with the neocolonial and racist origins that still pervade the spaces that have been dedicated to conservation, environmental studies, scientific research, archaeology, and recreation. Protecting the land is not enough; we are long overdue for a change that looks to Indigenous people to lead the way.

In Utah, like much of the West, ranching and preservation of the natural world on public lands coexist like oil and water. Ranchers have long feared that federal management will limit their rangeland rights. Unlike Johnson, some current San Juan County locals today vehemently oppose Bears Ears National Monument, which surrounds the 111-year-old Natural Bridges National Monument. This is nothing new—livestock operators opposed proposals to protect Grand Staircase–Escalante as a national monument beginning in the 1930s, and their outlook persists.

Beyond grazing, some locals are concerned that the monument will impinge upon activities such as energy extraction, ranching, hunting, woodcutting, and ORV (off-road vehicle) driving.

The dissent is unfounded, because national monuments are managed according to their purpose as stated in their proclamations, and Bears Ears specifically allowed these activities where they were already permitted pre-monument. The original proclamation did prevent new mining claims, oil and gas leases, and grazing allotments. The increased funding and the resulting management, educational programs, and rangers should aim to prevent looting and vandalism, and reduce recreational impacts.

To help understand this clash, I talked to San Juan County locals who were friendly and eager to share their opinions with a writer willing to listen. The responses ranged from opposing government overreach to calling for the reopening of the nearby uranium mines. My favorite comment was from a woman who lamented, "If god can give us a monument, I just want to know why he can't give us a freaking shopping mall?" Another woman gave me a #NoMonument sticker, which I displayed on my Jeep next to a "Defend Bears Ears" sticker, a symbol of my goal to learn about both sides of an issue rather than jump to a conclusion. The most important takeaway from these conversations was how much everyone in San Juan County seemed to care for and want to protect the local backyard, even if no one agreed about the ideal way to accomplish that.

With Johnson's resumé including rancher, miner, Mormon, conservationist, guide, explorer, father, he was the multi-use poster boy for public lands. If only he could mediate a round-table discussion to create a cooperative management plan with tribal leaders, Indigenous communities, ranchers, environmentalists, extractive industry CEOs, San Juan County residents, hikers and rock climbers, and Utah government officials today.

Johnson became an outback guru to Bernheimer, his desert disciple, who was nearly the same age. The experience quickly baptized Bernheimer in the complexity of the terrain, as he learned about both the earth beneath his feet and the way locals interacted with it. According to Johnson, there were two kinds of visitors: tourists and travelers. Tourists wanted to rush through an experience, which he disapproved of: "That ain't no way to treat this country. It wasn't made in a hurry and it don't get in a hurry, except in a stampede or an oil boom, and them things has nasty kickback." Bernheimer was determined to become a traveler. In a letter to his wife, Clara, Bernheimer boasted:

> We were seven hours in the saddle & not too fatigued. Does this not indicate to you that I am gaining in strength & endurance in this "near to nature" way of living, on the coarsest, simplest kind of food, sleeping under the sky so far five nights, drinking like a fish, water that city folk would not wash in … I am taking chances & going over dangerous places.

The rugged lifestyle was complimented by Johnson's genuinely pleasant demeanor. Bernheimer described him as an incorrigible optimist and perpetual sunshine. He had a reputation as a raconteur, natural entertainer, and singer. Dressed in overalls, a stovepipe hat, and round, wire-rimmed glasses, Johnson was the kind of guide who sang while he made Bernheimer biscuits directly on top of the flour sack. Bernheimer delighted in the cowboy culinary experience:

> My lunch is usually beans & they are fine, chipped beef, a bathtub of coffee, another tub of hot water or two, graham crackers, condensed milk & each a half tin can of Bartlett pears. Isn't that regal! At any rate, it is just the right thing for these here parts. I seem to flourish on it.

My stomach growls. I fold down the corner of the page I'm reading to scavenge for breakfast options. My cooler doesn't even need ice in these freezing temps. I crack open a can of ranch-style beans and pour them directly into the greasy pan with a few slabs of bacon. The smell wafts through camp, and Ralph walks over. I hand him a spoon and a bottle of hot sauce. We eat quickly, straight out of the cast-iron skillet.

After breakfast, Ralph and I decide to attempt some hiking. We drive up the paved highway, and I look out the window at the Bears Ears, atop Elk Ridge at an elevation of 8,400 and 8,900 feet. The silhouette of the two rust-colored Wingate Sandstone formations, crowned with green piñons and junipers, is so distinct that the Hopi, Diné, Ute, and Zuni place names each translate to a description of "bears ears": Hoon'Naqvut (Hopi), Shash Jaa' (Diné), Kwiyagatu Nukavachi (Ute), and Ansh An Lashokdiwe (Zuni).

A few years ago, Ralph and I sat on our tailgates near the Bears Ears after a hike. Still getting to know each other, he asked me why I felt so drawn to be here. I told him it was something different I felt here. That I could safely process trauma from my past. I never needed to hold myself together, as I howled in pain and joy. The solitude allowed nature to soothe my rattled nerves.

Learning to trust my feet in new terrain helped me regain the strength to rebuild my life. Writing about these experiences awakened my voice.

Ralph sat in his camp chair, the Bears Ears looming in the background. He explained to me that Bears Ears is seen by many Indigenous people as a place of healing, especially for women who have experienced trauma. Ralph gleaned this information about the Bears Ears from Eric Descheenie, a Diné Tribal member and former Arizona democratic representative. The Diné associate this area with Changing Bear Maiden, and Ralph explained that the "ears" represent where her body lies following a heated exchange that erupted after she was tricked into marrying wily old Coyote.

Diné people traditionally gather healing plants and medicines here, especially—though not exclusively—by and for women. Both Hopi and Ute people have different stories about the formations, but Ralph had not been given permission by tribal members to share them. He looks up toward the Bears Ears and takes a long pause before resuming, "Mother Bear is the guardian to the North, healer and watcher over the land and its peoples."

With tear-filled eyes, Ralph looked into mine resolutely and said, "I do not think it is a coincidence that you are here." My resolve to remain in Bears Ears deepened its roots.

Months later, I met two Diné women who worked on the ferry at Halls Crossing on Lake Powell. After letting me ride on the boat for fun, they invited me over to their employee housing complex for dinner and a shower. As they taught me to make fry bread, I asked them about the Bears Ears. They told me that some women go there to cry and heal. One of the women insisted that if I felt like I needed to go, I should trust my instincts. This has given me a clear reason to return this winter, not only for my personal healing, but as a penance to place. Among the many things I have gleaned while hiking with Ralph, his belief in repaying a karmic debt to places that provide pleasure, wisdom, and healing is something I am now devoted to as well. To dwell anywhere, there is always a cost. In lieu of rent or a mortgage, I vowed to give back and help protect Bears Ears by writing and advocating for it.

Today the Bears Ears are glossed in white snow, and I smile with gratitude as we drive past.

- - - - -

I lift my knees high to move through the deep snow toward the canyon's edge. We stop to take in the view and he wipes away beads of sweat dripping beneath his black leather hat. "This is the coldest hot I've ever been." I agree. My frozen feet and flushed face make simultaneous frostbite and sunburn seem possible.

A barbed wire fence is barely perceptible, hovering only an inch above the snowline. I grab Ralph's shoulder and climb up him like a ladder to avoid getting jabbed. He hoists a juniper branch over the other side to climb the phantom fence, leaps off and lands softly in the powder. The ground beneath us is a treacherous combination of snow, ice, and slickrock. We scan each precipitous step with juniper branches, our makeshift trekking poles. We don't want to wind up like Bernheimer's horse Wally who walked off a twenty-foot cliff in this canyon. It is of little comfort to me that Wally somehow survived.

A fluffy white rabbit hops in front of us, leaving tracks in the snow. We hike behind it until it vanishes inside its hole. I pause from watching my steps to look up at the other side of the canyon. The sandstone rim is bejeweled by daggers of ice, and the snow underfoot blankets all distractions; white contrasts with the salmon-pink walls to bring rock art to life. The etchings of an eagle with spread wings lurches from the rock. Cliff dwellings, woven into the pockets and folds of Cedar Mesa Sandstone, hide behind curtains of ice. Frozen hanging gardens adorn T-shaped doors like chandeliers. We leave footprints in the snow as we follow the handprints emblazoned across the frozen walls of time. There are no immediate translations for these images that we can draw from. Researchers like Ralph often prefer to not make assumptions, and descendant tribes connected to these images do not always disclose their meaning. The textures, forms, and colors delight and suspend our imaginations with the ice crystals.

Known habitation of Cedar Mesa dates back to 12,000–6,000 BC. Modern archaeologists call this the Paleoindian period, as indicated by a Clovis site located near here. This was followed by the Archaic period in 6000–2000 BC, when small groups of hunter-gatherers foraged seasonally on the mesa and left minimal traces of their habitation.

There was a substantial increase in population from the later BC years until AD 400, known as the Basketmaker II period, when people were heavily dependent on maize farming. They settled in camps on the mesas and in canyons, making colorful pictographs and manufacturing intricate baskets. Then, Cedar Mesa was depopulated from approximately AD 400 to 620, followed by reoccupation during the Basketmaker III period, AD 500-750. After another three-hundred-year hiatus between AD 1150 and 1290, the Pueblo II and III people repopulated Cedar Mesa. The advances of this period included firing more intricate pottery and a shift to varied agriculture, with corn, beans, and squash as primary crops. Dwellings and granaries were built within high alcoves using mud, stone, and sticks.

A widespread period of drought instigated a mass migration from the region around AD 1250, pushing the Ancestral Pueblo people to disperse across the Southwest. Their descendants, the Pueblo, Hopi, and Zuni people, continue to reside in the Four Corners and maintain strong cultural connections to these homelands of their ancestors. The Ancestral Pueblo did not vanish or abandon their dwelling sites—which are not ruins. This is where their ancestors continue to live, as they have since time immemorial. The timeline of set dates is merely the perspective of western scientists and culture.

Bernheimer's 1919 journal entries highlight the cultural sites and rock images of animals and human handprints he saw. He erroneously described the sites as "Aztec Ruins" and the people as "pygmies." It's cringeworthy, but the reality is that visitors, past and present, do not arrive with a baseline knowledge of the land and its connection to Indigenous people.

Bernheimer admitted to his readers that he was not an expert: "I do not even pretend to be even an amateur naturalist. I have simply tried to absorb what I saw and felt and heard." Between these early journal entries and the publication of *Rainbow Bridge* in 1924, Bernheimer began to fact-check what he wrote about cultural sites and Indigenous people with his guides.

He shifted away from the word *pygmies* and began using *Cliff Dwellers*, which was widely used among settlers at that moment. That term then fell out of favor and was replaced by *Anasazi*, a Diné term that is considered offensive to the descendants of the Pueblo people it describes, the Hopi Tribe and Zuni among them. Despite this it remained in use well into the last decade. Now *Ancestral Pueblo* is more commonly used to describe inhabitants of this area between about AD 750 and the time of Spanish conquest.

While affiliated tribes and academia now use this term, it continues the trend of describing Indigenous people with labels given by colonizers. The word *Pueblo* itself is a Spanish settler term that means "village." Each of the nineteen Pueblo Tribes has a way to refer to themselves in their own language. The Hopi Tribe uses the term *Hisatsinom*, and the Zuni call themselves *A:shiwi*. The Navajo prefer to be called *Diné*, which means, "the people," in their Diné Bizaad language. Navajo is a Tewa word, *navahu'u* which means "farmers of the valley," later altered by the Spanish as *Apaches de Nabajó*. Navajo people, particularly Navajo academics, also dislike the term Ancestral Pueblo because they rightly identify the people Bernheimer called Cliff Dwellers as ancestral to some of their own clans.

When Indigenous people lead in deciding how they and their homelands are referenced, it opens the doors for essential linguistic changes. So often, the language of the past is considered outdated, but perhaps we are not looking back far enough: to a time when people named themselves and their home according to the tone most familiar to their hearts.

- - - - -

After a few blissful days, Ralph needs to face the so-called real world and check in with his boss. To get cell service, we have to leave this sanctuary behind the sandstone fortress. So, we saddle up our packtrain—Ralph's white truck and my yellow Jeep—to climb out of Camp Snowball along the icy highway back to civilization. A distance that took Bernheimer and Johnson over a day on horseback, flies by in under an hour. We reach the cell service threshold, and my phone beeps immediately, jolting my nerves which are adapting to the serenity of living disconnected.

We stop to fill our gas tanks at the Shirt Tail Gas Station, a name that was inspired by Zeke Johnson. The legend goes that Zeke was driving his Buick at night. A nearby cowboy saw the lights, jumped out of bed and ran, in nothing but his underwear and shirttail, to console his spooked cows.

This is the only spot in Blanding that sells beer, so we pick up a twelve-pack. Waiting for my tank to fill, I reluctantly look at my phone. What would Bernheimer think about being able to send his wife Clara a text message? He wrote to her, "You have no idea how cut off from world news I feel," in a letter to her that he mailed after the trip. By the time it arrived, he was probably already back home in New York.

Unlike Bernheimer, there is not anyone or anything I need to go back to. Home is where I choose to be. There are few distractions out here, and I know which pockets of cell service are strong enough to submit my upcoming story assignments using the hotspot on my phone. There is only one text message, from my mom, asking me, "Where are you?" To which I respond, "Bears Ears." She instantly replies, "Good!" with a heart emoji. Though she has never been here, and only has a vague idea of where it is, she has come to associate it as a safe haven for me. I look up from my phone and Ralph is grinning at me—his boss permitted him to stay at Camp Snowball for the rest of the week. We hop back in our rigs and head home.

CHAPTER THREE

The Desert Is Home

The desert will take care of you. At first, it's all big and beautiful, but you're afraid of it. Then you begin to see its dangers, and you hate it. Then you learn how to overcome its dangers. And the desert is home.

—John Wetherill

It snowed all day, but we did not mind. We shook the snow from our robes from time to time, as we had been taught to do, so the heat of our bodies would not melt it and get us wet....The snowstorm continued all night. When dawn came, the snow was deep, but everyone was happy.

—Wolfkiller

Running sinuously for seventy miles, from the base of the Bears Ears into the San Juan River, Grand Gulch is frosted in glistening snow. Ralph stops to point out a line of bear tracks through the piñon and juniper trees. From where we are standing, they enter the canyon, cross the frozen creek, and climb out on the other side. Maybe the tracks are a sign, something to guide us. We contemplate following them but agree it looks too risky, aware of the slick surface of melting snow and ice beneath our feet.

Bernheimer's summertime expeditions passed through

Grand Gulch in 1919 and 1929, but the conditions today are far more reminiscent of his eventual guide John Wetherill's winter explorations here in the 1890s. Hailing from a working-class family, John and his brothers fit their explorations in between ranch duties, which usually meant they had more free time in winter. It's hard to imagine getting around in these conditions wearing leather boots—Ralph and I are wearing waterproof shoes with grippy rubber soles and still struggling. We tease each other for being such wimps, too afraid to follow the bear's tracks.

My interest in the Wetherills began two winters ago while commuting between Cedar Mesa and Mancos, Colorado. A local couple I met through a friend graciously welcomed me to stay with them as a respite from the snow. With a view of Mesa Verde from their loft, I read *In Search of the Old Ones* by David Roberts. The book introduced me to the Wetherills, whose Alamo Ranch could be seen from the south-facing window.

Southwest Colorado is the traditional homeland of the Ute people. The US government attempted to serve the Utes a series of treaties to terminate their rights to their lands, but the bands refused. In 1874, the land was stolen by the US government, and by 1895, white homesteaders were allowed to settle the area, pushing out the three local Ute bands and forcing them to move throughout the Four Corners. The Southern Ute settled outside Ignacio, and the Weenuchiu to Towaoc, next to present-day Cortez.

In 1881, the Wetherill family homesteaded in Mancos, alongside Mormons, local cowboys, and miners. At the turn of the century, the collision of people with vastly different beliefs and backgrounds made for community tensions. The Mormons were wary of the Wetherills because they were Quaker. The local cowboys and miners, and to an extent the Mormons, had notoriously tense relations with the Utes. These strained relations clashed with the Wetherills' Quaker faith, centered upon equality for all people and nature. The family avoided conflict and aimed to develop positive relationships with the neighboring Utes, Pueblo, and Diné people.

Today the town is colonized primarily by farmers, families, blue-collar workers, artists, packrafting river rats, and a few remaining cowboys. As the new girl in town, I knew my nomadic lifestyle chasing stories made me a little different from my neighbors, but I remained optimistic about fitting in. One weekend, I went to a hoedown and danced to live bluegrass music with a lanky Stetson-wearing man. He asked me what I did for work. I leaned in toward his cheek and said, "Write and run." He heard, "Ride and run," and asked me what my horse's name was. I explained what I did again. In response he twirled me off the dance floor and moved on.

According to the Wetherills, the Utes permitted them to graze their cattle within Mesa Verde, an area the local Utes were especially protective over. One day, Richard Wetherill, John's brother, and his friend Charles Mason were out searching for lost cattle. Their Ute friend Acowitz joined and guided them to a cliff dwelling that contained many walls and rooms. That site later became known as Cliff Palace in what is now Mesa Verde National Park.

The experience motivated the Wetherills to explore the other nearby ancient dwellings, and the boys soon began neglecting their ranch work to pursue their obsession. Swedish scientist Gustaf von Nordenskiöld, the twenty-two-year-old son of an Arctic explorer, came to work with the Wetherills for two years and wrote the first scientific report about the Ancestral Puebloans. Nordenskiöld taught the cowboys cutting-edge European excavation and cataloguing techniques; his intent was to both study and protect the sites they encountered. Both were nebulous concepts at that time. Without laws protect cultural sites, they were extremely vulnerable to looting, vandalism, and archaeology itself. The meaning of the word "protection" was limited to the morals and perspectives of each individual who encountered ancient dwellings and artifacts.

On every hike with Ralph I learn as much as we laugh. His knowledge about archaeology and the history of Bears Ears is on par with any book in my Jeep. As we trample through the snow, Ralph explains to me that the late 1800s were a peak period for looting because of economic insecurity. "People look for things they can sell when they are desperately in need of money." Times were hard thanks to the "Great Die Up" in 1887, the result of a devastating series of blizzards and a deep freeze across the West, causing millions of cattle to die across the West. Then came the first stock market crash, known as "The Panic of 1893." To supplement their ranching income during this period, the Wetherills led research expeditions. Afterward they displayed artifacts at the World's Fair and sold some collections to museums. They viewed selling objects for public scholarship versus private ownership as the line defining ethical collection and unethical looting.

In 1889, the Wetherills' father, Benjamin Kite, wrote to the United States National Museum, requesting federal support to make Mesa Verde a national park. He hoped this would protect the cliff dwellings from looting and prevent tourists from destroying them. The letter passed through several hands, including those of John Wesley Powell and archaeologist William H. Holmes, who denied these requests. The decision may have been rooted in Holmes's racist belief that there was nothing important to be learned from Indigenous people. He wrote:

In the inevitable course of human history, the individual races will probably fade out and disappear, and the world will be filled to overflowing with a generalized race in which the dominating blood will be that of the race that today has the strongest claim, physically and intellectually, to take possession of all the resources of the land and sea.

The resultant race will not have of the Native American blood even this one three-hundredth part because they are decadent as a result of conditions imposed by civilization. As diagrammed by the ethnologist of the far future, the career of the Indian will appear as a lenticular figure—beginning in nothing, ending in nothing—a figure of perhaps universal application by the historian of mundane things.

Later, Holmes made another hateful diatribe: "The complete absorption or blotting out of the red race will be quickly accomplished....If peaceful amalgamation fails, extinction of the weaker by less gentle means will do the work." There are not enough expletives available for me to respond adequately to this horrific quote. I hesitate to share it, primarily out of sensitivity to Indigenous people who continue to face the traumatic legacy of institutionalized racism. But it is necessary to call racism out rather than sweep it under the historical rug.

The racist foundations of American academia and scientific institutions undermined the question of how to protect Indigenous history and cultural sites, by criticizing the value of studying them at all. Archaeology in the early twentieth century disguised colonial plunder as research, education, and conservation. Ultimately, the methods of study and protection back then displaced cultural objects from their location of origin, which had been defending them naturally for long periods of time. This removal separates them from their historical and locational context, disturbing the intentions and beliefs of the Indigenous people who left the items there. It's akin to digging up someone's grandmother's grave, taking her jewelry, and keeping it in a safe in another country. Apart from asking who are we protecting these cultural materials from, we must ask who are we protecting them for?

As Southwest archaeology gained more notice, the legality

THE DESERT IS HOME

of digging up sites—especially burials—in the name of science and profits was starting to be questioned. The Wetherills gained a complicated reputation that ranged from being glorified as discoverers of known Indigenous cultural sites to facing accusations of being pot hunters, looters, and grave robbers. These claims were tough to legally determine since there were not any laws to deal with this stuff yet.

On the way back to Sweden, Nordenskiöld was arrested with a collection of cultural items. He claimed that he was taking them for further study and to protect the materials from looting. The charges were dropped. Nordenskiöld then took the human remains and funerary objects overseas, where they were curated at the Museum of Culture in Helsinki, Finland. All of this may have prevented someone from buying the pot just to look at on their shelf, but still reflected a belief that scientific institutions were superior and safer than the location of origin.

The legal line was finally drawn in 1906 with the creation of the Antiquities Act, which made it a federal crime to collect or destroy prehistoric or historic objects on federally owned land. It restricted excavation and collection of archaeological sites to permitted researchers and institutions, making unauthorized excavations a misdemeanor. John Wetherill adjusted and began guiding authorized research trips, including the Bernheimer expeditions, under the permit granted by the American Museum of Natural History.

In 1990, the creation of the Native American Graves and Repatriation Act (NAGPRA), gave descendant tribes rights to receive and repatriate previously excavated items from museum collections. The caveat is that NAGPRA gives tribes access to museum collections only when there's established affiliation. Anything dated to the Basketmaker era or earlier on the Colorado Plateau is considered unaffiliated.

The items that Nordenskiöld took from Mesa Verde would finally be sent back to the descendant tribes of the Pueblo people for repatriation and reburial in 2020. While this is an important legal step, it will never resolve the issue that these items should not have been removed at all. Nor will it expedite the endless backlog, often uncatalogued, of items waiting in basement drawers to be returned.

- - - - -

Ralph and I still cannot find a safe way to cross the canyon. The air is warmer than yesterday, and the slushy snow is slower to move through. We spot a granary tucked high in an alcove, where the Ancestral Pueblo people crossed this snowy canyon to reach their stored corn. Today the granaries are the only visible reminder of their presence. Snow conceals axe heads, projectile points, and pieces of pottery resting on the ground where they were left centuries ago. The feather blankets, sandals, baskets, and bone beads that were removed now sit in a museum basement, or worse.

Despite the Antiquities Act, looting continues to plague southern Utah. Many items at Edge of the Cedars Museum in Blanding have been retrieved from locals who either have been busted or decided to relinquish items passed along from a deceased relative who had a penchant for pot hunting.

A few weeks ago, a local Mormon family whom I met previously in Cedar Mesa, offered to let me stay with them during a blizzard. I obliged and enjoyed a home-cooked meal and carrot cake prepared by two middle-aged sons who were visiting. The guys started talking about their childhood explorations while showing me their artifact collection of arrowheads, beads, pendants, and yucca cords displayed in a glass box; forcibly removed and locked away.

I asked them if they ever considered returning some of the items to the Edge of the Cedars Museum. That way they could be studied or returned to local tribes rather than collect dust in a basement. My question was never answered, as they continued their show-and-tell. It was difficult for me to bite my tongue, but I try to be respectful in other people's homes even if their beliefs differ vastly from mine. My gut told me that pressing the issue may not be a safe thing to do.

That night, one of the sons offered to sleep on the couch so I could rest in a real bed. The respite was short lived. At two in the morning, he crawled into bed with me. Startled, my voice cracked, as he put his hand over my mouth. I was terrified and trapped, but I fended off his advances. Shocked, he blurted, "But I made you carrot cake!"

Like looting irreplaceable artifacts, some people believe they have the right to take whatever they want.

I left the room and went to the couch, lying wide awake until morning. The whiteout conditions and icy roads made it too dangerous for me to leave in the dark. At first light, I crept outside to my Jeep and drove home to the snowy canyons that would protect me once more.

- - - - -

Ralph and I decide to not risk our lives following the bear down the icy cliff. We turn around and laugh at each other's sunburned faces. As we trudge through the snow we fantasize about dinner plans, with a debate between fusilli, Ralph's specialty, or fajita burritos, mine. We settle on Italian, since we already ate breakfast burritos. We still use Ralph's favorite ghost pepper hot sauce on the pasta.

Even sitting around a hearty fire with a full belly, my teeth chatter. Ralph's thermometer reads twelve degrees, but laughter almost warms our bones when we nickname my coat Furrnando. As the fire dims, we agree it's too cold to drink another slushy beer. I crawl into the Jeep and tuck myself into bed, keeping my boots on for extra insulation. Under my down comforter and zero-degree sleeping bag, I dive into the copy of the book *Wolfkiller* that Harvey Leake passed along to me.

The introduction, written by John Wetherill's wife Louisa, describes how the Wetherill family moved from the Colorado mountains to the sand-swept Navajo Nation in 1900. It seems strange that the Wetherills would move from one community where they were the outliers, to one where everyone spoke a different language. Harvey Leake told me that the move was prompted by his family's value in a simple life and connection to nature, which felt more aligned with the Diné people than with the mainstream American culture of progress.

Unsurprisingly, the Diné people were wary about the new white settlers moving onto the reservation. To introduce them-selves, John hosted a feast of rabbits and discussed how his plans to open a trading post would enhance the community's access to supplies. After the feast, Hoskinnini Begay, the son of a highly respected Diné elder, told them they were welcome to stay. In time, the Wetherills became a welcomed part of the community, where John and Louisa were known as "Hosteen John," a Diné name of the highest respect, and "Asthon Sosi" or slim woman. Hoskinnini grew close to the family and considered Louisa his granddaughter. He entrusted her to manage his estate after he passed away.

Louisa and their trading partner, Clyde Coleville, primarily managed the trading posts, first in Oljato and later in Kayenta. Louisa's work and immersion in her new community helped stave off her loneliness while John was away guiding and explor-ing alongside both Diné and Paiute men. Their residence in Kay-enta helped to connect the white tourists that John guided with the Diné and Paiute people and their culture. Pack trips began at their home with shared meals, traditional gatherings, and time spent among community members going about their daily lives. Bernheimer described the interactions between the Diné people and Louisa at the Trading Post as thoughtful, joyful, and con-tent. Another guest noted that the Wetherills' doors were never locked and that they welcomed all guests regardless of race.

Louisa further committed herself to her new home by learning as much as possible about the Diné people. She explained, "I'd have studied the customs of any people in any place where I lived. Otherwise, it wouldn't be home." As a friend and ally, she listened and learned from her neighbors, and assisted them in the ways they requested. They often turned to her to help resolve health problems or personal disputes. Louisa documented and published these experiences in her book *Traders to the Navajo*.

Her willingness to advocate for her neighbors extended beyond the home front. Louisa traveled by train to advocate for her neighbors, including acting as translator for two Paiute men who were wrongly incarcerated. She helped collect several hundred varieties of desert plants and document their traditional Diné names and medicinal uses.

Wolfkiller was among the Wetherill's neighbors, and upon his request, Louisa translated and documented his stories. The manuscript collected dust until 2007 when Harvey published it. Wolfkiller's philosophies greatly influenced the Wetherills, especially "Path of Light," which echoed their Quaker belief in "Inward Light," that can help guide individual decisions even before they are intellectually clear.

Pressing my headlamp on, I open *Wolfkiller* to reread the passage: "When I was a young boy, about six years old, my grandfather and mother started me on the path of light."

Young Wolfkiller lamented doing his daily sheepherding chores in the bitter cold and winter winds. He wished to sit inside around the fire instead. His other worries included white colonialism, changing Diné culture, and local inter-tribal conflict—complex stuff for a six-year-old. Wolfkiller's grandfather overheard him whining, and began to tells him stories of past hardship that the Diné people encountered and overcame, including drought, famine, warfare, and poverty. His grandfather reminded him, "There have been times in our past when people have suffered more than I can tell you—times when we had more enemies than we could count."

He continued, "We must give up something for everything we receive. I must give up the comfort of the hogan fire and face the wind if I am to find my (lost) horse."

During these trying times, the Diné men recognized that focusing on negativity, the black path, leads to nowhere but the dark. The people came together to work toward a solution—choosing the path of light, which means selecting positive thoughts, being satisfied with one's life, and taking actions that lead to the outcome you need. This philosophy focused on the role of the individual as part of the collective: "A good thought will bring all of our people good, and an evil thought will be evil to all."

Snowflakes fall, clouding the Jeep windows as I turn the page. In the winter, Wolfkiller's mother woke him at dawn to go out and roll in the snow and told him, "The snow will be with us for several moons now, and if you roll in it and treat it as a friend, it will not seem nearly as cold to you." Though I am not tempted to get out and roll around in the snow tonight, living out in the elements is honing our friendship. The first time I slept in my Jeep, I worried about freezing to death inside the wheeled metal box. Now curling up for twelve hours on the dog bed I use for a mattress to hibernate is just a natural part of life. Winter, like sleep, is a pause for restoration and healing.

In the daunting terrain of personal and actual wilderness, self-care means stay alive. Sleeping inside my Jeep through this single-digit temperature night may appear like an odd way to protect myself, but not everyone is afforded the privilege to choose this freedom.

A so-called normal life never suited me anyway. When I was a kid, I absorbed every story I heard like a sponge. My play-time included cleaning up and saving my stuffed animals from the Exxon Valdez oil spill. At night, I preferred to sleep in the backyard; being outside grounded me and gave my imagination enough space to run wild.

Surrounded outside by sandstone walls, the cold desert is a hideaway that protects me when it is most quiet and still; here I can be left alone and undisturbed by my past. Is that not what a home is for? Protection from the elements, be it a storm or a predator. I peek my head out of the covers, my breath against the cold air fogs the frost-covered windows, the moonrise illuminates the canyon walls protecting me.

CHAPTER FOUR

Rainbow Chasing

As all roads lead to Rome, so in the more confined area of our western wanderings all our roads led to Rainbow Bridge.
—Charles L. Bernheimer

Ch-ch-ch-ch-cha. The Jeep grinds to a stop in the middle of the two-lane highway. It's as if Sunny, my stubborn old yellow mare, knows that we are near the end of the paved road, where her services are no longer required. There is no traffic so I am not as panicked as I should be. Instead, the stillness beckons me to look away from my problems. My gaze drifts away from Navajo Mountain, glazed in snow, toward Piute Canyon, a deep orange gash below the road. The scene releases happy tears from my eyes and riffles down the nerve endings in my arms. It's a joy to be here.

I manage a precarious U-turn and limp the Jeep to rest next to an old water tank, the words "Bull Shit" in red graffiti across it. On the back of a paper scrap I scribble, "I'll be back in a few days," and set it on my dashboard before taking off. My doors remain unlocked because the latches are broken. I leave the keys in the ignition for good measure.

Lately, mechanical issues are so frequent that I dream of

replacing the Jeep with a mule or burro, despite Bernheimer's warnings that nonmotorized travel came with its challenges:

> We have plenty of trouble with our animals, and it is a real western scene when they have to be rounded up, roped, and drag, at times when they become unusually head-strong, two or three of the men all around. The animals slip their loads often by knocking against tree branches, rocks, and each other in order to strip off their load.

Sunny bucked me off in the same spirit. I walk away from the Jeep carrying my backpack, eager to finally retrace portions of Bernheimer's 1920 expedition, the first of his three consecutive trips to Rainbow Bridge.

The paved highway I drove to get here eliminates a seventy-mile, three-day stretch of travel from the Wetherill Trading Post in Kayenta, Arizona. With a hiking permit from the Navajo Nation, my trek now begins at the Rainbow Trail, on the north side of Navajo Mountain, *Naatsis'áán* in Diné. It ends eighteen miles later at Rainbow Bridge National Monument. It is not the exact trail used by Bernheimer, but there is some overlap. A chilled breeze blows down from the mountain, into its ribcage of sandstone spines and canyons, but the snow down here is melted. I kick red dust behind me.

Today I am with two new hiking companions—Brent, a photographer from Colorado, and his nine-year-old husky mutt, Phil. For the last few weeks, we have been getting to know each other on hikes. Brent's sun-reddened cheeks and shaggy blonde hair are sheltered beneath a trucker hat and sunglasses. In addition to his backpack, he carries a camera case across his chest. It looks heavy. Phil trots alongside us wearing a little red backpack filled with his food. It lifts my spirits to be around him, one year after Herschel, my mellow coyote-esque dog, passed away suddenly.

For the journey to the stone rainbow in 1920, Bernheimer grew his team. He hired John Wetherill, who had been guiding people to Rainbow Bridge since 1909 and was the custodian of the national monument. Teaming up with Wetherill and his first hired guide, Zeke Johnson, Bernheimer reasoned, "I have with me the best man south of the San Juan River and the best man from the north of that river."

Bernheimer recognized that having two leaders can be problematic. He declared that Wetherill and Johnson would gain that role depending on whose turf they were on. In rainbow country, the lead went to Wetherill. Bernheimer was immediately impressed by his new hire:

> Mr. Wetherill is, of course, a genius and has a sixth sense which one riding behind him feels guides and directs him. He has not made a single mistake in his guidance of our party and is a thoroughly high-bred and highly educated man such as I rarely ever met. No subject seems strange to him, and in most of them, he is a master.

Serious Wetherill was quiet with a dry sense of humor, the opposite of outgoing Johnson. Among Bernheimer's early impressions of Wetherill were that he was adventurous, generous, well read, and modest. He held an impressive knowledge of geology, geography, and anthropology, gleaned from personal experience and the men he rode alongside.

Wetherill and Johnson's distinct dispositions complemented one another but led them to occasionally butt heads. Bernheimer recapped a dispute over the treatment of pack animals:

> Johnson, our quick, brilliant, yet gentile friend, who was under great tension kept mumbling: 'But my horses cannot do without water until noon tomorrow, or later.' Wetherill, who never spoke more than twenty-five words at a time,

felt what was on Johnson's mind and coldly remarked, 'A desert horse can work without water all twenty-four hours.'…Right here was the dividing line between the viewpoints of the two men.

Differences aside, the team members readily adapted to teamwork, and Bernheimer celebrated their mutual respect. Bernheimer maintained the same ethos in the desert as he did with business and public affairs in Manhattan. One of his *New York Times* articles, "The Advantages of Arbitration Procedure," aimed to reduce wasted energy, funds, and time resolving labor disputes. With these skills, Bernheimer noted any incongruity among team members and encouraged their quick resolution with teamwork:

> Fortunately, on all of our journeys my relationship with my guides and between these men and myself could not have been better. Each man had his particular duties assigned; but when these were too heavy the other men unhesitatingly put their shoulders to the wheel.

The addition of Earl Morris in 1921 shifted the expeditions toward formal permitted archaeology. Morris's boss, Dr. Clark Wissler of the American Museum of Natural History (AMNH), persuaded him to join Bernheimer on the premise that he could use his spare time to explore sites and scout for future research. Anything he found during those trips was donated to the museum in Bernheimer's name. Morris was instrumental in convincing Bernheimer to make sure serious research was a priority and not just a sideshow attraction.

Morris was born in Farmington, New Mexico, after his parents moved to the Southwest from Pennsylvania. His father struggled to find work to support his family during the economically depressed 1890s and unabashedly took to pot hunting and selling antiquities to make a living. While Morris inherited his father's interest in digging up the past, he went on to pursue archaeology legally by earning a degree at the University of Colorado Boulder.

In 1904 Morris's father was murdered by a business associate. Those who knew Morris noted that his personality intensified after that, turning inward and introspective to himself and beneath the surface of the desert's crust. His mother became a recluse after the tragedy and lived with Earl for the rest of her life.

After college, Morris and his mother lived at Aztec Ruins National Monument in Aztec, New Mexico, where he served as custodian and was employed by the AMNH. Morris traveled for work across the Southwest and also went south of the border to the Mayan site of Chichén Itzá, in Mexico's Yucatán Peninsula. Known to be a workaholic, Morris's employment was enough to sustain him, but by accepting the role as lead archaeologist on five of the Bernheimer expeditions, he gained important financial support.

On expeditions, Morris kept himself busy at all hours, sometimes hiking three or four hours away from camp to explore by himself, while keeping extensive field notes of locations, artifacts, and analysis. Photos of Morris wearing a black felt brimmed hat and khaki trousers covered in dirt conjure images of Indiana Jones. Some claim that the character was influenced by Morris's look and notoriety, although Steven Spielberg denied this. Morris was an archaeological celebrity regardless of Hollywood's portrayal, and his inclusion further heightened the credibility of Bernheimer's trips.

Bernheimer united a trio of that generation's savviest Southwest explorers, creating a Led Zeppelin-caliber supergroup:

Irrepressible Johnson kept us singing, telling Mormon stories, and applying his peppery, refreshing repartee.

Wetherill, after supper, added his local coloring by his unlimited knowledge of the country about; Morris started his many mooring questions about basket making and pottery making aborigines that lived hereabouts; and I added my own wisdom based on the experiences I gathered as a cliff dweller from Manhattan.

To round out the team, Wetherill hired both Diné and local Anglo cowboys to manage the pack animals and equipment. The lineup of men typically rotated from year to year, with a few guys returning for more than one trip. Wetherill frequently hired Diné men they met along the trail. The first time this happened, Bernheimer was unsettled by the seemingly tense conversation, spoken in Diné, that he could not understand. They agreed to pay each Diné man one dollar to help with water and feed for the rest of the trip, the same as Wetherill's monthly salary at Rainbow Bridge. According to Bernheimer, everyone was happy after that.

In 1921 the Diné guides were Shadani, Necloeybadani ("the laughing man's son-in-law"), and Not-si-san ("Navajo Mountain"). Not-si-san joined the outfit at the last minute as a trade for ten dollars' worth of coffee and sugar. He was a strongly built man with a mustache who frequently led the packtrain, helped the team avert several disasters, and knew where to find good drinking water. During the later stages of the 1921 journey, Dogistlanibega ("Many Whiskers Son") helped guide them to a canyon near the Colorado River.

Nineteen-year-old wrangler James Albert Smith and his brother Jess joined the lineup during the years 1920-1923. Al was a "strong cowpuncher, cook, athlete, and a general good all-around man." The brothers were born in Iowa and moved to Mancos, followed by Kayenta, just as the Wetherills did. I was able to get in touch with his daughter, Barbara Ohlwiler, who recalls that Al was known as a daredevil horse wrangler.

Tragically, Al died of multiple sclerosis at age thirty-five. Ohl-wiler was only one and a half when he passed and says that she has been told all her life how much she is like him. When I shared a photo of Al taken during the Bernheimer expedition with her, she told me that it was a treasure because she has few photos of him.

Both Wetherill and Johnson, like Bernheimer, were in their fifties and sixties during that period. Morris was thirty-one on his first trip, and the cowboys were even younger. When it came to physical tasks, experience mattered more than seniority and Bernheimer let his hired hands take the reins: a few black and white photos show him hiding in the bushes while his team handled a fallen horse in the Colorado River. Unlike his seasoned guides, Bernheimer knew his limitations, and called himself "The Tenderfoot Cliff Dweller from Manhattan."

Aside from his generous financial support, which contributed significantly to the livelihood of his team, Bernheimer served as the scribe. His field notes document not only the terrain, but also insights about the other men, who, aside from Morris, wrote next to nothing about themselves. Along with his book, Bernheimer's published articles in *Natural History Magazine* (1920) and *National Geographic* magazine (1923) informed the public, to the best of Bernheimer's ability, about the Southwest's Indigenous people, culture, and history. While his stories lacked research expertise, he exposed readers to a reverential attitude toward all people. Bernheimer, who was Jewish, celebrated the diversity of his team and, when united, referred to the outfit as the "rough-and-ready 'soul corral'":

There were gathered Jew and Gentile, Mormon, Quaker, and Polytheist, but all were enraptured by a single thought, each was speaking to his Creator in his own way. On that evening I believe I was lifted more nearly heavenward than ever before.

Even though I am grateful for the new hiking companions, I am cautious about who I let into my life and adventures. In the past, I was naive about the dangers around me, not just in the desert itself, but in the company I chose. The words, "You can trust me," are just as likely to lead to disaster as they are to safety. Memorable mishaps include running out of food on a forty-mile backpacking trip; getting stuck in a canyon on a nineteen-degree night while wearing shorts; drinking unfiltered mud chased with the worst mezcal money can buy; and hitchhiking across Monument Valley on a logging truck, only to discover that the car waiting had been fully stripped and impounded. Prior to, or during, each instance, my gut told me to walk away before things went awry, so I am as much to blame for not being prepared or voicing my concerns. It was a rapid education in self-reliance, the dangers of dating in the desert, and that a good story or mystery uncovered is never worth my well-being.

On the first morning camped with Brent, our differences are perceptible. He gets up much earlier than me to start packing. I wake up and roll over, still in my sleeping bag, and brush my teeth right there. Living outside, especially when it's cold, has instilled habits of efficiency. I pack up quickly, but Brent is still meticulously laying out, reorganizing, and repacking his food, camera, and gear. He looks up at me and quips, "Are you in a hurry to get somewhere?" I suppose he has a point. We only need to cover six miles today. I set down my pack and sit down next to Phil in the sand and pull out my notebook.

I watch and take inventory of his gear pile, which is much larger than mine. Though I am not a "gearhead," my minimalism is the result of budget more than cutting weight. I make mental notes to update my first aid kit; buy myself an aluminum spork so that I can stop eating my food with sticks; and replace my dim headlamp, which I found at a trailhead last summer.

Bernheimer was criticized by his team for his heavy loads

that weighed upwards of two hundred pounds. He spent a lot of time and money to ensure he looked the part for his Wild West adventures, and typically packed starched button-up shirts, leather leggings, riding breeches, ties, a felt brimmed hat, a red wool sleep cap, and traditional pajamas. He adopted the cowboy style of wearing a cotton bandanna, which kept him cool if worn loose and provided "a cheering warmth over the entire body if tightened." In addition to his wardrobe, Bernheimer brought a humidor for his cigars and was known to pack a bit of whiskey, despite Prohibition.

Fully repacked, we hike slowly. Around a sharp bend, a massive alcove swallows us. I crane my neck up to admire the swirled ceiling of the amphitheater, overcome by this world of eroding stone. We exit the cave and follow the stream below, watching our footing on smooth water-polished stones, until something unusual catches both our eyes on a heavily varnished wall. We veer away from the stream to investigate. The script reads: "John Wetherill 5/26/1918." Back then, carving names into stone was de rigueur for cowboys and explorers as a form of record keeping. Today, we know it's vandalism.

Next to Wetherill's name, in faint scrawl, is another name: "Clyde Whiskers," and the date "July 18, 1975." Inscriptions over fifty years old are considered historic, so this one misses the mark, but I sense this is more intentional than graffiti. I look down at Phil, who is lying down and panting while enjoying the wall's shade. "Did you write this, Mr. Whiskers?" Phil wags his tail in response to his new trail name.

The warm midday sun reflects off the water in the creek. We drop our packs to sun ourselves on the slickrock, stretched out with the collared lizards. Phil curls up behind us in the warm sand. The murmur of water rolling over smooth stones lulls my eyes shut. The fine blonde hairs on my arm stand to attention and wake me as clouds drift in on a chilling breeze, cloaking the sun. I had momentarily forgotten the chill of winter, but the remedy, to pull on a jacket and greet it like a dear friend, is now forever ingrained.

Refreshed from the nap, we pick up our backpacks and hike through Surprise Valley. Navajo Mountain towers above, standing guard. I dash ahead and scramble off-trail, up a dome of slickrock to admire the scene from above. The creek runs across the valley, flush with green grasses, red Indian paintbrush wildflowers, and silky white sego lilies. We pass an old Diné hogan, cut logs stacked up against each other to create a shelter. It's a reminder of the Indigenous people who walked here long before tourists and who still call this home.

The 1921 expedition encountered several Diné families living throughout these canyons. Later they paid a visit to their guide Dogistlanibega's home site and melon patch. They watched his three children playfully herding sheep and goats. Next to the homesite, there was a playhouse and toys, including tiny handmade clay pots and bowls. Today, a few families still graze their animals here seasonally, while many others remain connected to their histories that live here.

Bernheimer commissioned Morris to write an article about the 1921 trip in *Natural History Magazine* titled, "An Unexplored Area of the Southwest." Considering that the families and children they encountered on the expedition were descendants of many generations of people who had already explored here, did Morris's title simply mean unexplored by scientific researchers? Even that is a stretch, as several research parties were focused on this area during the same era. Morris's article even acknowledges that this region was not unexplored, by describing old mining inscriptions. He also acknowledged that the Dominguez-Escalante Expedition, led by two Spanish Priests, and the Mormon Hole-in-the-Rock pilgrimage also passed this way. Perhaps "unexplored" was simply a buzzword that he hoped would engage readers who were unfamiliar with the desert. The words we select when we write about experiences in these landscapes mark the changing perspectives of generations. We still have a long ways to go.

- - - - -

Past Surprise Valley, the terrain descends from the montane piñon-juniper forests toward sleek, naked Navajo Sandstone. The temperature steadily rises. Spring is further along down here; the bare oak branches are sprouting green buds before our eyes. Warm air contrasts with the cool water splashing my feet as we enter a canyon known in Diné as *Tse'naniahi Bikooh*. The sheer orange walls swathed in deep rust-colored streaks swallow us, as ancient etchings of bighorn sheep lead us around the curves. Bernheimer described this canyon with such awe, that only by hiking here ourselves do we understand that he was not exaggerating,

> The entire nine or ten miles from Surprise Valley until the Bridge was reached, is a round of surprises. Bridge Canyon is continuously, awe-inspiring, deep, cavernous, and concaves some two hundred feet or deeper by two hundred to three hundred feet openings, and when that occurs on both sides, one has the effect of walking or riding in the inside of a sphere with but a slit left open above for the sky.

Phil looks back at me, his tail wagging to ask me why my pace lags. I dread the moment we will reach Lake Powell's backed-up waters. During the construction of the Glen Canyon dam in the 1950s, efforts were made to protect Rainbow Bridge from water damage. The case was bolstered by Rainbow Bridge's status as a cultural site, revered by the Diné, San Juan Southern Paiute Tribe, Kaibab Paiute Tribe, Hopi Tribe, Pueblo of Zuni, and Ute Mountain Ute Tribes. The efforts failed, and when the dam was completed in 1963, forty-six feet of water pooled beneath Rainbow Bridge at Lake Powell's highest water level.

Today, drought and evaporation have sucked the water in Lake Powell down to record-low levels, liberating this passageway to the bridge so that it looks almost as Bernheimer would have seen it. The trail traverses a glossy-pink bedrock channel flowing with crystalline water until we reach a wooden cattle gate that ushers us toward the national monument. As we near the 290-foot golden arc I crane my neck skyward to take in the full view.

Near the bridge, two copper plaques embedded directly into a red sandstone wall pay homage to Nasja Begay and Jim Mike, members of the San Juan Southern Paiute Tribe, for leading the first research trip to Rainbow Bridge. In 1909, two separate parties set off nearly simultaneously to reach the fabled site. The party formed by Professor Byron Cummings of the University of Utah was led by Nasja Begay and John Wetherill. A US government survey party led by William B. Douglass enlisted Paiute guide Jim Mike along the way.

Before their journeys even began, Cummings and Douglass already had a professional rivalry. Cummings was a self-taught archaeologist who made efforts to learn from local Indigenous people, while Douglass was a representative of progressive academic institutions. Ever the peacekeeper, Wetherill unified the teams when they crossed paths, and everyone proceeded together to Rainbow Bridge on August 14, 1909. Black-and-white photos show the men from both parties sitting together jovially as one team in front of Rainbow Bridge.

Afterward, Douglass and the media debated which party member "discovered" Rainbow Bridge. Meanwhile, Wetherill denied credit and later explained in a 1938 interview with *Desert Magazine*, "Nasja-begay—the Pahutes—led us to Rainbow Bridge. The Indians found it long before the white men came."

Wetherill's wife Louisa wrote that the dispute over the so-called discovery weighed heavily on her husband who disliked the pointless controversy. Burgeoning student archaeologist Neil M. Judd, of the Cummings party, acknowledged:

> I have often been asked how we first learned of Rainbow Bridge and who really discovered it. The real discoverer was some unknown Indian in the unrecorded past.

While the word *discovery* continues to be misused in its association with this piece of history and many similar accounts, the word itself is not inherently the problem. A discovery means, "to shed light upon something." That perspective makes space not only for the positive aspects of history and the world around us, but also for revealing the murky, darker things often left out of textbooks. In the age of technology, where so many "frontiers" have been reached, the opportunities to re-examine the past, the world, and ourselves are limitless—and so are the discoveries to be made.

Journalists and media have a pernicious affinity to use sensational headlines to capture the reader's attention. In 2018 an East Coast–based writer for *Men's Journal* interviewed me about my Bears Ears hiking guidebook. Upon publication, he included the ghastly title, "Meet the Woman Who Knows Bears Ears Best." The superlative was aimed at clickbait instead of what I actually said in the article: "I've seen a lot, but I also feel like I've seen nothing." Without question, if any group of people know this place the best, it is the Indigenous people whose ancestors have lived here since time immemorial. Knowing how insulting that title was to Indigenous people, I called the journalist in tears, demanding he change it. He refused.

In response, an op-ed in the *Salt Lake Tribune* criticized the journalist for exemplifying white privilege and erasing the experiences and knowledge of Indigenous people. I fully support her opinion and would never want to be associated with something like that. The sad thing is, I was not given a choice and yet was blamed for it. Even though the op-ed writer did not take issue with my interview responses, because once again the headline mentioned me, not the journalist, I was at the forefront of public criticism.

In the online media age, many publications aim for high click-through rates even if it sacrifices truth. And those decisions are rarely made by the writers themselves, but rather by those at the publication. I have learned to push back against harmful headlines assigned to my stories before publication, and the editors I continue to work with are very receptive and even grateful for the input.

- - - - -

In 1927 John Wetherill sought to help people discover the real story behind the 1909 Rainbow Bridge Expedition. He spearheaded an effort to honor Nasja Begay by installing a bronze plaque near the bridge. It took thirty-eight more years for the National Park Service to honor Jim Mike, when he was 104 years old. During the ceremony, they finally gave him the fifty dollars he was still owed by Douglass for his guiding services. His plaque was not installed next to Begay's until 1980, after Douglass had already passed.

The media recognition of the Cummings-Douglass Expedition placed Rainbow Bridge in the public eye and onto USGS maps, leading to its designation as a national monument. A few months later, Wetherill began guiding tourists to the bridge, the first being New Yorkers Robert B. Townsend and his sister Eleanor, who was one of six women to make the pilgrimage that year. Among the early celebrity visitors were President Theodore Roosevelt and author Zane Grey, with Bernheimer on their heels.

Rainbow Bridge was once a remote destination adventure, accessible only by adventurous travel by packtrain, river raft, or on foot. With the creation of Lake Powell reservoir, motorized boat tourism significantly increased its accessibility. In 2019, the National Park Service reported that 200,000–300,000 people reached Rainbow Bridge annually, mostly on a fifty-mile boat ride across Lake Powell from Wahweap Marina, near Page, Arizona. What was once earned by sweat and adventure by all involved, now simply requires one afternoon, an entrance fee, and a short one-mile walk. This ease of access looks to be challenged by declining lake levels, which will force continued extensions and maintenance of the boat ramp.

Though most who travel to Rainbow Bridge are unaware of this history, much of its popularity is still built upon the legend and lore associated with those early tourists one hundred years ago.

- - - - -

Rainbow Bridge inspired Bernheimer to spiral into contemplation of creation itself:

Imagine a structure so massive that the evolution of the ages have merely brought to the surface its muscular structure, divesting of its weak and useless particles....How did this all happen? What forces were at work and how did these apply their cyclopean strength?...Here the earth ball is in complete nakedness, an open textbook of creation.

To help me learn more about Rainbow Bridge, Harvey Leake connected me with his friend Leo Manheimer, a Diné hiking guide who has spent four decades living and exploring around Navajo Mountain and Glen Canyon. Manheimer says that Rainbow Bridge is one of the cornerstones of Diné religion. These beliefs are so sacred that they are rarely spoken of, even among the Diné. Some knowledge can only be shared at certain times of the year.

As a young boy growing up in the Shonto and Inscription House chapters of the Navajo Nation, Manheimer listened to his grandfather Mike Calamity, a medicine man, tell stories and prayers about Rainbow Bridge, called *Tse'naa Na'ni'ahi* or *Na'nizhoozhi* in Diné. Yet it wasn't until adulthood, when he moved to Navajo Mountain with his wife, that Manheimer made the pilgrimage.

He took his first backpacking trip to the sacred rainbow in 1979, carrying a wool blanket and plastic bags filled with canned food down the Rainbow Trail. That was the same year that Harvey Leake first hiked there, although it took several decades for their paths to cross. The experience changed the course of Manheimer's life, and he has guided hikers to Rainbow Bridge ever since. Manheimer insists, "I've experienced it by boat and by land. And personally, there's more reverence in being able to do it on foot. [When] you go by boat, you miss all of the scenery—the high vistas, the nice mesas, the canyons, the water."

For our efforts on foot, Brent and I are rewarded with a quiet afternoon alone at Rainbow Bridge. Standing at the foot of the rainbow, its curvature frames Navajo Mountain, still covered in snow, contrasted against a cloudless cobalt sky. I admire the pathway of wind, water, and time that shaped Rainbow Bridge and the landscape surrounding it.

Bernheimer and his men camped near the bridge, which is not allowed today, so we walk back to where Phil is lying in the shade, patiently awaiting our return, because dogs are not allowed within the monument. He greets us, and we hike to Echo Camp, once used by tourists and cowboys. Today it's still outfitted with the same rusty wireframe cots and an old pantry next to a campfire ring. It's a little creepy, but since there is nearby water, we decide to stay the night.

We joke about the camp being haunted as we lie on our bedrolls and listen to the guttural cries of toads calling. Phil digs a shallow dog bed nearby under a juniper tree. I pull out my copy of *Rainbow Bridge*. Bernheimer reflected that his last look at Rainbow Bridge during that trip was so sentimental he could not find the words to put down on paper. I do not write anything down either. Nor do I want to think of the hike back to the Jeep. My mind is already dreaming of more exploration here.

CHAPTER FIVE

The Other Side of the Mountain

The month of June 1922, saw us once more on the trail: a paradise for the fault-finder, for here he would have plenty to find fault with, in the 'Land that God forgot.'
—Charles L. Bernheimer

Determined to put his name on the map, Bernheimer returned to Rainbow country in 1922 with a lofty goal to find a southern route to the bridge so he could then circumnavigate Navajo Mountain. Along the way, he noticed that his "new trail" already appeared to be in use:

In a few places we found stones where nature would not have placed them. They must have been so arranged by human hands at some time in the dim past. They were indicative of direction but not of any footing passable at the present time.

Leo Manheimer thinks these trails may date back to the Basketmaker and Ancestral Pueblo eras, and that they continued to be used by the local Paiute and Diné people, who likely improved them during what is known as "The Fearing Times" or "The Long Walk." In 1863 and 1864 the US cavalry, led by Kit

Carson, forcibly marched ten thousand Diné people upwards of four hundred miles from their Four Corners homeland to concentration camps at Fort Sumner and the Bosque Redondo Reservation in New Mexico. A bold band of some two dozen Navajo led by headman Hoskinnini, meaning "The Angry One," evaded capture by residing in the canyons behind Navajo Mountain. Hoskinnini was the father of Hoskinnini Begay who later befriended the Wetherills in Kayenta.

Bernheimer clearly did not discover a new route, but his writing did popularize it. He hoped it would become the primary trail to Rainbow Bridge. Within two years the Richardson brothers, traders on the Navajo Nation, built Rainbow Lodge at the trailhead and hired Diné men to blast a road to it. They advertised their tours and accommodations to tourists with the promise: "Yours may be the great adventure but for a fraction of the time and money expended by the famous [Bernheimer] expedition." At one hundred dollars a pop, it was still not an affordable vacation for most people.

Within a few decades Rainbow Lodge diminished in popularity, and it burned down in 1951. Today its dilapidated foundation and fallen walls mark the start of "The Bernheimer Trail," which Bernheimer considered less fatiguing. I am calling his bluff—the terrain is rough and steep.

One week after our first trip to Rainbow Bridge, Brent and Phil follow behind me up Bernheimer's steep and shadeless trail. We talk very little, and sweat a lot. The view from the other side of the mountain spans an expanse of hypnotic canyons casting their spell on me, assuring that I will never tire of these desert explorations.

At the top of Yabut Pass, the saddle that rides between Navajo Mountain and the adjacent mesa, we stop in the shade to rest and eat cold pizza wrapped in tinfoil. I offer the crust to Phil, who snatches it out of my hand. Instead of eating it, he digs a small hole, sets the crust down on the ground, and carefully covers it and tamps the dirt down with his nose. I call out with laughter, "Hey, I would have eaten that, Phil!"

It's all downhill after lunch. The descent into *Nizaadninah Bikooh*, Diné for "the long uphill canyon," drops 2,500 feet. Significant rockfall makes for tricky footing on the loose slope, and it is hard to imagine getting twenty pack mules and seven saddle horses down such a precipitous rock jumble. Bernheimer noted that total concentration was required on the descent, along with full trust in his horses, Carrie Ann and General Lee.

Our mouths are as dry as the sand beneath our feet, and we are already out of water. Bernheimer's notes caution us that we will not reach water until the bottom of this drop, a full eight miles from the trailhead. I sure hope he is right. The trail flattens out into a wash, and I focus my eyes down on the dry creekbed. The thirsty minutes drag on, until relief sparkles from a pool of water surrounded by tall grasses. Bounding woodhouse toads and buzzing mosquitoes abound in this thriving, isolated ecosystem. Phil lies down in the water while we gulp down several cups each and refill our bottles. The sheer 2,000-foot wall of No Name Mesa to our left offers welcome shade from the intense midday sun.

Well watered, we hike for a few more miles, until it is obvious that we have reached Bernheimer's "Painted Rock Camp." We set up our tent on a sandy clearing surrounded by piñons and junipers, next to the creek. My shoulders relax in relief, and I take a moment to sit down and let my bones sink into the earth.

Following our trip to Rainbow Bridge two weeks ago, my finicky Jeep tried to convince me to stay near Navajo Mountain. I limped it to the Inscription House gas station, where word about my situation spread quickly. Local Diné guys with toolboxes, transmission fluid, and curious eyes trickled in to help. A man named Stan generously suggested I marry his brother as a solution. "You could live here and drive his Kawasaki motorcycle! He has many cows and goats, too." He was surprised that I turned him down.

With the Jeep moving again, Brent urged me to come back to Colorado with him. I wanted to stay in the desert, but I knew something was very wrong with the Jeep. My fingers gripped the steering wheel tightly the entire drive, and I hoped that I would not need to reverse, or use second and fourth gears. Once across the state line, the Jeep completely quit on me. I learned that I needed a new transmission and that the repair timeline was unknown.

I have been camped indoors with Brent and Phil ever since. The abrupt shift to being indoors after choosing to live this winter outdoors is hard to swallow. Surrounded by domestic comforts, fancy cocktails, and gourmet dinners, I find myself contemplating, "Do I want to live like this?" It's hard to know if it is the environment or the new relationship with Brent that makes me question this. It feels like a rushed, if not forced, way to get to know someone.

With plenty of remaining daylight, we leave our packs at Painted Rock Camp and set out to explore. A set of colorful images painted on a sleek orange wall beckons us to admire an ancient art gallery—human figures drawn in shades of yellow and red ochre. One has a perfectly round face adorned by what looks like a feather. The others are headless bodies with V-shaped chests and intricate designs. There is even a tiny red dog. Perhaps a family portrait of a pack that once dwelled here.

Past the panel, the canyon abruptly narrows. We ascend steep switchbacks up Redbud Pass, which Bernheimer named for the small trees now bursting with regal purple flowers as they do every spring. This trail was constructed by the 1922 team to reach Rainbow Bridge. What Bernheimer does not mention, or perhaps did not know, is that this pass already was well traveled and had a name, *Tsegiizh At'iin*, meaning "trail through a rock crevice." Based upon Wetherill's correspondence with Bernheimer before the trip, I gather that he saw an opportunity to use his financier's funding to make improvements. The magic of the way Wetherill guided clients was in withholding some details to increase their sense of adventure, and in letting them make discoveries from their own experiences.

For five days, Bernheimer's squadron worked to widen the trail using TNT and dynamite to blast a passage wide enough for pack animals. The use of explosives was his team's idea, but initially it did not appeal to Bernheimer, who was concerned about injuring the horses and mules hauling the materials. While the men worked, Bernheimer served as general contractor at the job site, taking in the scenery while everyone else broke a sweat. Among his efforts, he chiseled "Bernheimer Trail" into the sandstone wall near the pass that was completed on July 5, 1922. The completion of the pass allowed Bernheimer to attain his goal of reaching Rainbow Bridge from the south and connecting it with the North Rainbow Trail.

On this trip we do not plan to continue to the bridge; instead, we are devoting this trip to exploring our surroundings near camp. I periodically open up Bernheimer's book to compare images and notes with my surroundings. Without that insight, a passage like Redbud would not hold the same significance. We are walking through a story, written by nature and humans, in the earth's history book.

Last light funnels into Redbud's stone hallway like a warm spotlight. Free of the coats and layers I was burrowed in all winter, I press my bare skin against the blood-red sandstone wall. I am at home between two walls, not four. The final embers of evening light fade, and we head back down the pass to camp.

- - - - -

I open my eyes and look up at orange sandstone and azure skies overhead. A smile stretches across my face. I roll over, stand up, and walk over to the creek to scoop up water in my cooking pot. The first round is boiled for coffee, then we experiment with cooking a new breakfast, dehydrated hashbrowns and gravy. We sit in the grass and share the hearty, salt-laden meal. There is no hurry to our movements this morning.

Bernheimer loved to indulge in what he called "camp loafing," which afforded him more time to write than the busy days of packing up camp and covering miles. On the 1922 trip he volunteered to loaf at camp with Johnson, who had an injured leg:

> In this, I was perhaps a bit selfish, for I knew camp loafing is no sacrifice, that it has a peculiar charm all its own....I explored every nook and corner of the ancient lair and for diversion watched the circular traps of the antlions or the polliwogs and water-beetles in the rock pool.

During the layover, Bernheimer dreamed up a story about a petrified wood chip, written in the style of a bizarre bedtime story he may have told to his daughters at home in Manhattan. Whenever I pick up a striated piece of fossilized wood glinting in the sunlight, I am humbled by the story it tells of a once living tree memorialized as stone over the course of a million years.

We decide to walk off our full bellies by following the creek downstream. The walls surrounding us narrow, and the ground transitions from silky sand to sculpted bedrock. Water flows through fluted pink sandstone and over a pour over, cascading into a pool below. The water serenading us with the sound of the canyon being shaped by water. When Bernheimer's team reached an impasse in these narrows, they observed logs jammed into the rocks to assist passage, an ancient canyoneering method still used today. The drop looks too tricky to bypass with Phil, so we turn around and head back to camp.

- - - - -

Our neighbors, the painted human figures, greet us when we

return to camp at dusk. They watch us set up our tent and boil water from the creek. In between slurps of ramen noodles, I crane my neck skyward and let my eyes climb the impenetrable fortress of Cliff Canyon until they reach the top of No Name Mesa.

Wetherill observed a faint set of ancient steps cut into the rock at the base of this mesa and was obsessed with his hypothesis that ancient people once inhabited it. On July 7, 1922, the team doggedly scouted and pursued several dead ends. Bernheimer wrote:

> We climbed on one baldhead after another....Resting in the shade we noted a deep gash to the west of us in the rock and decided that this was a better route to take than the one Wetherill and Morris had chosen. We had a general panoramic view (I made sketches in all directions) and thought before any such enterprise as ours is undertaken, just such survey is essential in advance of all else.

Equipped with some ropes, a bit of water, and handpicks, Johnson bravely led the group to a chimney-like gap filled in by boulders, with just enough space for a man to squeeze through. They dubbed the portal Johnson's Hole.

The following morning, the determined trio of Wetherill, Morris, and Jess Smith set off for another attempt. Johnson, Al Smith, and Hosteen Chee stayed at camp with Bernheimer, who lounged in the shade at Johnson's Hole and carved "American Museum of Natural History, New York, 1922 Expedition" on the wall.

The men returned at seven in the evening covered in blood. Bernheimer's book includes a photo of Morris's pants ripped to shreds. What is known to have happened within those eleven adventurous hours is limited to this vague secondhand account from Bernheimer, who recorded their post-climb debrief:

There were countless awkward holes in the chimney-like cleft which they had to squeeze through besides dodging falling rocks, sliding fifty feet at times down steep and slanting grooves where foothold was impossible. Without a drop of water, no food except a box of seedless raisins, they had finally reached the top of No Name Mesa only to be disappointed. They found no trace of man prehistoric, historic, or contemporary, ever having been there. There was nothing but the suggestion of an ancient cairn.

The incongruity in the report drives my curiosity wild. The cairn reveals an undeniable human presence on the mesa.

Author David Roberts further nudged my intrigue about No Name Mesa. We met a few weeks ago at the Celebrate Cedar Mesa event in Bluff, Utah. After getting to know David and his wife Sharon over drinks at their rental house, they invited me to stay with them for a week.

Each day, David and I got up early to write and then sat down again in the evening with a glass of rosé or an IPA. During the day, David and Sharon drove me around Bears Ears, while David pointed out his favorite sights. His wide-eyed gaze exuded his understanding that the trip could be his last one as he battled cancer. Our conversation topics oscillated between writing and Southwest adventurers, including Bernheimer. Afterward we stayed in touch, and his correspondence instilled a sense of urgency in me to tackle some of Bernheimer's adventures. In one email he wrote:

Matt (Hale), Vaughn (Hadenfeldt), and I spent an exhausting and exhilarating day NOT finding a way up No Name. The first chimney we tried is the one the guys got up in 1922. We shoulda pushed it! Despite their report, I'm convinced there's something on top. Tell Brent to quit his job.

(Job?) Life is too short not to plumb No Name Mesa. I don't know anybody who's been on top. You could do it.

There is not enough time for us to explore No Name Mesa on this trip. As we gawk at the massive wall, my curiosity is fixated on more than a way to get there—I want to see what is on top. There is only one way to find out.

CHAPTER SIX

Torn Up Pants Mesa

To turn back was impossible. Confronting us was the unknown.
—Charles L. Bernheimer

I look down into the vortex of intersecting rock faults and joints. It's hard to make any sense of the jumble, like standing too close to an oil painting. I take a step back, and the puzzle looks much clearer. There is one passageway that might lead to the summit of No Name Mesa.

The November air is brisk. Hints of the first snowstorm prod my sense of urgency. I have been gone for too long. In the months since the spring trips to the Rainbow Bridge, writing assignments have pulled me far away from canyon country, to Boston, the Middle Fork of the Salmon River, Patagonia, and Tahiti. Even on tropical beaches and glacial fjords, I dreamt of the desert. These pangs signaled clearly where I wanted to go home to after my travels.

It is a relief to look up once again at No Name Mesa in the twilight. It has remained the primary objective I have been itching to take on this fall. Brent is less enthused about my sense of urgency. I told him that I would be fine going on my own or with another friend. In response he squirmed and shifted directions, insisting I go with him and no one else.

Now because of his schedule constraints, we only have three days. There will not be any camp loafing on this trip. For dinner we quickly eat powdered mashed potatoes while we make sure our gear is in order. I accept that if we don't have something we need to reach the top, it means we are probably not on the right route. We smash puffy down jackets into our packs among our minimal snacks and water. The provisions seem sufficient, considering that in 1922 the guys only brought a box of seedless raisins.

The two-person tent is too big without Phil laying at our feet. We left him behind with friends just in case No Name Mesa requires climbing moves harder than a doggy climbing grade of 5.10. Tucked into our down sleeping bags, we laugh about his buried pizza crust. When we hiked back up to Yabut Pass on our last trip here, Phil remembered exactly where he left his snack, dug it up, shook the dirt off, and then proudly ate it.

I turn off my headlamp and fall asleep swiftly, knowing the mystery of what awaits on top will finally be out of my head and into my own hands.

- - - - -

The air temperature drops ten degrees when we veer into the narrow, shaded chasm lined with bare-limbed Redbud trees. I zip my jacket up higher with gloved hands. My toes are as useful as ice cubes in my boots, and I cannot feel them as I hop over the boulders strewn between the walls.

We reach the dead-end rock jumble that forms Johnson's Hole. I scour possible perches from which Bernheimer spent a day carving his preposterously long expedition memorial. This should be our most obvious clue that we are heading the right way, yet we cannot find it. This contributes to our already lingering doubts about the path ahead, stemming from another significant discrepancy. Bernheimer's book *Rainbow Bridge* and his 1923 article in *National Geographic* magazine contain different photos labeled "Johnson's Hole." With both images in hand, we compare them to our location. In the book, the angle of the stones look similar to this spot, but it is not an exact match. The photo in *National Geographic* mirrors exactly where we are standing right now.

Morris, the skinniest man on the trip, made the first attempt to squeeze through the hole. The opening is so small that I must slither up through it without my pack. My head pokes out the other side into the sunlight. I squeal, "It goes!"

We push and pull the packs through one at a time. I try to ignore visions of being crushed by the precariously piled boulders. On the other side of Johnson's Hole, the gap between the walls is so narrow that I can touch both sides by outstretching my arms and legs. As Brent takes a wide step across the frigid pools, his pants rip in half at the seams. "Way to keep this historically accurate," I laugh. The Diné name for No Name Mesa is *Tł'aaji'ee' Nahasdlaad Dah'azkani*, and is also called "the torn up pants mesa." How many people besides Earl Morris have torn their pants here too?

I awkwardly pull myself up between chockstones, and then stem between the closely spaced walls. It's a relief to have both feet planted on firm ground. Once my nerves settle, I am surprised that we are suddenly at our junction. The steep passageway is filled with loose rock and tops out between two sheer cliffs. It looks counterintuitive to take this route to reach the summit and we head in the opposite direction.

As we slog our way up the loose scree, rocks tumble down behind us. Deep breaths expel my fear, and sweat dripping from my brow obscures my vision. We traverse a narrow, exposed ledge, as wide as two feet placed together. Neither of us slips, falls, or sheds blood like the 1922 team. I worry this might mean the worst is still ahead. With our heads down, we press on. At the saddle, we momentarily pause to catch our breath. There is no way to see what is next until we shimmy around the wall to see what awaits us. A moment like this is only a brief celebration—we have a long uphill walk ahead.

Along the flanks of the summit slope, we take a short break to chug water and devour gummy bears, pretzels, and chunks of cheese. We are grateful to have more than raisins. I gaze across Lake Powell, and my imagination soars over the bronzed waves of Glen Canyon, to the confluence of the once free-flowing Colorado and San Juan rivers. Despite the adventure we are on in new terrain, the view incites a desire to hike farther still.

Near the summit, I must use my hands to balance gingerly on insecure boulder piles. We move slow, one step at a time. I do not know that I am on the summit of No Name Mesa until I look up from the ground and across the mesa top stretching before me. The topography of No Name Mesa is rolling, with a slight upward tilt. At its center are two ridgelines composed of gargoylian, darkly varnished stone blocks, striped across the mesa like a dragon's back.

We now hold the key to this fortress frozen in time. If there are truly no artifacts here, I might just curse myself forever for placing my feet on No Name Mesa's unblemished soil, surrounded by dams, highways, coal power plants, and uranium mines. In the lair between the ridges, we enter into a forested piñon-juniper valley where I spot an unusual pile of rocks. I gasp, "It's the ancient cairn!"

In *Rainbow Bridge,* Bernheimer details Wetherill's disappointment in only finding what looked like an ancient cairn atop No Name. But doesn't a cairn indicate that humans passed this way? Why did it not instigate further investigation? Were they completely jaded by more dramatic archaeological finds?

If this is indeed the same cairn that they spotted, I'm impressed that it still stands almost one hundred years later. The square blocks of stone, descending in size, are neatly piled on top of one another in an unusual style. The moss-covered edges hint at its antiquity. We find two more cairns, directly across from each other on either side of the mesa. Their alignment adds to the sense that they were not built here by accident. Beneath them are the sheer walls of No Name Mesa. As we continue walking along the ridgeline, we come across a collapsed cairn. Did Morris and Wetherill even explore this far? My mind drifts away from the Bernheimer team's nonchalance to my own questions of who built these cairns; when; and why. It's a mystery to me, but the cairns offer assurance that there is an answer.

We walk the full perimeter and down the center of No Name Mesa. By midafternoon, the clouds building tell us a winter storm is closing in. We decide to make our way down, in hopes we can get back to camp before dark. I curse the short winter days and tempestuous weather. It would be nice to camp up here tonight considering the effort we made. Brent forges on, and I lag, as I tend to do when I want to linger in a special place.

Colorful flakes on the ground catch my eyes. I stop to kneel down and take a closer look. Morris reported that he did not find any potsherds or lithic flakes up here, but at my feet lithics are scattered all around, chipped from red chert, orange agate, and clear quartz glinting in the sunlight. It seems impossible that Wetherill and Morris could have missed this. Or did they consider details this small irrelevant? In the 1920s these scattered fragments of stone from making projectiles were considered inconsequential and were rarely documented on survey maps with more than a dot.

A few minutes later we spot an old, faded pull-tab Coca-Cola can. Tucked beneath a fallen log and partially covered in dirt, its once red logo is now only faintly recognizable. The lid style dates the can roughly to the 1970s, and the can's presence tells us that someone else has been up here. Either that, or it was carried up by a raven—they do like shiny objects!

So much for David's theory that no one had been on top of No Name Mesa since 1922. It's not unlike Wetherill's belief that no one had been up there since ancient times. Perhaps this was simply a theatrical play by Wetherill, keeping his mouth shut to entertain Bernheimer with the belief that his team made a "first ascent."

Sensational titles helped Bernheimer's magazine articles keep pace alongside tales of adventures from that era's famous explorers, including "First Crossing of the Polar Sea," "Ascending Mt. Blanc," and "Sailing the Seven Seas in the Interest of Science." The words "first," "discover," "unknown," and "unexplored" were used liberally back then. They might be the 1920s version of "epic," "adventure," and "gnarly," which are similarly used to hyperbolize outdoor activities today in order to excite readers, secure publication, and increase revenue.

Bernheimer unabashedly wrote about his desire to feel like a true explorer and a peaceful conqueror. All of this is deeply entrenched in the man versus nature ethos that is often associated with, but not limited to, wealthy white men in their pursuit of exploration and adventure. Bernheimer exemplifies this sentiment when he writes about his desire to be the "first white man" to travel to certain parts of the desert. Although Bernheimer acknowledged the presence of Indigenous people there before him, in the tradition of American adventure literature, he glorified the importance of a white person showing up thousands of years later. David's prompt, no doubt adopted from his mountaineering experiences, for me to be the "next person" to reach the top is of the same tradition.

Modern English is influenced by the fundamentally racist foundations of the language. This violent dialect remains omnipresent in sports, adventure, and exploration, where words like "killing it" and "domination" and talk of "destroying" one's opponent are commonplace, even on the elementary school playground. No matter how we perceive ourselves, language influences our emotions, attitudes, and actions. Word choices can desensitize us to violence and trauma, past and present. We must choose to see this for what it is, if it is ever going to change.

I question our motives to climb No Name Mesa. It was sat-isfying to confirm the presence of human marks here, but we are not archaeologists trained to use that information. In the big picture, seeing the top has no more benefit to the world than climbing a remote peak. We climbed, we left our footprints, and we left. Why have I been so obsessed with doing this all year? What do we gain and do with this experience? How does it ben-efit anyone else or the land itself? I suppose contemplating the purpose of our presence is a piece of the puzzle.

On the way down, a rock rolls under my foot. I catch myself from slipping, throw down my pack and sit down to rest and drink some water. Something white blinks at me in the black-brush. I kneel down onto the ground to get a closer look. A white projectile point stands out against the red soil. With a gentle tug, I pick it up to caress its scalloped edges and T-shaped head. There are points all over the desert, but to me, this one is precious. I let it linger in my hands before placing it back into its impression.

CHAPTER SEVEN

Writing On the Wall

It was the desert we grew to love so well, the strange and desolate, the mysterious and colorful desert with its scorching heat and bitter cold. Its loneliness, its siren beauty haunts me now.
—Clyde Kluckhohn

Deep breaths steady my nerves as my fingertips grip ancient, shallow hand- and toeholds chiseled into stone. Once my feet are firmly planted inside the cave, the words "Clyde W," written in charcoal, stare back at me from the curved wall. I turn to look over the edge of the cliff, and yelp down to Phil, "Mr. Whiskers—I found your name again!" He wags his tail and continues to whine, as he does every time he watches me climb up something without him.

I now dream up imaginative tales about "the legend of Clyde Whiskers" while I hike. Maybe he was a bored sheepherder or a bandit escaping the law; maybe he just wanted to practice his signature. I have seen his name before, far to the north on some boulders relatively close to Camp Snowball. Though I only glanced at the name then, it etched itself in my mind. Sometimes it takes a while to understand why certain details stick with us and others do not. If only the writings on the walls could talk and tell us their stories.

The first time I saw Clyde Whiskers's name, I figured it was just graffiti, as is so common across the Southwest. But then the name repeatedly appeared on trailside boulders and on more canyon walls. One rendition reads, "Clyde Whiskey Bottle," another simply says "Clybe." Vandalism tends to be a singular occurrence—two lovers carving their initials in stone or a drunk houseboater memorializing his spring break. Instead, the frequency and time span hint at something different. In Clyde's defense, the earliest of his inscriptions are dated within the fifty-year cutoff that deems them historic objects rather than vandalism. Each time I see Clyde's name, or John Wetherill's, or an ancient handprint, I contemplate what it is about human nature that compels us to leave our physical mark on the world around us.

To attempt to find out, I send out an email search party for Clyde Whiskers.

Within an hour, the phone rings—it's a call from Logan Hebner, the author of *Southern Paiute: A Portrait*. He recounts his brief encounters with Clyde during that project, before redirecting our conversation: "To understand anything about Clyde Whiskers, you need to understand what happened to the San Juan Southern Paiutes."

The San Juan Southern Paiute homeland spans the Utah-Arizona border, from south of the San Juan River in Utah to north and east of the Little Colorado River in Arizona. For a portion of every year, the San Juan Southern Paiutes traditionally traveled along a loop starting near present-day Tuba City, Arizona, and encompassing the land between Navajo Mountain and White Mesa, Douglas Mesa, and Allen Canyon to the north—areas within and surrounding Bears Ears National Monument. The migration around their 9,000 square miles of territory allowed for hunting, foraging, and protection.

The Paiute Strip was designated by the US government as an official reservation for the Tribe in 1907, but this recognition was temporary. In the 1920s, the Paradise Oil & Refining Company began prospecting for oil in the region and lobbied to eliminate the Paiute Strip as a reservation in the 1920s. Secretary of the Interior Albert Fall officially removed the San Juan Southern Paiute title to the reservation to allow drilling for oil in 1922. Fall was later convicted and jailed for taking bribes from oil companies in exchange for leases on federal lands during the Teapot Dome scandal. This land grab occurred when the San Juan Paiutes were away from their seasonal territory because the government incorrectly assumed that no one inhabited it.

This land grab overlooked that the San Juan Southern Paiutes are some of the region's most tenured present-day Indigenous inhabitants. Bernardo de Miera y Pacheco of the Domínguez-Escalante Expedition was the first European to document the San Juan Paiutes in 1776. The Paiutes may have been here as early as AD 1300, and archaeologist Christy Turner said it is reasonable to think that the Paiutes on the north side of Navajo Mountain lived contemporaneously with the Ancestral Pueblo. The San Juan Southern Paiute people hold no oral history of ever living anywhere else.

The Diné migration into the Navajo Mountain area is punctuated by The Fearing Times, when the remote canyons provided refuge for people avoiding capture by US cavalry. Many Diné families recount stories of their ancestors being here much earlier, which is also indicated by tree-ring data derived from hogans on Black Mesa. When the captive Diné were released from Fort Sumner in 1868, the folks hiding out at Navajo Mountain were well established, which attracted an influx of people looking to rebuild their lives.

During this time, the Paiutes were strained by the Mormons settling on their homelands. Firearms often intensified disagreements, and the minority Paiutes were often discriminated against by the overwhelming presence of white, Diné and Southern Ute people. At this time, some Paiutes were assigned to the

Weeminuche Reservation, but two small bands of Paiutes and Utes in San Juan County led by Posey and Polk preferred to continue living nomadically. As a result, they did not receive federal government rations, and accounts by Mormon ranchers claim that the band often killed and ate the rancher's cows to survive.

In a more extreme case, Polk's son Tse-ne-gat was accused of murdering a sheepherder who had quit his job and was traveling with a substantial sum of cash. It took the local Sheriff a year to locate and arrest Tse-ne-gat. The attempts to arrest him led to a standoff between San Juan County and the Polk-Posey band, igniting the Posey War, or what is known to some as "The Last Indian War" in 1923. When the two convicted men escaped from their sentencing, the San Juan County Sheriff rounded up all the Paiutes and Utes in the Polk-Posey band and held them captive in corrals and in the Blanding school basement. Posey, the leader of the band, escaped on horseback and was chased down by the sheriff and other Mormon locals to the edge of Comb Ridge.

There are countless versions of this tale, but it was first explained to me by a seventy-year-old Monticello local, who was riding an ORV past my campsite. He pointed to the top of the sandstone monocline above Camp Snowball. Legend goes that Posey rode his horse straight down the cliff, where there was a faint stock trail led to the bottom of Comb Wash. As he raced with his horse down the trail, his pursuers shot him in his rear end. Posey kept riding and hid out in a cave, where he perished. However, the version told by Jim Mike, one of the Paiute guides on the 1909 Rainbow Bridge Expedition, explains that Posey escaped without any wounds and was later poisoned. Mike said that the bullet wounds were inflicted posthumously, "so they could make a history out of it or something."

Unrest about the Paiute Strip continued throughout the 1920s, as the federal government increasingly considered annexing it to the Navajo Nation, who wanted to extend their livestock grazing range. Before the 1929 Expedition, Bernheimer and his team attended a meeting at a hotel in Blanding to discuss and protest the future status of the Paiute Strip. Bernheimer was in the early stages of proposing a national park that encompassed portions of the Paiute Strip, Glen Canyon, and Rainbow Bridge on the Navajo Nation. He thought the park held a better chance of designation if the Paiute Strip remained in the public domain. Both he and Wetherill also felt that the Navajo Nation's aim to extend their grazing range was based upon flawed planning, and that the range could not sustain such increased impacts.

The debate dragged on for years, with meetings held between the Navajo Tribal Council, the Bureau of Indian Affairs, and the United States federal government. The San Juan Southern Paiute Tribe was notably not included in these discussions, in part because they were frequently on the move traveling long distances. The Diné maintained a more centralized lifestyle, grazing their sheep locally, and were more experienced in dealing with the white man's politics. A young Diné student who had returned from the Sherman Indian School even wrote a petition to the federal government to return the land, positioned as a social justice movement for the local tribes.

In 1930 the federal government ceased to recognize the San Juan Southern Paiutes as an official tribe. Then in 1933 and 1934, the former Paiute Strip and other Paiute Tribal homelands were annexed to the Navajo Reservation, "for the benefit of the Navajo and such other Indians." The new legal document erased, on paper, the Paiute's and, for a time, the Hopi Tribe's legal rights to their land. The San Juan Paiutes returned home after their migration season to find Diné families coming to their homes and telling them to leave, with federal backing to do so.

However, "such other Indians," does refer to the Paiutes, and it means they have a legal right to occupy this land, as determined by a federal court. Today, the San Juan Southern Paiutes still do not have reservation lands that are exclusively their own.

Tribal lawyer Robyn Interpreter explained to me, "I don't like to refer to the Paiutes as reservation-less, because they have a legal right to be on the lands that were added to the Navajo reservation in 1933 and 1934. The problem they suffer from is that the Navajo Nation does not want to recognize their rights, and they are still treated as second-class people within the Navajo Reservation system."

In 2000 the San Juan Southern Paiute Tribe signed a historic treaty with the Navajo Nation that would grant them 5,400 acres of land that would not disturb Diné homes and businesses. The treaty has still not been enacted. The hold-up: the treaty must receive official acknowledgment by the US government through congressional legislation. Today most San Juan Southern Paiutes live on the Navajo Nation at Willow Springs and Tuba City, Arizona, or near Navajo Mountain, Utah.

Logan Hebner recorded Paiute oral stories about this, including those told by the deceased Bessie Owl, who lamented:

> It really bothers me sometimes, how we lost this land to the Navajo. This land, it's not Navajo; it's Paiute. I don't consider it as a Navajo reservation. It's a lease, a lease from the government, that's how I think of it. I wonder about it, always think about how we would ever get the land back, get a reservation of our own. I was happy when we were recognized as the San Juan Tribe. My husband and I went over to be a part of it. It was a happy moment. But after we got recognized, the Navajo only gave us a little portion of land because they were grazing it.

Many of the Paiutes Hebner interviewed did not speak English, but Clyde Whiskers did, and he helped translate. Clyde was one of the few Paiutes with a cell phone, and, Logan remembers, "He'd call me late at night about his frustrations about what happened to his band of San Juan Southern Paiutes." He was an outspoken member of the Tribal Council and was instrumental in their regaining tribal recognition in 1989. Clyde even carried an embossed calling card proclaiming: "Let It Be Known by All That Clyde Whiskers Is A Member of The San Juan Tribal Council."

"So why do you think Clyde signed his name so much?" I ask Logan.

Without a pause he muses, "I don't really know, so I'm just making shit up, but perhaps he felt like the Paiute names were being erased from history and erased from the land."

I recall one carved on a boulder near Camp Snowball that states in bold letters, "CLYDE WHISKERS SAN JUAN SOUTHERN PAIUTE TRIBE."

Beyond the writing on the wall, the answers I seek about Clyde Whiskers will not be found in any history books, but there is one archive that holds promise. My search takes me north to the offices of the Utah State Historical Society in Salt Lake City, housed in the former Rio Grande Depot train station, built in 1897. Today it is a museum and archive of Utah government and historical documents, including the only file created for Clyde Whiskers. Inside, I spend forty-five minutes explaining to the bookkeeper that her computer catalog is wrong. There is indeed a file for Clyde Whiskers, compiled and stored by James (Jim) Knipmeyer, a historian who specializes in Colorado Plateau historic inscriptions pre-dating 1900. He also took an uncanny interest in the modern mystery of Clyde Whiskers.

The curator rallies one of her colleagues, and after another lengthy round of digging, they roll up a massive cart piled with boxes and wish me good luck. I have fifteen minutes to look for the file before the building closes. I race the clock, navigating the files with tunnel vision, confident in my eyes—if I can find this name etched into obscure sandstone walls, I can pick it out on a labeled manila file folder. My eyes latch onto the folder labeled "Clyde Whiskers," and my heart leaps in the same way it does when I see this name in the desert. I look at the clock and run to the scanner—I'll copy the documents now and sift through them later.

Outside the building, I sit down on a bench to examine my photocopies. Within the folder is a list of known Clyde Whiskers inscriptions, the details, dates, and locations spanning forty-nine years—a lifetime among these canyons.

But I still want to know more about Clyde Whiskers. For the sake of a complete investigation, if not closure, I dig up a phone number for the San Juan Southern Paiute Tribal Council. The phone rings, and a receptionist picks up.

"Hi, my name is Morgan Sjogren, and I am working on a story about one of the former members of your Tribal Council. I'm wondering if you can help me locate any records or connect me with anyone who possibly knew him." I am relieved that my nervous and unusual inquiry comes out intelligibly.

"Hmmm, well, that's not my job. Who are you looking for? Maybe I can help you."

"Clyde Whiskers."

The woman immediately snickers, "Oh, Clyde. Yeah, he's still around."

"Wait, like you mean he's still alive?" Imagine her confusion in hearing my excitement that some guy she sees walking around Tuba City all the time is still living. She confirms that it's true, and I thank her profusely. I put down my phone and start packing the Jeep.

The highway that cuts southwest through the Navajo Nation passes distinct geological features—the terminus of Comb Ridge monocline, the distant Bears Ears buttes, Monument Valley's red spires, and Agathla, a jagged black volcanic plug. These are the familiar markers on my commute across the desert.

I arrive at the San Juan Southern Paiute Tribal Offices in Tuba City and check the address. The strip mall is not the location I envisioned. I pull out my notepad and scribble a message with my phone number and walk inside. Unsure whether a reservation is required to be here, I am quickly put at ease by the familiar sound of the receptionist's voice. Sheepishly, I hand her the note. She smiles and assures me that she will get it to Clyde. I remind myself that, now that I have done everything I possibly can to track down Clyde. I can move on from this mystery in good conscience.

The muted pink-and-orange hues of the painted desert fade in my rearview mirror as I drive away. Then my phone rings. Without looking at the number, I pick up.

"Hello, Morgan? THIS IS CLYDE WHISKERS."

Is this a dream? Slamming on my breaks, I pull over—when the canyons call, you listen. Clyde's voice is strong and clear. He sounds eager to talk to me. We agree to meet at McDonald's in Tuba City the following Saturday. I enter Clyde Whiskers into my phone contacts and hope this isn't another dead end.

Clyde proceeds to call me every day, and then hourly on Saturday, to confirm that I am still meeting him. Each time Clyde calls, a photo of his inscription pops up with his caller ID. I assure Clyde I would not miss this meeting for anything.

On a hot August afternoon, I walk into McDonald's but don't see any men over sixteen years old. I call Clyde again and walk back out the front door, where a short, stout man with white hair and a sparse goatee answers his phone: "Hello Morgan!"

He looks up at me with a big toothless grin as I say, "Hi Clyde!" into my phone.

We both laugh as we hang up. I am completely in awe, meeting the man whose name has popped up on so many of my desert hikes.

We decide to head across the street to the Hogan Restaurant, where we can sit down for a proper meal and talk. Salisbury steak for Clyde and fry bread topped with ice cream for me. Clyde looks at me across the table and asks, "So how did you find me?" I explain the long saga, to which he interrupts, "Yeah,

I been everywhere." He then shares a flurry of locations where he signed his name. "It's what I did. I wrote my name everywhere." Later in his life, on a Grand Canyon river trip with other San Juan Southern Paiutes, Clyde learned about the modern consequences and ethics of carving your name on public lands. "We don't do that anymore," he assures me, "It's what we used to do, not anymore."

I have a head full of questions, but I am simply interested in listening to Clyde, the once elusive canyon scribe. In between bites of his dinner, he tells his stories. "Yeah, my uncle Angel Whiskers taught me to write my name, you know." He continues, "The Navajo keep erasing our names out there. Navajo Mountain used to be Paiute Mountain, you know." The mountain is known as *Kaivyaxaru, Tucané,* or *Ina'ih bi dzil* in the San Juan Paiute language.

Clyde talks about his parents losing their land to the Navajo, and he reminisces about his youth grazing sheep on the flanks of Paiute Mountain. He recalls the horror when he first saw the waters of Lake Powell flooding his homelands. As newcomers came to rename and reshape the land that the San Juan Southern Paiutes called home, Clyde wrote his name. In later years, Clyde took to more formal writing, spending ten years helping compile the San Juan Southern Paiute Tribal Constitution. Clyde is no longer a member of the Tribal Council, but he remains engaged with tribal politics and is eager for the day when the San Juan Paiutes have reservation land of their own again.

Clyde sighs, "They don't put Paiutes in books like they do Navajo, you know." In response, I reach into my belongings with an offering of my own, "Clyde, they didn't leave the Paiutes out of this book." I hand Clyde a copy of Hebner's book about Southern Paiutes, opening the pages to show him where he is even mentioned in a few stories.

As he looks through the black-and-white photos, he smiles

when he spots family members, "Yeah, I knew her, Bessie. And that's Jack and Mary Ann. And I remember Logan, too."

There is a plastic grocery bag on the table that Clyde brought with him. He reaches into it and pulls out some papers. He explains, "One time there were these other guys out at Paiute Mountain writing stories too. They wrote about me. I never met them, even though I was out there. Maybe you know them?" He hands me the paper across the table, and my eyes widen—it's a photocopy of David Roberts's Mystery Canyon story from *In Search of the Old Ones*. Within the chapter, Roberts wrote that he was "beguiled by a defiant 1986 inscription (he) found along the Rainbow Bridge Trail: CLYDE WHISKERS PAIUTE INDIAN," and another next to it simply marked "AW." Roberts went on to ask:

Had a young Angel Whiskers scratched his initials to declare to the world and the Navajos that this was still Paiute land? Could AW have been Angel Whiskers, once headman of the San Juan Paiutes, perhaps Clyde Whiskers's great Uncle?

"Clyde, I know David!"

He puts down his fork and smiles, "Then you can tell him about me, and that AW is my uncle, Angel Whiskers."

Clyde pulls out his wallet to show me his official San Juan Southern Paiute Tribal Card. He says he received it years after the Tribe's federal recognition in 1989. As he thumbs through his wallet, the name on his driver's license catches my eye: Clyde Kluckhohn Whiskers. Clyde Kluckhohn was a young adventurer who, inspired in part by Bernheimer, explored the Southwest by horseback on a shoestring budget in the 1920s. He went on to write two books about his explorations, *To the Foot of the Rainbow* and *Beyond the Rainbow*. Both books include Kluckhohn's encounters with Paiute people around Navajo Mountain. After these trips he pursued anthropology, forging an acclaimed research career at Harvard University.

"Clyde, were you named after Clyde Kluckhohn, the adventurer and anthropologist?"

He doesn't know if his parents or grandparents ever met the other Clyde, but confirms, "Yeah, he was famous, you know. In books."

"You are, too, Clyde. You're in a lot of stories. too."

He clutches Logan's book with his right forearm, the word "Clyde" tattooed in script letters across it. Clyde's eyes well up. "This is like a dream. The dream is right here."

CHAPTER EIGHT

A San Juan Southern Paiute
Holiday Party

I shall dance tonight
When the dusk comes crawling
There will be dancing and feasting
I shall dance with the others
In circles
In leaps
In stomps
Laughter and talk will weave
Into the night
Among the fires of my people
Games will be played
And I shall be part of it

—Lavern Owl

Clyde calls me every few days now. Each time he greets me, "Hello Morgan, it's Clyde Whiskers," followed by his whereabouts, "I'm in Tuba heading to Navajo Mountain." Now whenever I drive through Tuba City, I meet up with him at McDonald's. He eats chicken nuggets and I slurp down an ice cream cone while we trade stories. Hearing Clyde's voice always seems to bring a smile to my face.

On our last visit, we went to the Tuba City flea market

together. Clyde stopped to joke around with each of the vendors selling blankets, pottery, and fry bread. While we walked around I asked him about two of his inscriptions. One declares "Clyde Whiskers + Diana," and it is right next to another that reads "Clyde Whiskers & Mary Manygoats." They are dated just one day apart. A big grin pulls Clyde's cheeks back to his ears while he tells me about his girlfriends. He wistfully talked about Diana, a Mormon girl from Blanding. They had stayed in touch for years, though they no longer converse. Then Clyde changed the subject and asked me if I knew about Posey. He is one of Clyde's heroes, and Clyde's family holds land in Allen Canyon that was granted as a peace settlement after the Posey War.

The next time Clyde called me, he invited me to the San Juan Southern Paiute holiday party.

- - - - -

I rub my gloved hands together to stay warm while I wait for Clyde to meet me at McDonald's on the morning of the party. My battery is dead. When he arrives I explain the issue, and he says he will help me later because we are running late. I hop in his little sedan and Clyde notices that I smell like a campfire. "You still sleep out even when it's cold like this?" he asks. I did not ever expect Clyde Whiskers to question the sanity of my lifestyle.

On the way to the party, Clyde jokes, "I don't know. I think someone is trying to sabotage us. We're lost," as he makes a U-turn into the high school parking lot. For Christmas Clyde asked me to print him a copy of a photo of us together from our first meeting. He parks the car and I hand it to him along with a signed copy of *In Search of the Old Ones*, from David Roberts. His eyes tear up and he laughs.

We walk through the basketball courts to the gymnasium, where a large San Juan Paiute seal is posted at the doorway. The Tribal Council meeting rules are displayed: "No Talking About

Politics." All holiday parties could benefit from this. Traditional American Christmas carols are playing on high volume from a karaoke machine as families gather in clusters and greet each other by saying, "Mike," San Juan Paiute for hello.

Everyone sits at long communal tables, and we are served steaming plates of chicken, corn, chile peppers, and mashed potatoes. Evelyn James, the former San Juan Southern Paiute Tribal Vice President, is sitting next to me. She speaks fondly of her childhood herding cattle in Glen Canyon's tributaries before the government built the dam and flooded the land, further displacing a tribe with no reservation land. She lamented, "We had to enroll as Navajo when I was a young girl, but it wasn't right. We have a separate culture and language."

Without tribal recognition, the San Juan Paiutes lacked the funding, grants, and assistance provided by the US government and Bureau of Indian Affairs to other tribes. To fund governmental functions, the Tribe leases their gaming rights to other Arizona tribes. This injustice pushed Evelyn to pour herself fully into efforts to regain federal recognition, "It was a tough fight; just like having a baby, I had to protect it." In 1989 the Tribe was officially recognized once again. Evelyn recalls the day with pride: "We went from nobody to somebody." She laments that both the Navajo Nation and San Juan Southern Paiute Tribe have extended the case to review the treaty for their reservation.

Clyde is a stellar wingman and introduces me to as many of his relatives and friends as possible. He nudges me from my seat and takes me over to the Owl family, to meet his aunt, Mary Ann, who is eighty-five years old and wears her hair cloaked in a pink floral scarf. Clyde converses with her in San Juan Southern Paiute, and though I do not know what they are saying, I understand that less than three hundred people speak this dialect. This is their most potent link to cultural continuity. Most San Juan Paiutes understand other Paiute dialects and Ute, and are likely to speak Diné, English, and occasionally Hopi.

Rather than blend or simply adopt words for modern concepts, the San Juan Southern Paiute continue to expand their
language's vocabulary, creating words for things like televisions
and vehicles. Earlier Evelyn explained, "Young kids will never
know words that used to be spoken. Now we have words for
almost everything. For example, a newer word is "telephone."
People used to travel long ways to tell someone news. Now we
call phones "the talker," *ah-pa-ha-nip*, you spell it just like it
sounds."

Lavern Owl, Mary Ann's daughter, points out that language
retention is and will continue to be a struggle in the future, "The
kids only speak Paiute at home, not in school." There are generations of children living without an officially designated homeland. As we talk about this, two young children on stage sing
Christmas carols in San Juan Paiute and English.

Lavern grew up in Navajo Mountain where her father, older
brothers, and cousin Clyde tended to sheep in Piute Canyon and
Oak Canyon, which the Paiutes call "where water runs." She now
resides off the Navajo Nation in northern Arizona, to ensure that
her son gets the best education possible. She says it is common
for members of the San Juan Paiute community to move away,
for job, education, and housing opportunities. Lavern spoke
candidly about this, "When I grew up, I had to move away (from
Navajo Mountain) and start my own life because there are no
jobs....We can't just build a house on the Navajo Reservation
without our own land. We need a place to go home to. This is
where our home is and has always been." Lavern begins to weep,
but she resolutely states, "This is still where I will always call
home."

I ask Lavern about living as a Paiute among the Diné. She
speaks lovingly of her family's neighbors, especially her mother's late friend Stella Drake, who would join her family to plant
corn in Piute Canyon. She says it is very common for Paiutes and

Navajo to intermarry: "This is just history, and we can't erase it. We live among each other now."

- - - - -

Lavern and I exchange phone numbers at the party, and a few days later we use "the talker" to continue our conversation.

Throughout her childhood, Lavern's father, Jack Owl, taught her about the strength of San Juan Paiute history:

> Nasja Begay is my great-great-great-grandfather. He led the 1909 Cummings-Douglass Expedition to Rainbow Bridge with John Wetherill. He became well known with that history. He wanted to share that history with the world. He's (Nasja) never been forgotten, and my father won't be either. Our history is strong. Zane Grey writes about Nasja Begay in the book *The Rainbow Trail*. You can read about him in his stories about trail rides and travels.

Lavern's mother remembers Paiute healing songs and beliefs about the power of Rainbow Bridge, and she told Lavern, "When Owl's son (Nasja Begay) reached Rainbow Bridge, he was afraid to go under it because the bridge is so sacred to the Paiutes. It is a place for power, no one should travel underneath it."

Lavern further explains that Nasja Begay is a Diné name that means "son of owl," and that his Paiute name was Muu'puuts, which means "owl." She admits that she was very young when her father told her of these stories and that, like most kids, she may not have always been listening. But what she did hear from her father, she remembers: "What I know is what I know. My siblings have their own way of knowing that history. We all have different ways of knowing."

I reflect upon the copper plaque of Nasja Begay at Rainbow Bridge, and now understand that it is also a portrait of Lavern's relative displayed on a wall in their family's home. Lavern's parents both experienced the dramatic environmental changes that are the result of human attempts to control nature, including hotter temperatures, changing grasses, and a dam on the Colorado River. In an interview with Logan Hebner, Jack Owl lamented, "The land now, it's different. It's dying....The spirit is different."

Lavern then tells me that she found a picture of Nasja with President Theodore Roosevelt, the two of them standing together, and that "It was from an online story by a guy named Leake."

I tell Lavern that Harvey is my friend and the great-grandson of John Wetherill. She gently cries, "It would have been a great honor for my father to meet Harvey."

The threads of history weave the present together.

Since her father's passing, Lavern has taken a greater interest in learning about her family's history and that of Rainbow Bridge:

> When I was young, I didn't really care about this. I remember my father always talking about Rainbow Bridge. As I'm getting older, I realize I should have just sat and listened to my father tell the stories. Now I know why my dad stood for this. It's not a joke. He was not just a man. He was SOMEBODY. People might think my dad was a great councilman, but we have this history. WOW. We come from a very strong history. This is why he stood for Rainbow Bridge. I am proud to be a descendant of Owl's son, Nasja."

Where US records and lines on the map neglect the San Juan Paiutes, this history holds their place in time and terrain. Jack Owl worked tirelessly to gain federal recognition and reservation lands for the Tribe until he passed away in 2018 from a heart condition. He was ninety years old. The following year, the National Park Service and Glen Canyon National Recreation Area honored Jack Owl for his forty years of service and contributions to the Rainbow Bridge Native American Advisory Council.

Lavern's voice quivers but then picks up strength and passion: "We had that bond, I have that in my heart. I still have it. He's not gone, he will never be forgotten. I have to carry it in my heart. I miss him, I miss him a lot." Her voice cracks, "Nasja Begay is still here. My father is still here. We are still here. But very little people know. He wanted the Paiute people to be known. To have a reservation."

In the quest for recognition and a reservation, the San Juan Southern Paiute have patiently endured, not only hardship, but as a people and culture. Never have they abandoned their land, their language, their identity.

Lavern firmly says, "We exist. We are here."

CHAPTER NINE

Better Living Through History

We'll go on.

—John Wetherill

"**M**organ. Things are getting crazy out here. They say it's a virus. Everyone is buying all the food."

My heart sinks as I listen to Clyde on the phone.

"Clyde, this is a pandemic. It is very serious. Do you have enough food?"

As of March 2020, local and national governments worldwide are encouraging, and in some cases mandating, that we stock up on essential supplies and "shelter in place."

Clyde pauses and then assures me that he bought flour and beans, before adding, "Don't worry, I can always just eat a horse like we did in old days, you know." Clyde always finds a way to make me laugh. I plead with him to stay somewhere safe and to limit going out in public. How do you tell a nomad to stay home? Clyde is a man whose pride and joy is centered on his travels.

Countless times he tells me, "I've been everywhere!"

Now I beg him, "Go nowhere!"

He calls me again late at night while I am asleep. I try to return his call the next morning, but he doesn't pick up. This is very uncharacteristic. A week later, Lavern Owl texts me. Clyde is in the hospital, but she does not know where, or why. I pick up my phone, as determined as I was last summer to find Clyde. There's no record of him at the Tuba City hospital, so I give Flagstaff a try. The receptionist asks me for the patient's full name and date of birth, both of which I've memorized thanks to Clyde memorializing them in stone. "Clyde Kluckhohn Whiskers. Birthday March 12, 1948."

The nurse responds, "What is your relation to the patient?"

I waste no breaths: "My uncle." The nurse confirms that he is there in the ICU.

I hang up the phone and sob. I am scared for Clyde. I am scared for all of us. This virus is real.

I compose myself and exchange more text messages with Lavern. She replies, "We need to stay strong for Clyde." Later in the evening, there is more bad news: Clyde tested positive for COVID-19 and slipped into a coma.

On the morning of April 3, 2020, Lavern calls. I brace myself. Clyde is gone. Just like that, the virus infects us all.

- - - - -

When the pandemic began, I was at Brent's home in Colorado preparing to head out to Cedar Mesa. Instead of leaving, I adhered to the state requests to stay home, as well as San Juan County, Utah's COVID travel restrictions for nonresidents. Then my Jeep broke down, and I really could not go anywhere. I was imprisoned in my grief; homesick and isolated.

With good health and mountains near the front door, who am I to complain about anything as the world suffers? After all, some people are stuck inside studio apartments in New York City listening to the nonstop wailing of ambulances, in a city where the death toll is so high that refrigerated trucks are being converted into makeshift morgues.

To stay put is to stay safe, but I am not so sure. For many animals, myself included, there is safety in movement. "Sheltering in canyon" sounds far better to my psyche. My vision for surviving the apocalypse involves wilderness retreat, not Netflix and chill. I was a deeply emotional kid. To release and process whatever I was going through my mom often took me to the beach, even letting me ditch school on occasion, to decompress and revive my spirit. I came to understand the healing properties of sun, sand, sky, saltwater, and nature. The desert now fulfills that same need. I mourn the life I want to live.

Brent is annoyed by my agony. "Bears Ears isn't your home, you know. You can't just live in the desert." He doesn't understand why I want to be out there when I can stay in his house. His critique unsettles me. Between the time of my first Jeep breakdown and the pandemic, our relationship moved swiftly into challenging terrain. Now, when I am unsure if this relationship should proceed, it is not possible for me to go.

These days are drawn out with uncertainty, and too much time to fill. I cannot bring myself to bake sourdough bread, start a garden, doom scroll on Twitter, knit a sweater, or binge watch shows on Netflix. Phil shows me the ways of an animal living indoors. We lie in the yard and watch ants in the grass while we stretch. Squirrels and magpies tease us with their freedom while we stare at them from the windows. Random bursts of jumping around or howling at the moon are rarely contained.

I shelter from my present anxiety behind the pages of history. Time travel is the ultimate social distancing. Members of Bernheimer's team lived through the 1918 flu pandemic, the Great Depression, and both world wars. Somehow this comforts me and helps me view the future beyond this global chaos. Writing and reading are lifelines that channel my longing for the desert into arduous journeys of the imagination. When I am not on a sunny slab of slickrock, my fingers and psyche can always take me there.

Long walks with Phil soothe my restlessness. The nearest hiking trail encompasses a meadow held close by Entrada Sandstone that kisses the foundations of 13,000-foot peaks. This is the location of a Basketmaker site that Earl Morris studied in the 1930s. Morris was invited there by Zeke Flora who wanted him to examine a mummified young woman that he excavated. Because of a local quarantine, Morris could only interact with Flora and look at his initial findings through the window of Flora's house. It's a detail I would have overlooked until now. The mummy became known as Esther, and she was sent on a museum tour across the United States, before being displayed at the Mesa Verde National Park Museum from 1939-1970. In 2013, Esther was finally reburied during a ceremony led by the Hopi Tribe and Pueblo of Acoma. Her remains are closer to home, but not where she was originally laid to rest. I walk past the disturbed site, and the weight of my homesickness is light by comparison.

A pandemic affects everybody's equilibrium. Louisa Wetherill documented the effects of the 1918 flu pandemic on the Navajo Nation in *Traders to the Navajo* with a chapter painfully titled, "The Year of War and Death." When that virus took the life of Nasja Begay, she wrote:

> Nasja-Begay, the Paiute who had led the white men to the Rainbow Bridge, had died of flu at Navajo Mountain. While his family were coming down from the mountain, his wife had also died. The other five had kept on, and at last, stricken with influenza, had wrapped themselves in their blankets and waited for death in the Monuments. Only the child had survived.

Both of the Wetherills caught the flu. John Wetherill was riding out in the desert when he fell ill. He almost did not make it home alive. Louisa's memories reveal one harrowing perspective of what this period was like on the Navajo Nation:

When the Wetherills themselves recovered, they returned to the task of caring for the sick, of burying the dead. The Government school was turned into a hospital, and from Tuba City, seventy miles away, a physician and nurse came for part of the time. Dying Navajos begged to hold Asthon Sosi's (Louisa's) hand.

One hundred years later, the Diné, Hopi, and Paiute homelands are among the hardest hit parts of the country during the coronavirus pandemic. In early April 2020, the Navajo Nation ranked among the highest in positive cases per capita of COVID-19 in the United States. The Navajo Nation, with a population of 173,000 people residing on tribal lands, only has four hundred hospital beds. This puts pressure on surrounding communities like Flagstaff, Arizona, and Gallup, New Mexico, to provide care. Nearly 40 percent of homes on the Navajo Nation lack running water, which compounds issues with recommended illness-prevention measures like hand washing. This means that families must leave their homes more frequently to haul water, increasing their risk of virus exposure. Likewise, the Nation has only thirteen grocery stores, limiting the provisions and supplies available. To adapt, many families are able to rely on traditional farm plots, cattle, and sheep herds to sustain themselves, and Native communities have developed strong mutual aid networks.

The nearby San Juan Southern Paiute people face these same circumstances but are even further neglected by government assistance programs due to the lack of sovereign tribal land and the accompanying infrastructure. With such small numbers, every member of the San Juan Southern Paiute Tribe lost to COVID is a notable percentage of the population. And with the elders, like Clyde, being most affected, the Tribe is losing its language carriers, storytellers, and oral history books.

To help, I am collaborating with the San Juan Southern Paiute Tribal Council to help their efforts to provide pandemic relief to their community. The small donations funds are used to purchase once commonplace items like hand sanitizer and paper towels, which are severely backordered. It can take weeks for orders to arrive at the office in Tuba City for distribution to tribal members. Among the purchases are shelf-stable foods like dried beans and Blue Bird flour, which my friend Yermo Welsh delivers to the isolated Navajo Mountain community.

If I cannot be in the desert, my heart still can be. If there can be no memorial service for Clyde, I can extend my hands and energy to help his community. This pandemic is one of the most trying experiences of our lifetime. Leaning into past moments of healing and hope generates better living through history. Clyde Whiskers has now joined a team of explorers who live on through their stories and the landscapes they passed through. He taught me that history is not only written in books and that canyon walls can literally become our friends. We dwell, as always, in the unknown. The next chapter is uncertain, but the rocks already know the way.

CHAPTER TEN

Road to Aztec

I don't know. I'm making this up as I go.

—Indiana Jones

Steam rises through the willows on the edge of the highway, a winding two-lane road that parallels the Animas River. In between Earl Morris's far-flung travels across the Southwest and Mexico, this road was his commute to the home that he built on site at Aztec Ruins National Monument. To fill my time while I am in Colorado, I am veering off Bernheimer's trails and taking the 45-minute road to Aztec for a glimpse into Earl Morris's life, and to help historian Fred Blackburn document historic inscriptions.

Fred and I first met up in 2019 at a diner in Cortez, Colorado. I had driven from Cedar Mesa and still smelled like burnt juniper smoke. Fred leaned over a plate of greasy bacon and announced, "Oh, so you're doing time in Cedar Mesa. I've already done my time." From 1974 to 1979 Fred was one of the first Bureau of Land Management (BLM) rangers on Cedar Mesa. Back then, they still patrolled the canyons on horseback, primarily to protect the ancestral sites from looters. Fred described this as his "Vietnam" because the many cultural clashes that exist in San Juan County, Utah, make land management there especially contentious.

After moving on from the BLM, Fred, his wife, archaeologist Victoria Atkins, and local archaeologist Winston Hurst conducted research to locate the origins of objects excavated by the Wetherills in Cedar Mesa and Grand Gulch. Using historic inscriptions and photos, the team of volunteers successfully restored the contexts of these cultural sites and early archaeological work.

Most of the names at Aztec are carved and written into the wooden beams, adobe walls, and windowsills by tourists and local visitors to the site between the 1890s and 1920s. Fred's objective is to piece together a more recent human history of Aztec and the tourists who later came to this site.

During my previous visits, I studied photographs of inscriptions and then replicated, by hand, the nearly illegible names written in cursive and utter scrawl. These meetings with Fred at Aztec are training sessions for my eyes, sharpening them as tools to take with me to read names and spot ancestral art etched on the sandstone walls. Fred chuckles, "Oh, you're screwed now. You're going to see things all over the desert."

Another major focus of this project is for Fred to pass down his knowledge to the next generation of researchers. His assistant is a fourteen-year-old girl named Moriah, who was born and raised here in Aztec. Dressed in an official park service shirt and ball cap, her eyes absorb every possible detail through her wire-rimmed glasses.

Moriah was visiting the monument with her parents when they bumped into Fred and struck up a conversation. She recalls Fred asking if she could read cursive, the predominate handwriting method used in most of Aztec's inscriptions. Fred asked her to volunteer on the spot.

Moriah is now under the Monday-to-Friday tutelage of Fred, who has worked with her mother to coordinate and associate nearly every aspect of this project with her advanced learning needs, ranging from problem-solving and math to history and organization. "I told her she needs to start applying for colleges after this."

Fred talks like a tough guy, but he puts his big heart into everything he does, including mentoring students. He worked with high school students from Denver in Tsegi Canyon and Prayer Rock for several decades, guiding them in documenting cultural sites while earning school credit. He discussed a similar arrangement with Moriah's parents, who agreed and incorporated her assistant work into her homeschool curriculum.

Fred doesn't even look up when I walk into the office. He is looking at photo documentation, and sketching out a faint name to try and decipher it. Down to the wire, with funding deadlines ending in two days, Fred and his small team are nowhere near finished. I am here to help them as much as I can. Fred assures me that the remaining portals of study are the most intriguing. Today we will survey what he calls "The Socialist Room."

Victoria Atkins, Fred's wife, is here to lend her experience and help as the funding deadline fast approaches. Atkins is a former BLM archaeologist and an interpretive specialist at the Anasazi Heritage Center in Dolores, Colorado. She has coauthored and edited much of Fred's published work.

"Do you have an extra coat? The rooms get quite cold," she explains. "Oh, and here is a construction mask. You don't want to get hantavirus!" Victoria is bundled up in a thick wool coat. I grab my down jacket and beanie cap. Fred stays behind in the office, and the three of us head toward the habitation structures, where we will work in the underground rooms that are off-limits to the public.

Moriah leads us to the job site through Aztec's visitor center and museum, which now occupies the home that Morris built here. We pause for a moment to admire the beamed roof that brings to mind Aztec's ancestral construction methods. A glass case outside the building displays Morris's trowel and shovel.

We pass through a door on the other side of the building

that opens toward the Great House. The north wall, comprised of intricately stacked stone blocks, aligns with the sunrise of the summer solstice and the sunset of the winter solstice. All construction details here have meaning.

Victoria climbs onto the waist-high escarpment and walks up the inclined one-foot-wide wall. Moriah is next, and I follow. Then we take turns stabilizing a ladder for each of us to descend the wall. Victoria summons a key to unlock a wooden trap door. She lowers the ladder down into it and asks the two of us to hold her backpack, lighting equipment, and a folding chair while she descends into the dark underground rooms. Upon my turn to use the ladder, the cold air below tingles my extremeties while I take one last look up at the blue sky and sunlight above.

I duck down to follow the women through two more low hanging doorways into the very back room of this chamber. We are consumed in the belly of Aztec. The still air is eerie, and our movements immediately stir up dust. Victoria turns on a bright portable light and sets up the chair, while we begin a quick assessment of the room. Moriah leads the survey.

We scan every dimension of the drab gray walls and wooden beams for signatures, burns, dates, and carvings. In this room, most of the logs are relatively unmarked. Circular tree-ring samples cut from most of the beams are stamped with a serial number. "Workers Unite" is written in dark black lettering on the third beam. This is why Fred calls it "The Socialist Room."

We stop and measure the distance of each name from the main wall and the ceiling, and grapple to form a hypothesis of what it might say. Archaeology, far from the glamorous adventure portrayed in movies and imaginations, is a lot of time spent writing down tiny details in dirty places. There is only one inscription on the south wall. Holding the tape measure, I stand face-to-face with the name "Morgan." Moriah thinks this is beyond cool, and Victoria winks at me as she jots down the dimensions of the scrawl.

At noon, our underground Aztec labor union takes a planned one-hour lunch break, crawling through the tiny portals, back up the chute, and over the walls. Basking in the sunlight is an immediate mood booster. I cannot imagine living in Aztec's dark, cramped, and close-quartered rooms, which were occupied between AD 1100 and 1300. I would have preferred to live in a southern Utah cliff dwelling, enjoying a high, sun-drenched perch with sweeping views of canyons, clouds, wild-flowers, and water-filled potholes.

The break is too short, and though we are all enthused by the work we are doing, none of us want to put on our masks and return to the cold, dark room. We layer up and climb back over the wall, down the hatch, and through the door holes once more. Next, we survey the window vents. The rectangular openings only allow the dimmest light and tiniest flow of air to enter from outside. Each vent contains thirteen wooden lintels cut from the trunks of aspen trees. Fred explains that it is believed that these beams were transported down the Animas River from Durango, Colorado.

A circular core sample has been removed from each beam, and a serial number connects it to the sample taken. The earliest tree-ring dating in the Southwest was conducted by Professor A. E. (Andrew Ellicott) Douglass, a former astronomer who went on to pioneer the field of dendrochronology. Over the years, Earl Morris took numerous samples from the sites he worked at, even during the Bernheimer expeditions, and then shipped them to Douglass in Flagstaff. Douglass used the dates to define the timelines between the Basketmaker and Ancient Pueblo habitation periods.

The mundane task of documenting serial numbers moves swiftly—until we get to window number three. We cannot read the numbers. They are facing in the opposite direction, towards the open air courtyard outside the window.

I look inside the vent. The first lintel has a circle and a serial number, but then the beams appear blank. "Hmmm, can you shine a light in here?" I pull myself up and into the vent, craning my neck: "They're here but facing the opposite direction."

Moriah laughs, "Whoa, that's different from all the other rooms." The oddity is a major impediment to our goal to finish documenting the room before dark. We discuss options, but all sound clumsy and inefficient.

I suggest that we go outside to observe the vents from the other side of the window. Moriah's eyes widen through her spectacles and above her white dust mask. No one dissents about the idea. Victoria will wait for us in the room, while Moriah and I climb up the ladder and out through the vent.

Back in the fresh air, Moriah and I look at each other, unsure if this is the best decision. We smile, nod, and pull the ladder up to the high wall. I assure her, "We will just make one careful move at a time." If it doesn't look safe, we agree to turn around. We take turns climbing the ladder. Perched atop the wall, we pull the ladder up after us, drop it over the other side, and hold it steady for each other while we climb down. From our bird's perch we can see the visitors touring the monument.

Moriah worries, "What if they see us?"

I say, "Well, at least you're wearing a park service uniform! Routine tree-ring documentation; nothing to see here, folks."

We hoist ourselves and the ladder over another shorter wall. Once safely on the ground again we are standing outside the window vent we need to document. Moriah gushes, "Oh my gosh, this is so cool. It's like a real adventure. I've always dreamed of this." I hope that I am not being a bad influence, but if so, I like to think this is a formative type of education.

We peep inside The Socialist Room and can hear a man's voice booming from inside. It's Fred! "Where are the girls, Victoria?"

Our laughter gives us away. Fred walks up to the window and looks straight at us, startled but not surprised. As we had hoped, it was much easier to record the tree-ring numbers from this vantage. He is thankful that we found a way to get the job done.

The evening light dims. We need to be swift but extra cautious returning along the same route without headlamps. Halfway up the ladder, I pause and gaze down at the window vent and then at Moriah. I can vividly picture two women climbing these walls nine hundred years ago.

CHAPTER ELEVEN

A Drive in the Canyon of Death

Throughout the ensuing months, the lure of the canyon called imperatively …

—Earl H. Morris

My fingers grip the door handle, and my left hand holds on to my felt brimmed hat while I bounce around in the passenger seat of a topless red Jeep. I tilt my head up and watch the orange walls of Canyon del Muerto rush past me. Driving might seem easier than walking, but it was a lot harder for me to get here this way.

Any travel within Canyon del Muerto National Monument requires hiring an approved Diné guide. Not being a Bernheimer myself, this is not something I can usually afford. That is not a complaint—this requirement is an important regulation to decolonize outdoor experiences by directly supporting Indigenous communities and letting them lead visitor experiences through their homelands.

To expand my opportunities, I applied for a grant through Coleman USA, the company that makes those classic green propane camp stoves. The funding allowed me to plan this trip with Fred Blackburn and Dave Wilson, who works for one of two approved guiding services here.

Dave, dressed in a white cowboy hat and a pinstripe dress shirt, cruises through the ruts of the sandy wash as relaxed as if it were a smooth, paved road. His Jeep is waxed and polished for this Sunday drive. Fred, wearing a ball cap and oversized green T-shirt, sits in the back seat and keeps the stories rolling. Several are about the packtrain trips he and Dave took together over the years to recreate Bernheimer's expeditions on horseback. Fred romantically describes these as the last great archaeological expeditions to use packtrains.

Horses have always been a part of Fred's life—from his childhood in the San Juan Mountains, to his patrol days on Cedar Mesa. Now, he continues to hunt elk in the mountains with a traditional pack outfit. A few weeks ago, he invited me to help him prepare his horse and mules at his home. "You need to experience what it was like to get ready for one of Bernheimer's expeditions." In the front yard of Fred's house we saddled his mules, Elum and Belle, with wooden packsaddles, wool saddle blankets, and tarpaulins. The gear was nearly identical to what Wetherill, Johnson, and the cowboys used in the 1920s. Learning the knots and techniques felt like rigging for a river trip, only instead of a rubber raft, the vessels were adorable animals. Fred didn't think it was so cute when Elum, his most stubborn mule, took off on a walk down the street. After packing the train, Fred looked at me and said, "Now imagine doing that with forty more animals!" It certainly put the minor tedium of packing up camp on a backpacking trip into perspective.

Canyon de Chelly National Monument is located on the Navajo Nation in Chinle, Arizona, which is the northeastern portion of the state. Its 84,000 acres encompass the major canyon systems of de Chelly and del Muerto. It took me and Fred two and a half hours to drive here from Cortez, Colorado. Fred insisted that we take "the long way" through the town of Many Farms so that he could point out historical landmarks and routes that John Wetherill traveled on horseback.

In 1923, Bernheimer arrived at the railroad depot in Durango, Colorado where Morris and Johnson picked him up in a Model T to drive him to del Muerto. Bernheimer was not impressed; he detested what he called "prairie schooners," because of the time wasted getting stuck or dealing with mechanical issues. He believed that when riding a horse, "there is more freedom of motion, often more speed." The last time my Jeep broke down on the Navajo Nation, a guy at the gas station suggested that I trade it in for a wild mustang or burro because they'd be more reliable. I seriously considered the suggestion. A swift gray wild horse raced past my dead Jeep earlier that day, and looked far more reliable. Morris, on the other hand, loved his cars and hated dealing with the animals. Legends about Morris's Model T, "Old Joe," could fill a book. On the way to del Muerto in 1923, a rock ripped a hole in the oil tank, and he repaired it with a log from an old hogan.

In del Muerto, Morris convinced Bernheimer to transition away from glorified sightseeing trips to forge new trails focused on real archaeology. This increased the significance of Bernheimer's expeditions, while directly expanding Morris's field experience and career opportunities. Here, Morris looked to Wetherill to guide him in the delicate process of working at Basketmaker burial sites for the first time, stating, "Actual observation teaches one much more satisfactorily than someone else's publications, no matter how good the [latter] may be."

Morris was exhilarated about the research possibilities, so he obtained another research permit from the American Museum of Natural History and returned six weeks later. In his 1925 *National Geographic* article, "Exploring in the Canyon of Death," Morris sang of losing himself in the multicolored wilderness where "countless ages have caressed the cliffs" and history was "not written in formal documents, but in the results of their occupation, left in the caves by the succession of peoples who for unnumbered centuries dwelt here." The museum granted Morris enough funding to continue work in Canyon del Muerto through 1932.

Shortly after the 1923 expedition, Morris married archaeologist Ann Axtell, and the two spent their honeymoon camped out in del Muerto. This caught his friends by surprise because he was a workaholic who lived with his mother. Ann's spirit was a natural fit with Morris's unconventional life, which aligned with her childhood dreams "to dig for buried treasure, and explore among the Indians, and paint pictures, and wear a gun, and go to college."

Morris and Ann traveled for field work and lived in tents across the Southwest and at Chichén Itzá, on the Yucatán Peninsula of Mexico. In addition to working in the dirt alongside Morris, Ann painted large watercolor paintings depicting artifacts, pictographs, and Indigenous people. Ann wrote stories about the unique lifestyle of the archaeologist for a popular audience, publishing two books, *Digging in the Southwest* and *Digging in Yucatan.*

Ann's colorful memoir lends insight into the evolution of archaeological science that was shifting away from careless and destructive digging. In it she praises the importance of federal permitting. She emphasized the need to use techniques that caused as little disturbance as possible to cultural sites, at least by the standards of that era. Above all, Ann understood the connection between their research locations and the present-day Indigenous people, explaining this bond as living archaeology. I wish I could ask Ann directly what she meant by "living archaeology," but I can't help but note its resonance with the Indigenous perspective that cultural sites are places where their ancestors continue to live. Perhaps Ann learned this from the Hopi, Ute, Pueblo, and Diné people that she encountered during her travels.

The Morris's were both vocal about the designation of Canyon de Chelly National Monument in 1931. They hoped that it would help curb issues with looting and vandalism. Unlike conservation efforts that stripped Indigenous people of their land and rights, this monument would be co-managed by the National Park Service, the Navajo Nation, and the communities within the adjacent canyon systems of Canyon del Muerto and Canyon de Chelly.

Dave pulls over to point out his childhood home. "This is where I was born. And my father was born behind that rock." Today, eighty Diné families like Dave's continue to live here alongside the Ancestral Pueblo dwellings tucked in the large alcoves of 200-million-year-old de Chelly Sandstone. The history of this canyon is a tapestry woven with diverse cultural threads.

Archaic people hunted and gathered in Canyon del Muerto as early as 2500 BC. Around 200 BC, the Basketmaker people occupied the canyon, leaving colorful pictographs on the walls, followed by the Ancestral Pueblo people who built multi-story structures between AD 750-1300. Dave points out two stone structures on the canyon floor constructed between AD 1300 and the early 1700s by Hopi people. Then roughly four hundred years ago, the Diné made this their home.

The centuries that followed are documented in blood. In 1778 the Dominguez-Escalante Expedition marked Canyon de Chelly on the first Spanish maps of the Southwest. This was a period of unrest for the Diné people, as Spain, Mexico, and the United States all claimed hostile governance of their homelands, through use of force, in the next century. In 1805 the Spanish killed 115 Diné people at a site in Canyon del Muerto that came to be known as Massacre Cave. Regional conflicts continued through to the Mexican-American War in 1846. Then the US military attempted to gain control of Diné lands with an invasion led by Kit Carson in 1864.

Dave stops the Jeep at a monolithic buttress known as Tse'laa', or Navajo Fortress Rock. An estimated two hundred Navajos hid atop the 700-foot formation to evade capture during the Fearing Times. They sustained themselves with dried food and used ponderosa pine logs like ladders in the stone's cracks to descend the fortress and retrieve water at night. After they surrendered to the troops, they were forced to walk hundreds of miles to New Mexico along with ten thousand Diné people who were detained in a concentration camp for four years. Many died of starvation and illness during the Long Walk and under the harsh conditions of captivity. These acts of genocide and forced internment are embedded in every corner of the Diné homelands, even if history books choose to gloss over it.

A treaty signed in 1868 permitted Navajo families to return home, including to Canyon del Muerto, and this document officially formed the Navajo Nation reservation. The release treaty was negotiated by Chief Manuelito, who was born at the Bears Ears, further bolstering the Diné connection to that landscape.

- - - - -

Dave drives the Jeep down the bumpy wash for two and a half hours until we reach Mummy Cave. The large alcove arcs slightly in the middle, framing eighty rooms built for dwelling and ceremony that are flanked by a three-story tower. Fred looks up at the site and whispers, "It's like two eyes staring back at you." This is his first trip back in nearly twenty years. "I needed this," he sighs.

Fred and I step out to walk closer while Dave waits in the Jeep. Bernheimer wrote that his Diné guides also avoided the sites: "The superstition of the Indians is so strong as regards things found in ruins that not only will they not touch them, but there is always the risk that they may decamp."

The reasoning behind this was explained to me by Leo Manheimer. The Diné believe that spirits of the dead, referred to as Chindi, may still linger at a burial site or ancient dwellings. They believe that it is best to avoid these sites, and if you leave footprints, it makes it easier for the Chindi to follow you home and bring bad omens to you and your family. If a person is accidentally exposed, protection way prayers are done for you and certain plants and herbs are used to ward off any spirits that may have followed you home.

Whenever Morris exhumed human remains, he hid them from the Diné men on the team. Perhaps Morris was attempting to be considerate while fulfilling the job he was instructed and paid to do. But he was still blatantly disrespecting Diné cultural perspectives and brushing them off as superstition instead of important values. How would he have felt about someone digging up his ancestor's graves for work? Did he ever question the ethics and entrenched racism of his career?

The Antiquities Act formally protected cultural sites from both looting and vandalism, but it did not protect them from archaeology itself. Several decades later, two new laws would improve the management and ethical standards of this type of archaeological work. The Archaeological Resources Protection Act (ARPA) was created in 1979 to govern the excavation of archaeological sites on federal and Indian lands in the United States. Then came along the more effective Native American Graves and Repatriation Act (NAGPRA) in 1990. NAGPRA ensures that Indigenous peoples are consulted and, when appropriate, are on-site during archaeological projects to facilitate the respectful repatriation of human remains, funerary objects, and other sacred objects.

These laws, especially NAGPRA, dramatically changed the field of archaeology. Ralph Burrillo explained to me that he, like most archaeologists today, spends most of his time walking, taking notes, and writing reports. Digging in the soil is increasingly rare. Whenever recovery of human remains is necessary, the term "excavation" is no longer used, and current laws ensure that the descendant tribes are invited to oversee archaeological work that involves human remains, funerary and sacred objects.

A few months ago, Ralph worked on a recovery effort for

the first time in his decades-long career. The Tohono O'odham Nation was involved at every stage of the process, which was undertaken with so much reverence that photos were forbidden, and all sketches were drawn in pencil; pens are not even allowed at the site. Metal tools were off-limits, and instead, wooden chopsticks were used to gently lift items out of burial features. Then items were carefully wrapped in cotton batting and tied up with string. Tribal members oversaw the ensuing reinterment of ancestral remains. To comply with NAGPRA and ARPA, Ralph must remain tight-lipped about the materials they recovered. He succinctly described the experience to me as "intense," which may have been enhanced by the 120-degree temperatures at the site that week.

That's not to say this progression is perfect. Today recovery is seemingly only permitted when a construction project with lots of funding is interested in a plot of land. The company or agency is required to hire and consult cultural resource management (CRM) archaeologists who consult with affiliated Tribes to survey the site. If the CRM survey determines that cultural resources are present, and if the people interested in building on that site wish to proceed, and therefore remove the items of cultural significance, they hire and pay a CRM group that works with the local tribe to recover and repatriate artifacts. At the end of the day, big businesses are spending big money to relocate ancestral burial sites.

It begs the question, have archaeological ethics changed as much as we like to believe? In 2010, the Government Accountability Office reported that after twenty years key federal agencies were still not compliant with NAGPRA. Has the gray area of what is acceptable and permitted shifted to accommodate the people with the deepest pockets? What are today's "Bernheimers" doing to contribute to cultural preservation, Indigenous-led research, and to the tribal communities they affect?

A shadow is cast across Mummy Cave as the remaining

sunlight drenches its tower in gold. Bernheimer noted that large and ugly cracks threatened the tower, and he worried it might crumble in only a few years. After the national monument designation, the park service enlisted Earl Morris to restore the tower, built in AD 1284 by the Ancestral Pueblo people inhabiting this canyon. To do this, Morris studied ancient building and masonry techniques, closely replicating them in both style and form using the natural materials available in the canyon terrain surrounding the sites. Morris worked with a Diné team who reinforced the stone walls using adobe mortar from the canyon.

In the 1960s, the National Park Service's Southwest Archaeological Center's ruins stabilization mobile unit was charged with maintaining the structural integrity of the tower. *Popular Mechanics* magazine reported, "Unlike Morris, they were using a cement mortar mixed with mud," and the article celebrated that "this method was first used in airport construction." Among the modern restoration tools and techniques listed were cordless drills, log beams with steel cores, cement pumped under pressure, weatherproofing by electrolysis, and baking bricks with infrared rays.

Today, Indigenous archaeologists are leading the return to using traditional techniques and native materials. Hopi archaeologist Lyle Balenquah recently worked to stabilize a cultural site in Bears Ears National Monument for the Bureau of Land Management (BLM) with the Zuni Ancestral Lands Conservation Corps. The necessity of doing this is of utmost importance at increasingly popular and well-known cultural sites. In addition to visitors boating to the site via the San Juan River, a nearby ORV road has increased the site's accessibility, and now it has up to 20,000 visitors a year. Balenquah explains the process:

The use of foreign materials in reconstruction has negative consequences for the structures which are built from organic material. The philosophy in Hopi speaks of structures as being living entities because we gather these materials from the earth, the stone, the soil, the wood beams. They are assembled to serve a purpose, have a life cycle, and are born out of the earth. Once that purpose is done, they should be allowed to turn back to the earth from where they came. The use of foreign materials like cement and steel rebar does not allow that natural process to continue. Now we've completely reversed or changed how we approach the preservation process. At the sites we were working on this summer, we primarily used unamended soils, meaning the soils and mortar are gathered from around the sites, not within the sites themselves, but close enough that they were a good match.

Balenquah insists education is the best way to address these issues, including face-to-face interactions between visitors and Indigenous workers. The goal is to instill proper site etiquette and to emphasize the connection between modern Indigenous people and these places.

- - - - -

Back at the Jeep, Fred leans in through the window and talks to Dave. These two have been friends and cohorts for over forty years, and they joke that nothing has changed between them, except that they look old. Beads of sweat drip down Fred's smiling face as he hops back into the Jeep. Fred is seventy-one and speaks candidly about his health issues slowing him down. It's all relative, of course; when I picked Fred up for this trip, he was on his hands and knees alongside Victoria, turning over soil in his vegetable garden. Most people, myself included, can only hope to keep up with Fred.

Fred's grandparents immigrated to Ophir, Colorado, in 1920 from the Trentino territory of Austria, newly formed after World War I. The former Ophir Climbing School used to be his grandmother's house. His childhood stories are all about his rambunctious explorations and salt-of-the-earth upbringing in the rugged mountains surrounding what is today a luxury ski resort. His ingrained connection to the land around him led him to develop a resumé that encompasses such a broad skill set it could field an entire multi-use land management agency: miner, outdoor guide, BLM ranger, youth educator, wilderness therapist, archaeological researcher, and historian. Fred balks at stereotypes, as Johnson and Wetherill both did, using his expertise in all facets of multi-use land management to inform his work as a conservationist.

- - - - -

On the drive back, Dave brings the Jeep to a halt and points up to a procession of animals dancing above us on the alcove. I gasp, "Antelope Cave!" recognizing it from Bernheimer's and Ann's written descriptions. Dave urges me to stand up on my seat in the roofless Jeep for a better view. The life-sized pronghorns, orange outlined in white, were painted on an alcove wall in 1804 by a Diné and Jemez Pueblo artist named Dibé Yazhi, "Little Lamb." Next to the relatively modern antelope are much older Basketmaker pictographs depicting humans and animals.

Bernheimer was so enamored with the site that he returned several times and wasted several rolls of film attempting to photograph it. He later lamented that black-and-white photos failed to document the brilliant colors intricately streaked on the rock canvas. This was over a decade before the invention of Kodachrome film, which made color photography readily available to photographers.

As a solution, Bernheimer commissioned Ann Axtell Morris to paint a replica of the rock art. Bernheimer admired Ann's artwork and spirit; he called her a "brave little lady" because of her penchant to ride on horseback solo through the desert, once to the team's camp to visit her husband. Upon completion, Ann's paintings were displayed at the American Museum of Natural History in New York City. Her art is considered instrumental in the development of pictorial documentation methods and standards that are still used in archaeology today.

I lift the camera up to my eye and snap a photo of the antelope panel, followed by another of Dave smiling in the driver's seat. Mine are another set of hands recording, through a different lens, the stories living within the walls of Canyon del Muerto. I take the photos, and then Dave says we need to get going so he can be home before dark. When we pull away, the headlights of a red Suburban draw close behind us. I was not aware anyone else was in this canyon. Dave softly remarks, "That's my son. Always checking on his father." He stops the Jeep to greet him. His son follows the Jeep to escort us. A few minutes later, a young woman on an ORV rides alongside us—Dave's granddaughter. Two other trucks piled with Dave's relatives follow. He explains they are all checking on him to make sure he gets home safe. The strength of this family unit reverberates in the echoes of motors down the canyon.

After the tour, Dave invites us over to his house for dinner. His wife Fannie ushers us to sit at a table with a tower of fry bread and brings out two steaming bowls of mutton stew. I use my spoon to draw up lean pieces of meat and chunks of potatoes and carrots in a savory broth. As we eat, the rest of Dave's family arrives—his teenage son, two granddaughters, and the son who followed us home on the drive. Fannie fills Fred in about their children who are not here tonight, with whom Fred has hiked and traveled. Their oldest son died unexpectedly last year. Tears season everybody's bowls of stew. She brings out a memorial poster and photos honoring the champion bull rider.

Fannie wipes her eyes and asks if we want more stew. She brings us steaming cups of hot water and Nescafé. It's 9 pm, too late for caffeine if I hope to get any sleep, but I oblige.

Dave speaks to me in Diné and points across the table, and I respond by grabbing the plate of fry bread. He laughs and exclaims, "See, you speak my language!"

CHAPTER TWELVE

In the Shadow of the Bear

With a vision of the long, long road traveled by man through time, our present and its troubles shrink small; but in the light of this same perspective, we seem somehow tremendously dignified because of the length and difficulties of that journey.
—Ann Axtell Morris

With windows rolled down, the scent of ponderosa pine wafts into the truck. The Lukachukai and Chuska Mountains appear to blend into one expanse, but their Diné place names distinguish them: *Lók'a'ch'égai* means "white reeds extending out," and *Ch'óshgai* means "white spruce." My truck strains to climb up a steep bend in the winding two-lane mountain road. Fred cheers, "And until 1991 this used to be a four-wheel low dirt road." Long before that developed road even existed, Bernheimer noted that travel through these mountains was slow moving.

"Why don't you turn off on the next dirt road you see?" I ask Fred if there is a particular spot he is looking for; there is not—he says he just wants to help me get a better view. I turn left off the asphalt and onto dirt. Fred's eyes widen. "Now we are on an adventure!" I am uneasy about our rogue turn—what if this is private property? An oil and gas truck drives toward us, and

Fred nudges me. "Just stop and wave, like you know exactly what you are doing."

I stop, and the truck driver waves, but he keeps driving. Along the washboarded strip of dirt, Fred points out various cuts on the trunks of the ponderosa in this old-growth forest. Some are lightning strikes, but one is a carving taken to make a Diné cradleboard. He urges, "Slow down so you can see it better."

At a pull-out further up the road, Fred again asks me to stop. Without explanation he gets out and walks toward the edge of the mountain, and I follow. We thrash through the dense maples and over fallen tree logs until we are on the edge of a clearing that reveals a panoramic view into New Mexico and southern Colorado. Our line of sight covers Shiprock to Sleeping Ute Mountain. The lush emerald-green ferns glimmer over the redrock desert below. Fred takes a deep breath of the pine-scented air and sighs, "Oh my, the uninterrupted distances."

Fred refers to these mountains as a "refugium," which he explains is a biology term for a site of refuge for isolated, relict species in an area of high biodiversity. These mountains are where the Diné hunt deer and elk in the fall, and they also use it as a summer camp, providing forage and cooler temperatures for sheep at higher elevations. We drive past one family's summer camp and a roadside food stand, demonstrations of how the summer tradition continues.

We stop atop Buffalo Pass near a hand-carved sign: "Elevation 8482 ft. Help Keep Our Earth Clean!" A Navajo Fish and Wildlife sign a bit farther down the road states, "Respect and Protect Our Wildlife Resources," as a dozen or more large semi-trucks pass by, signaling the juxtaposition between wildlife conservation and resource depletion that humans subject the natural world to today. Since the 1960s, oil and gas leases have punctured the ground. Then there was an oil spill in 2005. Then helium extraction began in 2015.

In the 1990s, Diné environmental activist Leroy Jackson,

the leader of Diné Citizens Against Ruining Our Environment, protested logging of the old-growth ponderosa pines. Logging was a threat to the Blessing Way ceremony and was turning these mountains into what he called "tree farms." Jackson helped reduce the timber harvests on the Navajo Nation by 50 percent, which resulted in two hundred layoffs of loggers and millworkers. The next year, Jackson's dead body was found off a New Mexico highway. The cause of death remains unsolved; his family and friends suspect that he was murdered.

Our destination is the Red Rock Valley, nestled between Shiprock, New Mexico, and these mountains. This valley was the destination of Bernheimer's final expedition in 1930. We drive up to a faded pink trading post that Bernheimer used for resupply and mail. The hand-carved Red Rock Trading Post sign transports us to a bygone era of craftsmanship. The outside of the building is in good condition, and a family walks inside, confirming that the trading post is still in use. We drive away, and I immediately regret not going inside to buy a cold drink, so I turn around. I slow to pull over, but Fred has another idea, "You know what, hang a left here. Let's see how close we can get."

We draw closer to the small community at the foothills of the mountains. Fred reminisces about his fieldwork in nearby Prayer Rock District with the Jefferson County Open School of Lakewood, Colorado. The program lasted for eleven years, consisting of four one-week trips to Prayer Rock each year. Fred directed the high school students "on a reverse archaeological project that connected artifacts stored in museums with their locations of origin. The students conducted research, interviews, and fieldwork to pair objects recovered by Morris at Basketmaker III sites at Prayer Rock in 1930. All work was done in collaboration with the Navajo Nation, and their reports were displayed at nearby chapter houses.

Like Bernheimer, Fred kept copious journals and began work on a book about these experiences, *Prayer Rock: In the*

Shadow of the Bear, which he has not yet published. The title refers to the specific reverence for bears in this area. Fred says, "There are petroglyphs of bears everywhere on the cliff walls." Whether Fred chooses to publish his book or not, I am grateful to stand in the shadow of his work researching Bernheimer's expeditions.

Like the artifacts he documents, Fred belongs in his beloved outdoor museum. Here his stories come to life. One of the highlights with his students was finding an old dress shirt box stashed in an alcove with field notes on it—Bernheimer, that dandy and textile aficionado, even made a point to bring clean, pressed shirts into the backcountry. Fred also found Morris's cigarette carton: "There was frayed cardboard sticking out of a Mormon tea bush. It was an old 'flat pack 50,' which had fifty cigarettes in a box lined with foil and an embossed camel. Tucked inside the box were Morris's notes and a sketch of an alcove they had worked in."

Fred nudges me: "Normally, I would go visit my friend Alberta, but we don't have enough time. I want you to see something. Why don't you turn right here?" My anxiety climbs with the truck up the steep, rutted road, through the Chinle Formation, until it ends. Fred exclaims that the view is far better than expected, and immediately points out the distant caves studied by Morris in 1930. These are the same places Fred and the Jefferson County students researched as well.

Fred grabs the box of original black-and-white photos from the 1930 expedition to take me on a virtual tour. We take turns holding the pictures up into the sunlight, and we step back in time. A photo of Zeke Johnson on horseback scales the horizon line. Fred points out Royal Arch, the Obelisk, and Prayer Rock. The spindly red pinnacle was so named, according to Bernheimer's guide, because it points the direction for the Diné people to pray to the east.

The photos were taken by professional photographer Merl

LaVoy. He is considered one of the first internationally famous photographers, revered for his documentation of World War I, mountaineering feats, and Indigenous people around the world. LaVoy entertained Bernheimer's whimsical requests for self-portraits and movies among the birds and wildflowers, freeing up the rest of the team to focus on research.

Characteristic of LaVoy's style, he took photos of Diné people weaving, dancing, and at home. Fred holds up a striking photo of Diné Chief Blackhat facing Prayer Rock with his horse. He is cloaked in a patterned woven textile and wearing a stately black hat. From his research in Prayer Rock, Fred learned that the chief and his band lived in the Red Rock Valley and granted Bernheimer's team permission to camp and conduct research.

Bernheimer's 1930 field notes depict interactions with Diné people more thoroughly than notes from other years. The team that year included Diné cowboy Eugene Cappahausa, who spoke English. Perhaps LaVoy's photographic focus and Eugene's perspective helped Bernheimer better understand the other Diné people they encountered. In one touching scene, Bernheimer describes two Diné girls, age four and five, to whom they gave candy, prunes, and crackers. He then smoked a cigarette with the girls' father. They encountered a mother with a toddler strapped to her back, and a five-year-old boy with whooping cough.

While LaVoy and Bernheimer took photos, the rest of the team was hyper-focused on the archaeology, without distractions. Of primary interest were the valley's many high caves. At age sixty-five, Bernheimer lamented that his ailing physical condition made them difficult to reach. Both Bernheimer's and Morris's reports about the Prayer Rock area detail a high density of Basketmaker II and III sites in the caves, with findings that included *Olivella* (sea snail) shell necklaces—a trade item from people along the Pacific coast—and deer hide blankets. Morris continued to take tree-ring samples from wooden beams at sites for Professor A. E. Douglass.

In Prayer Rock's Basketmaker shelters, Morris uncovered an abundant collection of adult Basketmaker sandals with intricately designed soles. In 1998 researchers came across an unpublished report about these sandals. Archaeologist Elizabeth Morris, Earl Morris's daughter, and anthropologists Kelley Hays-Gilpin and Ann Cordy Deegan, studied the report's handwriting to determine that Ann Axtell Morris, not her husband, wrote one of the unpublished reports. The trio of women teamed up to complete the Morris's research and publish the book *Prehistoric Sandals from Northeastern Arizona: The Earl H. Morris and Ann Axtell Morris Research.*

Morris was so frustrated with how little they accomplished in 1930 that he returned in 1931 with the support of the AMNH. He decided to rename the previously recorded sites but did not document the changes. This inconsistency between site names complicated the task Fred's students undertook almost a century later, not only in matching up artifacts with their locations, but in lining up two different sets of site names. Fred always insists, "Document, document, document," because you never know what nugget of information will be helpful to somebody in the next century. Fred's journals from Prayer Rock alone fill a bookcase in his house.

In the distance, Shiprock beckons us both on toward home. The pinnacle is called *Tsé Bit' A'í*, in Diné meaning "rock with wings," referring to the two spindly black dikes extending outward from the dramatic formation created by a volcanic eruption thirty million years ago. The Diné creation belief states that the formation is the remnant of a great bird that carried the Diné people here from the north. When a lightning strike split the rock, it left some of the people stranded on top. To the Diné people, Shiprock is sacred, and for the reasons associated with this story, climbing it is prohibited.

One of the Bernheimer Expedition photographs is of a Diné man, presumably Eugene, sitting on horseback in front of Tsé

Bit' A'í. There is also a photo of Bernheimer and Morris posed next to the volcanic dike; Fred wants to recreate this shot, so we pull into the parking lot. The flurry of tourists looks puzzled when we walk away from the best vantage point of Shiprock and head toward the highway. Fred readies the camera, and I position myself near the boulders.

On the home stretch of our trip our chatter slows. I pull over at McDonald's so we can stay alert with some cold, caffeinated drinks. Only the very busy drive-thru is open; the lobby is closed due to COVID. We resume driving. Fred sips his vanilla iced latte and says in disbelief, "It feels like we've been gone for two weeks! Was this only a two-day trip?" Where we may have failed at time travel, we now found ourselves fully immersed in the present. I roll down the windows, letting the warm desert breeze energize us. We agree that Bernheimer would enjoy this ride.

PART 2:

The 1929 Expedition

CHAPTER THIRTEEN

Expedition Planning

The Urge of the Subconscious Wish: Boys will have ambitious dreams. It is fortunate that they do, for these often live on as smoldering flames buried in ashes for years, sometimes coming to the surface too late for realization.

—Charles L. Bernheimer

A year passed before I could start my journey. Perhaps it was just as well: there is no test quite like the erosion of time for finding out whether you really want to do something. If the dream dreamed can survive untarnished through a year of doubt and discouragement and frustration and all the drawn-out detail of research and planning and preparation, then you can safely assume that you want to go through with the project.

—Colin Fletcher

When I pulled the Jeep into a camp spot on Cedar Mesa, the battery immediately died. There was not even a murmur from the ignition as I turned the key. Unsure of whether to laugh or cry, I cracked open a beer and walked out to the edge of the mesa to watch the dancing fuschia and orange light over the crest of Navajo Mountain. This was my best problem in a long time. At last, I was stuck exactly where I wanted to be.

Phil had just died. For the last three weeks, energy drained from my body as I lay alongside him on his dog bed. At times it felt like I was dying too. Blood diverted from my stomach and my soul. I could not eat. I already understood the deep loss of losing unconditional canine love. Rather than fight it, I surrendered to the storm. Brent was irritated by my emotional state. Phil was his dog, and he wanted me to be the strong and less sad one, to support him. He began pushing me away, only to reel me back when his mood pacified, with a promise that tomorrow would be better.

While Phil was terminally ill, I attempted to leave. For good. I could barely look at his dog bed on the way out. Tears streamed down my face, and my vocal cords were numb from crying. Within three miles of leaving, the Jeep promptly overheated, and I returned to the house. I walked through the door and, upon seeing me, Phil's tail wagged up and down—a rare occurrence in his near comatose state. After that, I refused to leave his side until he passed.

It felt wrong to go, as if staying with Brent was somehow necessary to honor Phil. Entrenched in grief, we mourned the loss of Phil, and the laughter, love, and warmth he helped foster between us. Lately, the only thing we seem to agree upon when things are hard is that I should go to the desert.

I fell asleep peacefully under the stars, on the ground next to the dead Jeep with no thought about what to do about it. The next day, a friendly couple stopped and helped me jump-start the battery. Before hooking up the cables, the man looked at me and asked, "Are you sure you want to do this? Maybe your Jeep is telling you to stay here." I almost told him to stop.

With my wheels in motion, I resolved to recenter my life in the desert.

I sold my Jeep a few weeks later, along with my excuses. I spent all my money on a reliable truck so that I could resume my nomadic life and regain my freedom. And I finally decided it was time to retrace Bernheimer's 1929 expedition. After dealing with pandemic chaos, it no longer sounded daunting. The only thing that terrified me was sitting idle.

To envision the route, I read through Bernheimer's 1929 journals repeatedly, jotting down any notable locations and marking them on a map. As the territory covered by his team expanded, the idea of doing this by myself became daunting. It was not like I would be following the steps of solitary vagabond Everett Ruess. Though the ghosts of Bernheimer's team would travel with me, I craved an expedition team of my own.

So I emailed Steve Allen, who is the ultimate desert rat, expert backcountry hiker, historian, and lifelong explorer of Utah's canyon country. For years people have told me they could not believe our paths never crossed, but it's probably because we were both too far out in the desert most of the time. Within minutes of sending the email, he replied, "You need to come over so we can look at maps."

- - - - -

On a snowy evening, I arrive at his house. The pandemic has not abated, and gathering indoors is still questionable. Because I spend so much time outside, no one seems to be too worried about getting sick from me. The very thing that distances me from society allows me a semblance of normalcy in these times of plague.

He welcomes me inside to his library, where a dozen topo maps are spread out, wall-to-wall, across the floor. "How do I even begin to digest all this?" I ask him.

With a goofy chuckle he exclaims, "One step at a time, my dear!"

Stevo, as he is known to his friends, retired at age thirty-eight from the auto shop he owned in Fort Collins, Colorado. He moved into his van, got a post office box in Hanksville, Utah, and started systematically hiking desert terrain. His feet have covered everything from classic canyons to obscure mesas, wild rivers, first ascents of desert spires, and descents of technical slots. He's worked as a guide and written three hiking guidebooks. In the last fifty-five years he has walked over one hundred thousand desert miles, and counting.

Now at age seventy he continues to spend over six months a year living in and exploring the most remote pockets of Utah, documenting what he sees along the way. From roughly mid-January to late May, and again from August through December, Stevo still lives out of his camper van in between backpacking trips. There is no guidebook to living in the desert. The humans, like the critters who thrive there, all do so with their own unique adaptations.

During the heart of his desert seasons, Stevo leads scheduled trips with small groups of long-time friends. Many of his hiking partners travel from across the country and Canada to join these outings, ranging in length from ten to thirty days. He won't go on a shorter backpacking trip than that. Stevo's group trips are bookended by rugged weeks spent alone "nickel and diming" the vast terrain that he hikes through. Only for a brief pause in the hottest summer months and the coldest of winter does he hunker down and stay at his home in southwest Colorado. There he rests, fattens up, repacks, and prepares to get out for the next season. Somehow, he makes time to report on his hiking observations and send them to conservation groups working on various environmental lawsuits.

There are very few blank spots on Stevo's lifetime map—which is no hyperbole because he has recorded his footsteps along the way on a sizable collection of 7.5-minute USGS topographic maps. During each trip he plots his camps, notable sites, water sources, and routes, all drawn by hand. The maps are a work of art that could belong in a museum vault, but Stevo prefers that trusted people use his maps to keep exploring. I consider the maps he shares with me a great honor.

I pull Bernheimer's journals from my pack and read aloud,

while Stevo follows along using a highlighter to sketch general directions on the map. We skip the first section, in which Bernheimer took a road trip with paleontologist Barnum Brown in the Bisti Badlands of New Mexico before meeting up with Earl Morris at Aztec. I've enjoyed travels through this enchanting land of subtle curves and pastel-colored soils, but cannot afford to spend the gas money on a detour before this trip.

The primary terrain Bernheimer covered that year spans Bears Ears National Monument and Glen Canyon National Recreation Area. The lollipop-shaped route began in the town of Blanding, heading south toward Comb Ridge. The packtrain passed Camp Snowball on the way to Arch Canyon, where they craned their necks up at looking-glass portals eroded through high sandstone walls by the wind. From there they traversed the piñon-juniper forest atop Cedar Mesa, and then traveled down thirty-eight miles of Grand Gulch's mysterious sinews. They continued beyond the Clay Hills, crossed Lake Canyon, and then rode along the Colorado River, weaving their way in and out of its tributaries. They exited the river corridor by climbing up onto Grey Mesa where they rode overland to the confluence of the Colorado and San Juan Rivers. The team looped back on the Hole-in-the-Rock trail and studied sites in another Glen Canyon tributary.

After ascending Mancos Mesa they took a precipitous route back down to the Colorado River at the mouth of Red Canyon. They climbed rugged Chinle badlands up to Blue Notch and then down into White Canyon, which they followed to Natural Bridges National Monument. Kachina Natural Bridge served as their finish line. For the encore, an automobile picked them up and drove them through the Bears Ears back to the town of Blanding on a new road constructed by Zeke Johnson that year.

We sketch the outline one segment at a time. Some of this is familiar territory to me. I have backpacked Arch Canyon, Grand Gulch, and a few tributaries of Glen Canyon. The rest will be brand new. Stevo has hiked all of this, but never in a single trip. His enthusiasm is evident: "Ooooh, you're going to really like this section. It's STUPENDOUS!" More than once, we cross out the line and revise the route. The section Bernheimer coined "the blank triangle" challenges our plotting—its edges are now under Lake Powell. To adapt, I conspire to walk around the rims of the canyons, giving me a bird's view of what Bernheimer explored on the way to the confluence. Stevo warns me it is one of the most desolate and alluring landscapes I will encounter, especially in this time of drought. "You might find a pothole, but I wouldn't count on it." I don't care how much water I have to carry to get there.

Many of these areas were included in Bernheimer's national park proposal aimed at protecting the Glen Canyon region from developmental impacts. One hundred years later they reveal a century of human impacts and the current climate crisis instead. President Biden has yet to restore the boundaries of Bears Ears and Grand Staircase–Escalante National Monuments. Lake Powell is dropping to historic low-water levels. Plans are in the works to process uranium ore dangerously close to the nearby Ute Mountain Tribal community.

Several long stretches of the route are now paved highways. Walking them sounds like a torturous idea. I decide to cut the highways and Arch Canyon so I can spend more time in the wilder parts of the landscape. Retracing the past is impossible, the only steps we can ever take into the unknown future are our own. If we humans are ever to seriously address our relationship with the environment, and to reckon with what we have done to it, we are going to have to proceed differently than we ever have before.

Bernheimer's 1929 expedition route was approximately four hundred miles. We gauge that my version is three hundred. It's hard to know how long it will take, but based upon known terrain and my hiking ability, I plan for forty days, roughly the same as Bernheimer's trip. As a nod of faith, Stevo agrees to join me on a ten-day portion across Mancos Mesa.

- - - - -

I spread the maps out and study them daily. The expedition creeps into my dreams each night. I walk down a desolate stretch of sand. The ground sizzles. The potholes are dry. Tired, hungry, thirsty, and lonely, I have not seen or talked to anyone, except the ravens circling overhead, in months.

Bernheimer's route was so ambitious that, prior to the expedition, they considered taking an easier trip in northern Arizona instead. In retrospect, Bernheimer admitted, "Our journey was conceived on an ambitious scale…we tried once more to do too much."

I wake up in a sweat. Do I really want to do this to myself? Am I capable? There is nowhere to hide from what the desert is telling me, even in slumber. I am certain that walking a great distance is necessary to return to the path of light.

- - - - -

With cocktails in hand after dinner, Brent and I look at the maps together. He asks me if I think doing this is worth it. It echoes other criticisms he's made about my lifestyle: "People who do this stuff end up being hermits, you know." As if planning something like this is not daunting enough, my worries about the implications of being away so long are already stressing me out. By 1922 Bernheimer had run into this conflict with Clara as he was trying to plan his month-long trips. In his planning correspondence with Morris and Wetherill, he requested that they work on trip details while he persuaded Mrs. Bernheimer to let him go.

I invite Brent to join me for the expedition, but he is unsure if he has time to even hike a portion of it. My early memories of hiking with him to Rainbow Bridge and No Name Mesa are a distant mirage that I still reach for. Intermittent walks together through sensuously curved Navajo Sandstone rekindle a bit of that flame, but we frequently fall back into our patterns like we sink into the dilapidated mattress we sleep on at his house.

He mixes a second round of drinks, pulls up Google Earth, and zooms in on Glen Canyon. Although I have invited him to join me on the expedition, he is non-committal and reminds me that it overlaps with ski season. A few minutes later his eyes widen, and he changes his tune. He suddenly wants to join for a ten-day section. Brent's ambivalence leaves me on edge. I cautiously hope he follows through even though I know it might be emotionally better for me to go without him.

A phone call with Harvey Leake resets my confidence and eases my worries. He believes that my plan is about as close to the 1929 edition as is possible in 2021, with or without a horse. After giving me his blessing, he sighs, "I sure wish I could go with you, Morgan." We devise a plan for him to join me for three days in Grand Gulch. I purchase a permit for the two of us, which further commits me to this plan.

Expedition preparation consumes my days. Bernheimer's lavish packing lists used to seem ridiculous to me. Yet now I sit surrounded by more gear than I could ever have imagined needing. I overanalyze what tent and sleeping bag to bring, calculate how many water vessels and fuel cans I need, and decide what clothes to wear every day for over a month. I even indulge in buying a red nightcap like Bernheimer's. Guilt occasionally creeps in about the amount of synthetic and plastic goods that are supposedly necessary to survive in the wilderness. It seems like it counteracts any of my carbon footprint reductions I make with my simple lifestyle.

I make a spreadsheet to calculate food quantities. The overwhelming details make me lose my appetite just looking at it. Forty dehydrated breakfasts and dinners. Forty packets of tuna, trail mix, and bars for lunch, and enough snacks to fill in the cracks. At the market buying supplies, a five-year-old girl in a princess dress enviously looks over at the grotesque quantity of candy and snack foods in my cart. It is also overflowing with dehydrated meals, jerky, crackers, and dried fruit. I have picked up some items from Bernheimer's packing lists as well: cans of beans, jarred peaches, sardines, and ketchup. The final touches include blank notebooks, candy, and beer. The woman at check-out helps me haul three carts of food to my truck.

To carry the load, Bernheimer brought forty horses and mules. I have one backpack. I consider nicknaming it Skippety Ann, Oatmeal, or Spaghetti to pay homage to Bernheimer's favorite horses. Walking may be slower, but it alleviates me from another 2,500 pounds of food to pack for the animals. At night I collapse into bed, not into my notebook. I now understand why John Wetherill and Zeke Johnson never wrote about these trips. Getting ready for it is an expedition in itself.

In mid-March, I set an automated message on my email and cut the tether to civilization:

> *On an expedition in the desert. I am uncertain of an exact return date. Cheers to exploration!*

The only task left is to take that first step.

CHAPTER FOURTEEN

Water in the Desert

Our zeal and a throbbing vein for adventure would not allow us to be balked in our planning regardless of the countless obstacles we were bound to encounter.

—Charles L. Bernheimer

Stevo peers over the edge of the sandstone pour-off. He lowers his sunglasses, lifts the brim of his hat, and sighs, "You just don't mess around with water!"

Janes Tank, the water hole we have been hiking to for five days, is dry. Joel Arnold, one of Stevo's hiking buddies who was eager to join our adventure, chimes in, "Oh dear." The original plan was to resupply with precious liquid here and then traverse a series of canyons to an overlook of the Colorado River where the Bernheimer Expedition descended Mancos Mesa. This disappointing scene is now our paradoxical turnaround point.

Mancos Mesa is the largest isolated slickrock mesa in southern Utah. Narrow canyons cut through its colorful layers and unite with Glen Canyon, now Lake Powell. The purple-hued silhouettes of the Henry Mountains cast a rain shadow over the mesa's arid, sandswept expanse. This was not the starting point of Bernheimer's 1929 expedition, but it is one of the driest stretches, so we are attempting it first. March is typically a wetter month in this part of the desert—even snow is possible. But this extremely dry winter comes on the heels of the previous monsoon-less summer, and another lackluster winter the year before. The stark lack of water drains my hope for the rest of the expedition.

In 1929 Janes Tank was dry, but Wetherill was able to find a nearby pothole filled with rainwater and thus avert a crisis. The 1920s was a relatively wet period in the Southwest, and the overall global climate was cooler. Earth's average temperature has risen 0.14°F per decade since 1880, and 0.32°F per decade since 1981. Climate scientist Brad Udall put together a panel plot of the Colorado River watersheds since records began in 1910 that shows an upward trend in temperatures overall and a downward trend in precipitation. The period between 2013 and 2021 are the ten warmest years on record according to NOAA on Climate.gov.

In addition to water woes, it was difficult for Bernheimer's team to find feed for their animals here. Stevo estimates that back then there would have been upwards of four to five hundred cows on Mancos Mesa. The open range concept allowed ranchers and sheep farmers to graze an unlimited number of stock anywhere on public land. Then, in 1934, the Taylor Grazing Act was enacted to prevent soil deterioration and overgrazing impacts on public lands. The end goal was to stabilize the livestock industry, which was suffering from the overcrowding—the benefits to the land were only a secondary effect. The law established grazing districts and required stockmen to pay a fee for each cow/calf pair the rancher had on the land per month.

Old cowboys have told Stevo how horrible the range was pre–Taylor Grazing Act, and how much it has improved since then. The act is not a perfect solution to the problems associated with grazing on public lands, but it does reduce livestock impacts. By the 1970s, the BLM began managing the land according to specific rangeland resources, including riparian areas, endangered species, and cultural sites.

Enforcement today is nebulous. Stevo casually lectures as we trudge through the sand, "Government range riders used to monitor stock use on allotments. Now they rely on the honor system." Agency staff do periodically visit grazing allotments to assess utilization—how much grass the livestock have eaten in the current year—but it is difficult for them to require any changes in livestock use, regardless of the conditions. Stevo mentions a cattle fence we hiked alongside a few days ago, and explains how the cowboys used to "ride fence," meaning along its length, to ensure cattle were confined to a designated zone. This still happens today, but it is nearly impossible to monitor all of the fences.

Mancos Mesa is the home of a relict plant community, meaning native vegetation that was once broadly abundant but is now confined to a smaller area. This includes perennial grasses, shrubs, and cacti. Most plants have been munched down to the nubs by the cows, including the blackbrush and Mormon tea, which are not their preferred meal. Unlike wetter canyons, dry, exposed terrain like this has difficulty fully recovering from the cows who continue to use it as a salad bar. The remaining vegetation hardly even gets a chance to produce seeds and grow new plants. Since the 1970s, grazing has expanded, reducing the relict zone.

On the original 2016 Bears Ears National Monument map, Mancos Mesa is the boxy island separated from the main monument boundaries by Red Canyon. It was among the areas removed from monument protections in 2017. Still, it is protected as a Wilderness Study Area (WSA), which is a strong level of federal land protection. In theory, no new development or grazing leases should take place within its boundaries, but until the US Congress formally designates it as "Wilderness" it could be developed.

In the 1970s, the BLM recommended closing Mancos Mesa to both mining and grazing interests. But instead of withdrawing it from mineral entry, mining roads were constructed, and uranium exploration occurred anyway. It was finally designated a WSA in 1992, based upon Mancos Mesa's Wilderness attributes: excellent opportunities for solitude, cultural sites, native plants, and wildlife habitats. Unfortunately, the WSA designation happened too late to avoid the ongoing impacts from roads and overgrazing.

It's well known that hikers should avoid stepping on blackened cryptobiotic soils, the delicate living desert biocrusts made of algae, cyanobacteria, and fungi. Cattle grazing on arid lands are one of the most serious crust-busting offenders. This, coupled with eating away the native grasses that once thrived here, allows invasive and exotic species to move in. As we walk, Stevo says, "Early diarists to this country wrote of grass 'belly-deep on a horse.' Now those same pastures are covered with cheatgrass, big sagebrush, blackbrush, and Russian thistle, also known as tumbleweeds."

It's not like the cows are thriving here. In the last few days, we've seen small clusters of a dozen or so scrawny cows with protruding ribs and shabby hair. Most of the cattle are concentrated in the canyon bottoms, where there is some promise of water pocketed in sandstone potholes. The mass bovine bone heaps we've encountered in empty water holes tell the real story.

This does not mean that Mancos Mesa is a wasteland. It's a crucial yearlong habitat for a native herd of desert bighorn sheep that the state of Utah uses to transplant and repopulate other native habitats. Mule deer, mountain lions, foxes, coyotes, peregrine falcons, and chuckwalla lizards all reside here. Unlike humans and cattle, these animals have adapted to living in this arid mesa.

Two cows wander into our camp this morning; I reckon they are stopping by to see if we have any water to spare. We do not.

Stevo is right—you don't mess around with water. Even a seemingly tame activity such as backpacking can and will turn deadly without it. We each only have enough water to get back to our last known source. Most days we carry three gallons of water each, roughly twenty-five pounds, bringing the total weight of my pack to over fifty-five pounds. As we hike, we try to look up at the gorgeous scenery to distract us from the miserable loads we carry.

The clouds cast a somber shadow at Janes Tank when we decide to turn around. Joel apologizes to me for falling short of our goal. His sincerity is touching, and I am not disappointed at all. These group safety decisions are exactly the type of expedition experience I want. To shift the mood, I pull up a scanned black-and-white photo saved on my phone. Wetherill and Morris are sitting on the ground, shoulders slouched, heads tilted. Bernheimer stands between them, with perfect posture and a stately air of determination on his face. After a decade of traveling the backcountry alongside his desert guides, Bernheimer seems to be at the pinnacle of his confidence in his outdoor abilities, honed far away from his daily life among the skyscrapers of Manhattan.

We prepare to re-create the photo, adjusting everyone's hats and testing out our facial expressions to mirror theirs. I set up the camera on a rock and dash across the sand to enter the scene before the timer goes off. We do a few retakes until our serious explorer faces relax into smiles.

Scattered line camp equipment has been left here by local cowboys over the last century: lassos, metal bins filled with oats, saddle-sore balm, saddle blankets, horseshoes, and chains. Joel, an astute student of historic artifacts and antiques, identifies some of the more unusual objects, like an anvil for sizing horseshoes that was attached to a steel post. He explains that the equipment used by cowboys has not changed much in the last one hundred years, but that no one would bring horses here if there was no water. I wonder when the last time was that Janes Tank had enough water to make it useful for the cowboys. Nearby, a bighorn sheep petroglyph indicates that the use of this spot as a camp goes back much further.

Stevo reaches into his pocket for a printed page of stories about Janes Tank that he saved for this occasion. He tells us that this spot was named after an old mule named Jane who often wandered here from camp. We munch on trail mix and listen. The story is one told to him by local rancher Eric Bayles:

> Harrison (Oliver) was kind of a little short fellow, and (his son) Erwin was big and tall....Harrison comes in early one day choking to death and went up there and crawled in [Janes] tank and got a drink, and when Erwin come home, back to Janes Tank, he just started supper and tended stuff and wondered where his dad was. Finally, he went to get some water and there wasn't no bucket, so he went up there and his dad was in the tank, been in there all afternoon. He said, "Hell, kid, took you long enough to get here!" He was so short he couldn't get out of the tank.

These stories are published in Stevo's encyclopedic *Utah's Canyon Country Place Names*. It took him fifteen years to write the two volumes, but they reflect his lifetime immersion in the desert and its stories. His research is a mixture of boots-on-the-ground exploration, meticulous combing of historical archives, and talking to knowledgeable locals. In *"Place Names,"* as he refers to the books, one can look up just about any notable location in Utah's canyon country and gain knowledge on a wide range of topics, including place-name origins, history, famous quotes, and the region's defining geographical features. In some instances, these books may be the only written record of such information.

The books mostly cover English language names given after

the arrival of white settlers; this was primarily due to Stevo's time and language limitations. Fully documenting Indigenous place names is a monumental task that Stevo hopes Indigenous historians and anthropologists pursue.

Janes Tank was the spot that set Stevo's project ablaze:

Someone asked me about Janes Tank. I'd never heard of it. I scoured the maps. Nothing, I searched the literature. Nada. I queried my friends. Zip. Then I asked a local rancher and I got an ear full. It was an epiphany. I didn't know as much about the land as I thought I did. I'd been to Janes Tank on top of Mancos Mesa several times; I'd even camped there. But, I didn't know the name of this huge pothole that had been used for generations of cowboys as a line camp. I needed to learn more, not only about Janes Tank but about hundreds if not other thousands of other named places in canyon country.

The best of Stevo's outlandish tales are not written down. One evening on Mancos Mesa, while eating dinner, he opens up about the time he met an elderly Everett Ruess on the Navajo Nation. Ruess was a twenty-year-old wandering artist who went missing near Escalante, Utah in 1934. While many historians and reporters have attempted to solve the mystery of his disappearance and write about it, Stevo's story, enlivened by his intimate knowledge of the terrain Ruess roamed, made all other hypotheses I've heard fade away.

- - - - -

Detours were not an uncommon occurrence on Bernheimer's expeditions. Johnson promised the group that it would be smooth sailing to traverse Mancos Mesa. He spoke too soon. After Janes Tank, Johnson made a few wrong turns. In the heat and high winds, the weary team retraced their steps, over rough, waterless terrain. It took them a full day of toil to get back on course.

As if Bernheimer's notes were not confusing enough, sorting through the section where they were lost is comedy. Stevo chimes in, "It's great that Bernheimer and his team didn't write everything down because now we get to try and figure it out!" These challenges, not the desire to reach the destination, are the reason we pursue this game.

To avoid wasting time and water by getting off course, we frequently stop to look at our maps. On each paper map, Stevo adds lines, dots, and notes to fill in what we see on the ground. The land is not blank, and never was, but the maps share only a fraction of the information that our eyes see out there.

We eat another snack and discuss our options, which will be decided collectively. I appreciate the respect they have for my ideas—these guys have over forty years of experience hiking in the desert. I have not even been alive that long. I cringe writing that down in my journal, but I do so out of reverence for their wisdom.

Stevo asks me, "Do you think Wetherill and Johnson got along?"

It's a fair question to ponder. Scuffles between Wetherill and Johnson were not uncommon. "Hmmm..." my mouth stuck together with peanut butter, "Who would go on trips with people you didn't like every year for a decade?" Thankfully, our team synergy is smooth even when things don't go as planned.

The breaks are anything but relief as we shiver in the cold and driving winds. Assessing Bernheimer's interview with the *New York Times* after his trip, it's fair to say he was not overexaggerating how tough conditions can be here:

> The heat was intense. The nights were at times freezing; the sandblasts distressing; the fatigue was overwhelming. The water was for many days poisonously unfit to drink—

it smelled like ammonia—and there was nothing to do but go ahead and drink it or choose the [sic] alternative.... Sometimes it rained....Climbing perilous ladders or along trails scratched into the side of precipices or over slick rocks, steep and slippery, provided the most constant dangers of all.

A faint indentation through the sagebrush aligns with Bernheimer's note, "A trail here means where some cattle or cowpunchers' horses have at one time traveled—possibly several years before—and such trails are at best very deceptive in view of the sand drift." That this cattle trail exists up here is a testament to it still being occasionally used today, no matter how improbable that seems.

Joel declares, "Look, I see some of Bernheimer's footprints on the trail!" Stevo stops abruptly, picks up a stick, and draws a footprint into the sand, adding the letters CB in the middle. We've yet to spot any footprints besides our own. And those tracks are almost immediately covered up with sand by the howling wind, which has been our perpetual nemesis. I cinch my hood and wear sunglasses, even when it is overcast, to protect myself. The three of us laugh at how tan our faces appear set against our exceptionally white teeth—effects of our daily sand dermabrasion facial and teeth whitening.

The cattle trail parallels a massive dune that drops off into the canyon below. Bernheimer recorded this as a steep but pleasant descent. Dust rises like smoke from the sleek, sandy cornice, shaped by the wind, atop the peak of the 400-foot dune. The orange horizon leads our eyes toward the contrasting view of the jagged, snowcapped Henry Mountains. Stevo shouts over the wind gales, "Woohoo! Let's go straight down the gnar!" With skier's stances and trekking poles in hand, we drop directly down the face, weaving our way down like it is a powder day.

On our way back out of the canyon, we scour the ground

for subtle signs like piles of rocks, steps hacked into sandstone, crude ramps, and cattle-trampled paths. This is a move in our game of desert Chutes and Ladders. Instead of struggling back up the steep sand slope, a "chute," we hope to find a "ladder," meaning another constructed stock trail. The land no longer looks as untouched as it once did to me—there are literally trails everywhere. The early 1900s were the heyday of stock trails because the cowboys were desperate for every blade of grass they could find. So they built trails to improve access. Stevo says, "If a rancher could keep his cattle or sheep from starving for another week or two, perhaps that would be enough to get through a season."

On the edge of a cliff, Stevo points out a "Navajo fast route" in the cleft of sandstone. These were more simply manicured passageways—a rock cleared here, a footpath imprinted there—used by sheepherders to move quickly in and out of canyons, or to access water sources. We gingerly down-climbed a loose slab of rock, lowering our packs and roping up to avoid slipping down the steep ten-foot descent. Once around the Wingate Sandstone corner, a striking side-notched projectile point, pale pink in color, directs the way down into the canyon where there is one full pothole. We won't have to ration water tonight. We celebrate with hot cups of soup and Gatorade as hydrating appetizers before dinner.

At night it is so windy that it requires all three of us to set up and tether down my über-lightweight tent. I am stressed and embarrassed to need help with the simple task. Joel gives me a big hug and tells me it's going to be just fine. A thoughtful hiking companion is more essential than any fancy gear. When I crawl inside my tent, I discover that my sleeping pad is flat. Lying against the ground, I listen to the wind howl in my quivering shelter. On one trip Bernheimer's rubber air mattress deflated, and his team fixed it with chewing gum.

I toss and turn trying to get comfortable on the hard, cold

ground. Exhaustion eventually holds down my eyelids and restlessness, until I hear the pitter patter of raindrops on the tent. Now that we have plenty of water, of course it rains. For a moment I forget about my equipment woes and drift off to sleep, grateful for the gift of water in the desert.

I unzip my tent the next morning and the sand is saturated with water. Stevo is already sitting next to a newly filled pothole; in its reflection I can see the orange glow of the canyon walls drenched with sunlight. We bask in the warm light during breakfast until more dark clouds accumulate. We pack up camp and hike until the skies unleash again. In a matter of hours, our plans shift from no water to lots of rain.

We stop and take shelter at a large alcove, and unanimously decide to wait out the storm beneath it. A cup placed outside the cave fills with water in minutes. Ephemeral waterfalls cascade off the canyon rim into the creek below us, rushing and gurgling. Watching water fall is mesmerizing, listening is worship.

Stevo yelps like a coyote, "Well, it looks like your trip is saved, my dear!" With over two hundred miles ahead of me, that is a true relief. The fresh water in the potholes is a blessing I will be drinking for weeks to come. So will Stevo, who plans to spend the next two and a half months out backpacking. He admits that age may be slowing him down a bit, which is hard for me to imagine with the perpetual smile streaked across his face. He only has one complaint: "I envy how much of this desert country you still haven't seen yet, Mo."

The rain finally ceases, and the sunlight illuminates glossy canyon walls. It's barely five o'clock, and there is chatter about hiking for a few more hours. I speak up and vote for us to stay right here, to sit in reverence and appreciate the rain. The petrichor of nearly dried-up sagebrush and damp sand tickles my nose. Stevo picks up the tin cup, now overflowing with water. "You're right, MoMo, life is good. Look where we are. This isn't a backpacking trip—we are living in the desert."

CHAPTER FIFTEEN

#Bernheimer

Back at my truck, I have twenty-four hours to recover, clean up, and prepare to meet Harvey Leake at the Grand Gulch trailhead for the next segment. With a touch of cell service, I check in with my mom—communication with loved ones during an expedition would be unfathomable to Bernheimer. During my layover I also post a few photos from the last eleven days on Instagram with the caption:

> @running_bum_: The toughest part about this first stretch of the expedition is that it's over.

Bernheimer would have made an excellent Instagram influencer. In many of his expedition photos he posed alongside wildflowers, wearing his felt brimmed hat, bandanna, riding boots, and a wistful gaze. I can imagine one of his posts, coupled with a stately photo of the team on horseback:

> @ManhattanCliffDweller: A desert promenade among the purple sage with @EMorris @ZekeJ and @JW during the 1929 #BernheimerExpedition. #Sponsored on behalf of @ AMNH @Smithsonian @CarnegieInstitute.

Initially, my Instagram account, @running_bum_, was a fun way to share photos of my running and travel adventures. Upon moving into my Jeep and out to the desert, my account's following grew exponentially, almost overnight. It has since presented opportunities and challenges in equal measure.

I consider my work as an "influencer" as no different than another writer working part-time as a bartender. It helps me pay the bills so I can focus on writing long-lead feature articles and books that can take years of research and toil before any money is made. During a typical month I am juggling several content creation contracts, with at least one freelance writing assignment.

The behind-the-scenes work begins with negotiating the contract terms with a brand, and then finding a way for the client to ship me the product, be it a camp stove or a jacket, despite my remote locations. Once I pick up the gear, which sometimes requires me to drive across state lines, I keep it with me until I am in a scenario in which I would naturally use it. When the inspiration strikes, I pull out my two-year-old, badly scratched iPhone and set it up, using a tree or rock as a makeshift tripod. There are no fancy sets, cosmetics, or even showers. To get the shot, a timer on my camera and lots of practice help me capture running and action shots.

On set in nature, I am the photographer, lighting director, stylist, producer, and model. Afterward, I get into post-production mode and edit the photos and videos. Then my writer hat comes on, and I draft the copy, report to the marketing girl (still me) to add brand tags and messaging, and then submit to the client. Once they approve the piece, I share it to my account on a specified date and time, which often requires me to climb a high mesa or park at a certain spot to access decent cell service. Once it's posted, I turn off my phone and retreat into the wild, to walk or write, until the dance begins again.

These are all skills I have honed from my work freelance

writing, modeling, running professionally, living outdoors, and as the vice president of a marketing firm in my twenties. I am grateful that for this moment in time social media offers an outlet to combine these abilities with the outdoor freedom I need. When the opportunities shift from social media to whatever is next, I will still have these skills and be ready to pivot. Despite the effort and skill required, content creators and influencers are still stigmatized as people who don't have "real" careers, evidenced by the frequent eye rolls or air quotes used by folks who say, "Oh, she's an 'influencer.'" I have learned to shrug it off.

A nasty side effect of my online presence is relentless trolling, which has escalated to include sexual harassment, public blogs flogging my actions, and abusive personal emails. "Stupid Fucking Bitch" was the most memorable subject line. Some people have been motivated enough to write letters to my publishers and brand partners pleading with them to stop working with me. An author I respected as a mentor told me no one would take me seriously as a historian and writer until I stopped running around in my bikini. One woman continues to make aliases, fake accounts, and new emails to harass me, my friends, and my family. The motives of people who do this seem to originate from their desire to express their misogyny and hate, with the aim of silencing a voice other than their own.

Some of this stems from a belief that social media is at the root of evil in nature. In one article titled, "How Instagram Ruined the Great Outdoors," the author called me the most insidious of Instagram influencers, mocked my photos, and criticized me for attracting attention to Bears Ears. He further claimed that I do nothing to draw awareness to overgrazing or high-impact tourism, blatantly slandering me rather than reading a single one of my articles or Instagram posts that do just that.

Limited cell service protects me from the flying monkeys—strangers hiding behind their phones, determined to belittle, scare, or intimidate me. Into doing what? Quitting my jobs? My employers have all stood up for me through this torment, recommending that I not engage with vicious commenters. Repressing my urge to explain or stand up for myself, I ignore the trolls and kept living my life. Despite the support, all of this has taken a toll on my mental health. Imagine the most toxic work environment possible with no way to stop it aside from quitting. It's a form of job-related stress that I certainly was not prepared for, nor something I will ever accept. These tactics are an act of violence against my peace of mind.

While silence is my preferred response to anyone who makes an effort to harm me, speaking up might help someone else who is being trolled. It might even encourage an online bully to pause before hitting "send." Over 40 percent of Americans experience some form of online harassment or cyberbullying, with several studies reporting that women are disproportionately targeted for sexually oriented online abuse. The United Nations considers this a form of violence against women and has created online safety guidelines while also calling upon governments, civil rights groups, and online services to take action.

While there is no justification for hate and bullying, these experiences have pushed me to study and better understand how social media affects the outdoors and to assess my participation and role in those outcomes. It is essential to tread as lightly on the internet as we do on the land. On one of my very first trips to Bears Ears I took a photo with my hand placed gently upon an ancestral dwelling wall and shared it on Instagram. At the time, I was completely unaware that this is disrespectful at cultural sites and could inadvertently damage them. My post incited a full-blown social media flogging. I pulled it down immediately. The incident taught me how to visit cultural sites with respect, but that educating people in a gentler way is more effective. The outcome would have been the same if someone had sent me a kind and educational note.

Education is vastly different from shaming, the latter of

which is a major problem on social media. Some profiles are devoted to calling out or canceling people who are behaving badly outdoors, be it taking a fashionable photo in wildflowers or camping on a sensitive surface. Seeing images like this is certainly distressing, but the Leave No Trace Center for Outdoor Ethics (LNT) cautions that negative feedback or call-out culture is ineffective in educating the public or influencing their behavior, according to psychological studies.

In an op-ed article I wrote in *Backpacker* magazine, "Outdoor Shaming Needs to Stop," I weighed in on Leave No Trace's new "anti-shaming" clause:

Rather than positively influencing people, shaming is actually associated with greater levels of anxiety, depression, and social stress. Ironically, these are some of the ailments we seek relief from in the outdoors. All that is to say, that shaming either encourages people to otherize themselves by acting worse, or it excludes them from an experience they could really use. Which of those is a positive outcome?

Alisa Walsh, Leave No Trace's social media coordinator, explained:

Leave No Trace is sometimes turned into a weapon, wielded to shame rather than educate. Comments ranging from calling out someone's lack of knowledge or experience, to violent threats and personal attacks, are sometimes done in the name of Leave No Trace.

Despite the positive response to my article from conservation groups and other people who have been harassed, I still got shamed by a mob of online bullies. My course of action, supported by both the publication and the LNT, was to ignore them

and return to the desert where I could remain blissfully disconnected from the nonsense.

Each time I write or take a photo, I consider, and occasionally agonize, about its potential effects before sharing. If in doubt,
I simply do not post. A careless choice can leave a mark or send
the wrong message, not unlike a footprint in delicate cryptobiotic soils. Even though I explained in my Instagram post today
that I am on a long backpacking trip, I have kept many details
intentionally vague. I do not want a bunch of strangers to know
exactly where I am. That same safety tactic helps protect the
sensitive places I visit. Social media is often devoid of nuance,
which is why I like the element of mystery. When locations are
left to the imagination, the world becomes endlessly large and
wondrous.

Concerns about crowds infiltrating remote corners of the
desert are not new. A 1925 *Literary Review* blurb on the back of
Bernheimer's book *Rainbow Bridge*, lamented, "One's only regret
is that Mr. Bernheimer's book is likely to send hordes of tourists
to Rainbow Bridge, spoiling its present solitary majesty." Back
then, the books and articles Bernheimer wrote for *National Geographic* were one of the few ways to read about far-flung travels
and offered readers perspectives beyond their own worldview.
Today, that same comment is guaranteed to pop up on an Instagram post about an eye-catching locale, with the addition of a
few expletives.

The spectrum between maintaining secrecy and encouraging exploitation of sensitive areas has raised conflicting concerns
and perspectives throughout the last century. In 1963, following
the completion of the Glen Canyon Dam, Elliot Porter penned
and photographed *The Place No One Knew*. The premise was
that if more people had experienced the beauty of Glen Canyon,
there would have been more people protesting the dam. In the
foreword, Sierra Club President David Brower wrote:

> Glen Canyon died in 1963 and I was partly responsible for its needless death. So were you. Neither you nor I, nor anyone else, knew it well enough to insist that at all costs it should endure.

Of course Bernheimer, along with generations of Diné, Hopi, Ute, and Paiute people, would object to that title. But Brower was right about one thing—we are all responsible for protecting these places.

In 1921 the US population was 108 million, and in 2021 it is 330 million. Travel has been made easier, more accessible, and affordable. Population growth means more people everywhere, including the outdoors, which makes the resulting human impacts a legitimate problem. It also means there can be more people to speak up on behalf of protecting the wild world.

Steve Allen and I have discussed the present conundrum extensively. We've both written guidebooks and articles about Utah's canyon country, and these works inherently attract new visitors. We both have proceeded with these projects with the intent that guidebooks can be used as tools to help aid preservation measures.

Stevo's three guidebooks, written during the 1990s, aim to educate hikers about respectful visitation and encourage participation in protecting these landscapes. Guidebooks, like maps, help people access and navigate the outdoors, and these are the gateway to the experiences that encourage people to get involved with the protection of threatened places.

In 2017 and 2018 I wrote guidebooks to Bears Ears and Grand Staircase–Escalante National Monuments. I was motivated by the fact that both places are simultaneously experiencing more media exposure and visitation with less federal protection, management, and funding, which has created a precarious imbalance. With limited educational and informational materials available to the public after the Bears Ears designation, people were increasingly turning to the internet for information. And with this comes the problem of giving away too many details, like direct GPS links to cultural sites, while neglecting to provide information about cultural significance, safety, and visiting with respect.

Initially I was hesitant to write a hiking guide. First, I was brand new to the region, not to mention that there is a certain stigma against guidebook authors, even from people who use their books. The first time I met my friend Ralph Burrillo, he told me that he had sworn on his grave that he would never get involved with a guidebook. The next day, while talking on a hike, he had a change of heart. Ralph encouraged me to take the project on because he saw that I was genuinely concerned about the future of Bears Ears. We schemed how writing it could be an opportunity to ensure that the first guidebook to the new monument helped, rather than hurt, it. Cedar Mesa guidebooks have already been around for decades, but they do not reflect the monument designation, reduction, and boundaries-in-flux. We agreed it was possible to write a guide aimed at providing essential information to help mitigate the new challenges Bears Ears National Monument faced.

Ralph taught me about the "sacrifice site" strategy, today called "focal sites." The idea is to steer visitors toward hikes most easily managed by the Bureau of Land Management for visitation, and therefore distract them from more sensitive cultural sites. As my research confidant, Ralph helped me select hikes, careful to also point out what locations should *not* be included. My guidebooks educate readers about visiting cultural sites respectfully and about Leave No Trace ethics, and they include overviews of the monument reductions to help people understand what is at stake with fewer protections.

The goal of my guidebooks, like Stevo's before me, is to inspire hikers to become advocates to protect places where they recreate. Not everyone agrees with this approach. Some people hate guidebooks in general, fearing they will give away secret spots. Environmentalists have legitimate concerns about the impacts of increased visitation on the fragile desert ecosystem. Stevo told me that he has had people complain about his guidebooks, and then have the audacity to ask him personally for information about an area. This sense of entitlement is also expressed by people complaining about a crowded trail or national park when they are in fact a part of the crowd. It's a double standard about who gets to be privy to location information in the outdoors, known as gatekeeping. Who deserves to enjoy these places? The answer is, in short, everyone. Locals and longtime visitors are not more deserving of hiking the trails or a certain campsite than newcomers.

Social media has now stepped into the limelight for the ongoing debate over the consequences and ethics of sharing information about the outdoors. Today almost everyone has a smartphone that can broadcast GPS coordinates, geotags, and other location data to billions of people worldwide with a single click. The internet colonizes every inch of unmapped earth and our once private lives. There's no denying the correlation between social media and increased visitation to beautiful areas the world over. Unlike guidebooks that are intentionally sought by people looking to visit a certain place, social sharing apps provide a constant stream of information and inspiration about locations people may not have previously considered visiting.

In response, the LNT created guidelines, not black-and-white rules, for social media use outdoors. These include suggestions to consider what your images portray, to educate others about LNT guidelines, and to give back to the places you love. LNT suggests that people "tag a general location such as a state or region, if any at all. While tagging can seem innocent, it can lead to significant impacts."

Still, LNT emphasizes that they are not anti-geotagging. "Posting a photo that specifies your location along with appropriate Leave No Trace information can be a great way for others to educate and invite people into the outdoors. It empowers people to research safety measures, learn about the location's history and culture, and find out what to expect when visiting." Although this puts the ability and responsibility to educate in everyone's hands, the caveat is that one cannot assume that people will do that type of research on their own.

The Bears Ears Inter-Tribal Coalition takes a stronger stance against geotagging, and states in their respectful visitation guidelines, "Please do not reveal a site's location, GPS coordinates, or utilize geotags on social media as this can attract large foot traffic to an unprotected space." These guidelines are developed by Indigenous people based upon how they want their homelands to be treated.

People are often looking for something or someone to blame for overcrowding in the outdoors. Mainstream media increasingly villainizes social media use by posting headlines like "National Parks Officials Grappling with High Volume as Instagram Tourism Booms" and "The Paradox of Instagram Famous Wilderness." These clickbait stories often fail to provide a complete picture of the myriad forces driving visitation upticks.

Ralph explains misperceptions about visitation and social media data in his second book, *The Backwoods of Everywhere*. There's a strong positive correlation between ice cream sales and shark attacks, but it's because both are associated with sunny days, not because of any causal relationship between the two. Similarly, although the rise in visitation to public lands is accompanied by a rise in social media usage in general—and the appearance of public lands in photos on social media in particular—this doesn't mean the one is driving the other. Not necessarily, anyway. Instead, it appears to be more likely that the two are simply increasing at the same time rather than in response to each other. This is probably linked to a common lurking variable—escapism. Both the out-of-doors and social media offer means of escaping the everyday, and these days the everyday is pretty grim.

A 2021 study, "Bears Ears and Outdoor Recreation in San Juan County," demonstrates that visitation has indeed increased as a direct result of the monument, but the number of photos on Instagram and Flickr did not increase. This suggests that social media was not the primary contributor to the overall trend of increased visitation.

Other spots in the Southwest have certainly gone viral. The number of people taking the same photo as everyone else at Horseshoe Bend near Page, Arizona has increased from four thousand people annually to over two million in only the last few years. The Wave, located in the Paria Canyon–Vermilion Cliffs Wilderness, was once a local attraction until print magazines and, later, social media regularly began sharing stunning photos of it with the world. Visitation steadily increased until it exploded, and the BLM began regulating visitation with a permit system. Angels Landing in Zion National Park is the next major destination in Utah to be managed with a lottery permit system.

The effects of major advertising budgets on increased tourism cannot be overlooked. The state of Utah's "Mighty 5" campaign promotes Utah's five national parks: Zion, Bryce Canyon, Arches, Capitol Reef, and Canyonlands. The campaign's advertising budget of $3.1 million brought an average of half a million new visitors per year to these parks during a three-year run. During the ad period, Arches National Park was already actively trying to reduce visitation, which now exceeds the park's capacity. A line of cars often stretches for miles from the park, and a new timed entrance system is being implemented in 2022 to address the demand and associated issues.

The COVID-19 pandemic also plays a role in recent increased visitation to national parks and public lands. With travel restrictions and an emphasis on social distancing, outdoor vacations have had a greater appeal. With remote working and learning more widespread, more people are free to travel year-round than before. This compounds the pressures already being placed upon national parks, where staff fell by 14 percent and overall visitation jumped 20 percent in the last decade.

As a Band-Aid, the National Park Service encourages visitors in overcrowded national parks to disperse to other federal land jurisdictions, like BLM areas and national forests, where you don't have to book campgrounds in advance or secure permits. Ultimately this means that the NPS is ushering people to places with less management, less educational infrastructure, and scant funding, which sets these more sensitive areas up for significant impacts. For example, Bears Ears National Monument has only two BLM law enforcement rangers covering nearly two million acres. Kane Gulch Ranger Station is only open for limited hours during spring and autumn. During COVID-19, permits and information have only been available online, and permit holders are requested to watch an educational video before their trip. It's up to the honor system for them to follow through.

Stevo believes that when it is too crowded, or a permit is too hard to get, people will inevitably drive down the road and hike somewhere else. Based on his experiences, heading to the backcountry is certainly a viable way to disperse people and prevent overcrowding: "In the past ten years I have literally seen no more than ten people TOTAL in the backcountry." He is willing to walk much farther into remote country than the average backpacker.

I concur. We did not see any footprints besides our own over the last eleven days of backpacking. That does not mean that even a small uptick in backcountry recreation does not come with consequences. In an article for the Society for American Archaeology, Ralph compares the potential effects of the increasing backcountry popularity in Bears Ears with the much more thoroughly studied conditions at the Grand Canyon. "The desire to escape the crowds by pushing deeper and deeper into the Grand Canyon's imposing backcountry includes both intentional and unintentional visitation of archaeological resources, many of which bear scars as a result."

We are all part of the problem. And whether you learned about a place in a print magazine, or on a travel website, an Instagram post, or a regular map, you still leave footprints on the land. Therefore, a solution must be collective and must consider the current state of our culture and lifestyles to be effective. There is no denying that simply by being alive, humans alter the planet, and never as negatively as we have in the last century. As the blame game continues to point fingers from one user group to the next, solutions evade the lands that need them most. Recreation is arguably far less damaging than a dam or a strip mine, but the unmanaged long-term effects may have just as dire consequences. Increased funding, management presence, and permitting are all necessary tactics to address this.

The conundrum of our generation is to navigate the increasing complexity of protecting wild places. Social media is the frontier of this moment; uncharted terrain that will take generations to understand how it affects human consciousness, and our physical impact on each other and the planet. One hundred years ago, location information was routinely lost. Now nothing is.

The internet is not going anywhere. Rather than wage a war against it, or attempt to ban people from using it outdoors, we each must find the best ways to live intentionally with it. As long as social media and the internet exists, it is in our best interest to seek ways to use it as a conservation tool rather than simply gripe about it. After all, the World Wide Web churns out information, and photos, faster than our government churns out reactive federal land management plans.

People with a large online audience have an opportunity to influence other people about better outdoor ethics. It's a brilliant tactic utilized by social media celebrity "Pattie Gonia," a self-professed homosexual drag queen and activist who has 425,000 followers. Pattie frequently partners with conservation groups and outdoor brands to make entertaining, educational videos to raise money for important causes. During a 2021 campaign, they raised $538,920 for five BIPOC (Black, Indigenous and People of Color), Queer, and environmental nonprofits. In addition to increasing funding, teaming up with influencers is another way to both grow a conservation group's audience and expand the reach of their educational information.

Public lands management needs to consider increasing its online presence, as well as seeking opportunities to team up and educate through visitors with larger influence. These individuals are potential frontline advocates to educate people and recruit new stewards. The number of followers an account has directly correlates to its influence and ability to disseminate information. Consider that Glen Canyon NRA has 44,000 Instagram followers compared to a celebrity like pop star Miley Cyrus who has 155 million. A few years ago, Cyrus took a trip to Page, Arizona, and posted a photo of herself within a narrow slot canyon. Guess which photo is more broadly accessed and influential to the public? Bears Ears National Monument does not even have its own social platform. As a result, the education initiatives fall upon groups like the Greater Bears Ears Partnership, Bears Ears Inter-Tribal Coalition, and Utah Diné Bikéyah, which have 3,000, 7,000, and 17,700 followers, respectively.

Ideally, this internet consciousness needs to include land management and state tourism boards, whose platforms and advertisements encourage and set the tone for visitation. Likewise, it is prudent for conservation groups to invest in building up their content, audience numbers, and engagement on Facebook, Instagram and Tik-Tok so that their information is prominent when people do search on social media. This is not to say that viewing social media posts should replace learning about a place from topographic maps and talking to real people, including rangers, visitor center staff, and locals. The internet can nudge people in this direction. You know, like a guidebook.

In addition to education is the all-important need to support conservation groups, who do the heavy lifting of advocating policy changes and participating in lawsuits. Stevo is a practicing believer in "tithing for wilderness," an idea passed along to him by Ginger Harmon, a devoted environmentalist and one of the most experienced canyon rats ever. The concept: Every time you go on a trip, donate to one of the groups who is helping protect the land you are walking on. Signing up for a volunteer trip is another great way to get involved while out on the land. In southern Utah, that includes the Grand Canyon Trust, Grand Staircase-Escalante Partners, Great Old Broads, and Southern Utah Wilderness Alliance.

This is why I am compelled to devote the work I do as a writer and on social media to these places. The time required for research and exploration is something I have in full, compared to what I have in my bank account. While some of these writing efforts I share with the public, much of my time is spent penning public comments about land management decisions. As someone who cannot afford to make large donations, I support conservation groups by joining at the basic membership level, especially Indigenous-led groups like the Bears Ears Inter-Tribal Coalition, Utah Diné Bikéyah, and Tó Nizhóní Ání. These organizations still gain strength and traction through their collective numbers.

And this is what I admire most about Bernheimer: he sought ways to give back to the places he loved to explore—first by supporting local guides; then by funding scientific research; and, finally, by proposing to protect these places with a national park. Bernheimer can still be an influencer a century after his expeditions, encouraging folks to do as he did, whether through their financial contributions or writing an informative message alongside a photo of someone posing with wildflowers. There are so many ways to step up as a defender and ally of the places we love, and it is essential that we each use our abilities and tools available to inspire others to do the same. Asking ourselves how we can be a #Bernheimer is as necessary to prepare for our next adventure as packing a water bottle and map.

CHAPTER SIXTEEN

Near to Nature

[T]he important point is that a world of inter-dependent relationships, where things are intelligible only in terms of each other, is a seamless unity. In such a world it is impossible to consider man apart from nature, as an exiled spirit which controls this world by having its roots in another. Man is himself a loop in the endless knot, and as he pulls in one direction he finds that he is pulled from another and cannot find the origin of the impulse.

—Alan Watts

Entranced by the flickering light through the cottonwood trees, I tilt my head skyward to admire the twisting walls of creamy Cedar Mesa Sandstone. Occasionally, I look down to make sure I don't catch my foot on a root or rock. The miles roll by as Harvey Leake leads the way, easy on his feet with a lightweight blue backpack. It looks too small to have enough supplies for two nights.

Kane Gulch, a three-mile-long tributary of Grand Gulch once known as Wetherill Canyon, is well trodden by hikers year round and familiar to us both. "Ten miles of Grand Gulch is no ten-cent movie. It is a grand opera," I sing out to Harvey, quoting Bernheimer. Harvey has read these journals intently for decades and looks back at me, smiling. Interestingly, it was Bernheimer, not John Wetherill, who inspired Harvey, an electrical engineer by trade, to pursue an in-depth investigation of his family ancestry. While living in Seattle, he was browsing at Shorey's bookstore when he came across several books about the Southwest, and Bernheimer's *Rainbow Bridge* was among them. It inspired Harvey to take his first hiking trip to Rainbow Bridge in 1979:

> I embarked on a personal quest to understand the passion that compelled my ancestors to endure toil, privations, and hardships in order to immerse themselves in the archaeology, native residents, and scenery of the Colorado Plateau. I began to realize that my quest was not only teaching me about the rich history of my ancestors, but also something about myself.

That trip inspired him to take over fifty hikes to Rainbow Bridge thereafter, and countless trips through Grand Gulch. At age sixty-nine, Harvey frequently goes backpacking around the Colorado Plateau, enriching his stories and familial ties.

Matching our steady hiking pace, Harvey's baritone voice effortlessly projects over the gusts of wind. "Morgan, I'd like you to think about why someone like Bernheimer wanted to come out and do this every year." A clue about Bernheimer's motivations resides in a journal entry that celebrates what he called "near to nature" living: sleeping under the stars, eating simple food, facing the elements, and traveling on horseback. Harvey muses, "I believe it is in our innate human makeup to yearn to be close to nature. Bernheimer must have realized that the wilderness that needed redemption was in the human soul."

This prompt encourages personal reflection. I developed a longing for immersion in nature at a young age among the orange grove–lined suburbs at the edge of the Mojave Desert and Southern California mountains, all bounded to the west by the Pacific coast. There, my mom and I took up urban backpacking. We'd pick a different market, sometimes as far as seven miles across town, walk there with our backpacks, and carry our groceries home. It did not matter whether it was over one hundred degrees or raining. The elements were something to experience, not hide from. At night, I slept in the backyard under the sky-scraping sycamore trees, wrapping myself in warm air as a blanket; the coyote and bird song over the rumbles of motor traffic were my morning alarms before school. And on weekends we often visited my grandparents at the beach, where I spent hours at a time in the ocean. A pod of dolphins once encircled me when I was only eleven years old; their current swirled through my legs dangling off my board. I never felt the illusory separation between the animal and human worlds again.

Backpacking was the hook for Harvey to better understand his familial relationship to nature:

> I began to understand why John Wetherill and his more perceptive clients were so attracted to the region—the stunning scenery, the simple pleasures of sunshine, fresh air, and still nights under the stars, the intrigue of seeing new places and discovering what is around the next bend in the canyon, the mental challenge of finding routes across seemingly impassable places and locating life-giving water sources, and the satisfaction of pushing our bodies to new limits and learning how to cope with any challenges that came our way. Above all else, (they) were gaining the sense of freedom that comes from learning that nature is not our enemy.

Harvey's mother, Dorothy, was born in Kayenta, Arizona, on the Navajo Nation and was very close with her grandparents, John and Louisa. She lived with them at the trading post for a portion of her childhood, which profoundly impacted her and has rippled down to Harvey:

The concept of the path of light has always been a part of my life, although the phrase, itself, and my deeper understanding of it came from my reading of the *Wolfkiller* manuscript about twenty years ago. I have to believe that my perspective on life, which was influenced by that of the Wetherills, came to me through my mother, although I don't understand how it all occurred, nurture or nature?

The landscape was John Wetherill's utmost priority because he understood the value of protecting it and viewed the outdoors as his home, not separate from it. This perspective was enriched by what he learned from the Diné and Paiutes who lived with the land and contributed to his fascination with archaeology, which helped him learn more about earlier Indigenous inhabitants.

We round a bend, following a row of ten human faces painted across the sun-drenched walls. Grand Gulch is a family tree, whispering stories of ancient peoples whose imprints remain around every twist and turn. This sentiment was explained to me a few years ago by Hopi archaeologist and cultural resource consultant Lyle Balenquah:

> My ancestors, the Greasewood Clan, have an oral history about migrating, traveling specifically up through the Bears Ears. They lived a unique lifestyle, were some of the first people to farm in the Southwest and built architecture that people from around the world still come to see. For many Indigenous people, we all have that sense that we are working and living in these lands.

In the desert, the arid climate and land itself preserves history, so that it may continue to live and breathe. Maybe this is why so many people are drawn here. To observe the tradition of humans as a part of nature, not in opposition to it.

- - - - -

At dusk, Harvey and I stop to set up camp within view of a rock art panel. As we set up our tents, a family walks over to peruse the site and gather water from the spring. Elementary school–aged children scramble up the rocks, and their parents slowly follow them. This would have shocked Bernheimer, who sarcastically reported that many people had been there, meaning maybe one party a year. It was not always that unpopulated. Archaeologist R. G. Matson, who worked alongside Bill Lipe on the Cedar Mesa Project, hypothesizes that the Grand Gulch mesa tops supported an estimated average population of five hundred to eight hundred people between AD 200 and 400.

Today, Grand Gulch is one of the most popular canyons in Cedar Mesa. Between 2014 and 2019, there has been a 49 percent increase in overnight permitted use and a 78 percent increase in day use. Visitation numbers in the canyon today represent a more than 3,000 percent increase in human presence from the numbers of people living here about 1,800 years ago. To address this, a backcountry permit system is enforced in high-traffic canyons, including Grand Gulch, limiting overnight travel from each trailhead to twenty people per night.

Harvey and I cook our supper while we watch the families admire the images on stone. The kids are engaged and observant: "Look at this!" a boy gleefully exclaims, pointing at one of the anthropomorphic pictographs, painted in brown. "I wonder if they drew this one because…" The stories on this canyon's walls are teaching something important to these children. Hopefully it will instill deep respect for cultural sites and this landscape, as well as a lifelong motivation to protect them.

The Bears Ears Inter-Tribal Coalition has its own suggestions, guided by traditional Indigenous knowledge of the Hopi Tribe, Navajo Nation, Ute Mountain Ute Tribe, Ute Indian Tribe, and Pueblo of Zuni, for respectful visitation of cultural sites that emphasize a heightened sense of reverence for the land:

Approach the land with a respectful mindset. You will encounter interconnected natural, cultural, scientific, and spiritual spaces within Bears Ears. It is important that even before you step foot into this sacred place, you recognize that these are the homelands to many Tribes today; it is a region to be treated with intention and care.

These inquisitive children are next in line to absorb this philosophy and use it to help protect places like this. Harvey explains this as "the chain of knowledge," a concept passed down to him through his great-grandmother Louisa, who learned from Wolfkiller, who learned from his grandfather to preserve stories and knowledge for future generations. "Now, you are a part of this chain too, Morgan. We need to do our best to continue it, not just for a few of us, but in hopes it may help many."

Doing so is no simple task. How can we weigh the impacts and benefits of public visitation to best protect cultural resources? How do we forge the connection from education to stewardship and preservation? The answers to these questions may be as complex as the rock art we are all here to see.

Near the alcove ceiling, abstract polychrome pictographs were created by some of the earliest hunter-gatherers in the Southwest. While the meaning of the images is unknown to me, the segments of squiggly lines and circles evoke ephemeral wings like those of fairies or butterflies. Adjacent to these are distinctly Basketmaker pictographs. The human forms with triangular bodies, adorned with spotted breastplates, dance above later Ancestral Pueblo dwellings. Two golden spirals plastered on a blackened wall look out over the canyon and keep watch. Here, generations built upon the past to make it their home.

Harvey and I spend the remaining daylight hours in the alcove, sleuthing for his great-grandfather's initials. A faint "JW" etched in stone catches our eyes. It is diminutive and sits in an obscure location that does not disturb any of the cave's original markings. Although it is dated, the numbers are too faint for me to decipher. As far as historic graffiti goes, John Wetherill seemed acutely aware that leaving his mark was for documentation, not stealing the show or desecrating the rock imagery.

Since paper records of early expeditions were rare, these inscriptions offer important clues about late nineteenth to early twentieth century archaeology. After the exhumed artifacts were shipped off to East Coast museums, the items were often unlabeled, with little or no mention of their origins. Bernheimer was concerned about these poor documentation methods and hoped his funding would help John step it up.

Decades later, the inscriptions left at sites were still the most reliable location data, so archaeologists like Bill Lipe started using them to assist their research:

> As much as I curse the graffiti left by modern hikers in the Gulch, I'm thankful these pioneer archaeologists were afflicted by that human urge to record their passing. We'll keep looking for these faint old scribblings and may someday be able to reconstruct from them the course of that first Wetherill expedition.

In the 1980s, Fred Blackburn organized the Wetherill–Grand Gulch Project, which pieced together much of the puzzle created by early archaeologists.

Historic inscriptions themselves are a misunderstood classification of artifacts. If we consider a name carved on a canyon wall, rock, or tree today to be vandalism, what makes something a little older any different? To address this murky question, the BLM caches pamphlets written by two of the Wetherill–Grand Gulch Project volunteers explaining the historical value of inscriptions, and instructing visitors not to touch, deface, or add to any historic sites in the Cedar Mesa area.

These pamphlets are among the educational materials the

BLM places in metal army surplus ammo boxes for visitors at more frequently visited cultural sites.

An inscription from the 1892 Illustrated American Exploring Expedition, funded by a New York-based magazine to study and collect cultural materials in the Four Corners to display at the World's Fair, was recently obliterated from a nearby canyon. It is possible this was done by a well-meaning visitor who hoped to help remove what they thought was graffiti. Perhaps they assumed that '92 meant 1992. This is why education of the public is so important. Whether there is a mark or not, erasing the past is not possible, but learning from it always is.

- - - - -

Warm air flows up canyon during the day; as it grows cooler in the evening, it flows back down and settles. This is how canyons breathe. With this frigid breath settling in, Grand Gulch dips toward its projected low of twenty degrees. Harvey and I both eat dinner dressed in our sleeping bags. Our teeth begin to chatter, so we decide to turn in for the night.

My eyes are not fully open when I unzip my tent in the morning, until I notice mountain lion tracks in the sand encircling my tent. Before crawling out on all fours, I carefully scan my surroundings. The feline paced around Harvey's tent too. This is their home, so it's fair for them to scope out the guests and let us know that they stopped by. I wonder if the other families camped here have any sense that they also were being watched?

Bernheimer's musings about wildlife are inconsistent. He claimed that they did not encounter any animals in 1929, followed by a list of creatures they saw, including snakes, lizards, insects, birds, packrats, and frogs. He later explained in an interview with the *New York Times*, "Where fox, bear, wolf, and puma, sheep and goat cannot find food and water in sufficient or dependable quantity, man perishes. Subsistence lacks its foundation."

It is possible that Bernheimer saw far less wildlife than we do today because, at that time, killing off carnivores was common practice by ranchers to protect their cattle. The practice dates back to the arrival of white colonizers in the United States who imported a vendetta against any animals thought to threaten livestock, crops, or humans. On the expedition, the group chased a lone coyote on horseback and let cowboy Kenneth Helquist kill it because the hide would earn him six dollars, equivalent to almost one hundred dollars today.

The practice continues to this day. Last year, the USDA Wildlife Service killed off 62,537 coyotes, 434 black bears, 703 bobcats, and 276 cougars. Among these primary predatory mammals in southern Utah, there are very few incidents of them killing off cattle. Coyotes only occasionally venture away from their standard diet of rabbits, small game, and carrion. Mountain lions are known to prey on the coyotes—I once found a coyote skull with cougar bite marks piercing its temples on both sides. Coyote populations can handle the loss and have an evolutionary adaptation to produce more offspring when efforts are made, by any species, to reduce their numbers. Nature is already managing itself.

The ancient inhabitants of Grand Gulch likely coexisted with far greater numbers of these predators every single day. One petroglyph panel that Harvey and I visited yesterday had distinct lion paws carved deeply into the walls. Mountain lion encounters are rare and intimidating, yet I have had several in the desert and mountains. I am always awestruck by these powerful creatures. Among the lion tracks, on the walls and in the dirt, I walk in unison with the wild world.

Harvey and I wait for the sun to pop over the rim of the canyon while we drink coffee in our sleeping bags. It is instant relief and warmth when the orange sunlight washes over the canyon wall behind us. We pack up and resume hiking for a few more miles. Harvey will make an exit at the next side canyon so he can spend Easter with his family, including his mother, who is ninety-five. As we part ways, Harvey, ever the philosopher, reminds me, "It's not about the destination. Find a philosophy and work toward that."

I resume walking alone through the overgrown creekbed, crawling under fallen cottonwood trunks, over flash flood debris, and around boulders. The foliage is dense and prickly, and the trail meanders up and down the four-foot-tall creek banks, which are often so steep that I use my hands to hoist myself and my heavy pack up them. I squeal as I launch myself off the embankment to land in the wash below.

Despite this tiresome dance, I am overcome with a sudden urge to pick up speed. Not to rush, but as a test to see if I can keep pace with Bernheimer's packtrains. Halfway down Grand Gulch, Johnson and the wranglers took off early and accidentally traveled farther than planned. They covered roughly twenty-four miles in two days, by my calculations. Keeping a steady gait, I imagine the horses trotting alongside me.

Would Bernheimer have taken to backpacking? I think he would appreciate its aesthetics, and the thought of being fully reliant on oneself outdoors. But I bet he would still bring a mule to haul his gear. It reminds me of stories David Roberts told me about using llamas to pack steak and red wine into Grand Gulch in the 1990s when that was still allowed.

Amid my internal competition with the packtrain, I pause often to look at the stunning dwellings, granaries, and rock art lining the canyon. The wash widens, and my feet scoop smooth sand behind me. A thin canopy of budding cottonwoods is the only shelter between me and the sun. I arrive at a reliable water source with plenty of daylight and find a decent camp nearby. This is the warmest evening of the trip, and I comfortably sit barefoot in the sand without a jacket. I eat macaroni laced with dried green chile, and watch the sky shift from blue, to pink, to starscape.

Each night feels less and less like an adventure, and more like I am home. The drawn-out pace of days without distraction revolves simply around water, walking, eating, and camping. I cherish this peaceful evening because I know the desert's mood will shift again. Weather patterns cannot remain calm forever, and when they do become tempestuous, I remind myself of Wolfkiller's lesson. When it is cold, I wear all my layers at the same time and make sure to keep moving. When my pack is heavy, I am grateful because that means I have found enough water. When the howling wind rattles my tent, and nerves, I just deal with it.

Of the conditions in Grand Gulch, Bernheimer wrote: "The scenery is majestic, the quicksands the Villain (we had so much rain that he was ready to do his work), but the many cliff ruins that represent the most sought after 'fair lady' were rescued by the ingeniousness of our leaders and their experienced steeds." I disagree. Nature is not the villain here. She is the fair lady, and it is our responsibility to coexist peacefully within her domain.

- - - - -

The crescendo of canyon wrens singing awakens me in the morning. It means there is no wind. It is already so much warmer than yesterday that I unzip my sleeping bag to cool off. The task of simultaneously making breakfast and repacking my gear is becoming more efficient. I top off my water and walk across the bedrock toward yet another meander.

A few miles later, I reach a pond of water that is the size of a small motel swimming pool. I guzzle what is left in my bottle to prepare to refill it. When I dip it into the pool, I notice schools of squiggly red larvae. I optimistically assume I can filter most of the wigglers out with a bandanna, but they are so prolific the task is futile. I dump the water out and examine a smaller pothole nearby. It reeks of sulfur, and I doubt that this water is safe to drink, even if laced with iodine tabs. Bernheimer warned me about the alkali water here, lamenting that coffee could not hide the bad taste. Oddly, he suggested that the water's mineral content was good for your dental hygiene. I attempt to calculate how much water I have for the remaining miles as I dump the water once more and walk away with even less than I came here with.

To walk away from water in the desert is either an act of faith or the tempting of fate. I convince myself I can make it the next few miles without a sip, but then what? A stretch of pink bedrock dotted with water-filled potholes quickly answers the question for me. Relieved, I stop to filter once more, and this time it tastes sweet and refreshing. To celebrate, I lie atop the sun-drenched sandstone and drink up this moment of solitude.

CHAPTER SEVENTEEN

No Hero

We shouldn't be looking for heroes, we should be looking for good ideas.

—Noam Chomsky

Into each life it is said that some rain must fall. Some people have bad horoscopes, others take tips on the stock market. McNamara created the TFX and the Edsel. Churches possess the real world. But Indians have been cursed above all other people in history. Indians have anthropologists.

—Vine Deloria Jr

D ry leaves and branches crack and snap in the creekbed. I am no longer alone. A man clears the brush, carrying the water bottle he just refilled, and steps toward me. Tall and wiry, his jeans and a gold chain hang on his leathery skin. He lifts a cigarette to his mouth, and tilts his cowboy hat to greet me with a wide grin. "Well, howdy!"

We start to chat, and he declares, "I been to Grand Gulch every year since '75; this place is spiritual to me." A group of col- lege-aged boys trickle in toward the creek. These are his grand- sons and their friends. He proudly talks about their first trip here as a rite of passage. The boys, all built like defensive linebackers and adorned with tattoos, nod in respect.

He tilts his chin up to me and asks, "And where you comin' from?" It's complicated, I vaguely explain. The guy interrupts me midsentence: "You look like one of them Nat Gee-Oh people." My wide-brimmed khaki felt hat, wrinkled plaid shirt, and bandanna are starting to feel like a second skin. I forget that I am vaguely dressed like an old-fashioned explorer, with the exception of tiny pink shorts and running shoes. Laughing, I tell him that I am following in the footsteps of a Nat Geo writer from the 1920s.

"Oh, was it one of them Wetherills?" I laugh again and explain that John Wetherill was the expedition guide. He immediately fires back, "You do know those guys did a lot of bad stuff?" Now I'm on the spot. Another couple hiking down the canyon stops behind me and chimes in randomly, "Oh, and Richard Wetherill was murdered at Chaco." Suddenly I have an audience. I sense it's a tough crowd.

If only Harvey was here now, or perhaps it's better that he is not. Accusations and false stories about his family, gleaned without researching primary source documents, are upsetting to him. These folks, like so many others, probably read an article on the internet or an outdated book that slapped "grave robber," "pot hunter," or "discoverer" in front of the Wetherill name, without providing historical context.

Everyone's eyes widen when I mention that I was hiking with John's great-grandson just a few days ago. I do my best to explain that the Wetherill's early work pre-dated modern archaeological techniques and laws. The hikers are still listening intently, so I continue, presenting the early mistakes they did make, and how John Wetherill's work helped pave the way for the improved methods, regulations, and laws that govern archaeology today. As the regulations evolved, so did the Wetherills.

It's a lot of ground to cover, and doing so requires diverse perspectives for a more complete picture. All too often, what we read about history is from the lens of white people. For a different perspective, I asked Hopi archaeologist Lyle Balenquah if he would be willing to talk about this era of archaeology. He was understandably hesitant at first to make time in his busy schedule to talk about a sensitive subject. I am truly grateful for the honest conversation that followed.

Parked at one of my known cell service spots on Cedar Mesa, Balenquah began our call with his memories of growing up on Third Mesa. He remembers his grandfather telling him stories about disrespectful eighteenth- and nineteenth-century researchers barging into Hopi ceremonies and excavating graves. He explained that these were methods that were only beneficial for the explorers, who viewed the Hopi people as specimens and who did not give back in a tangible way to the Indigenous communities that they studied.

When he studied archaeology at Northern Arizona University, Balenquah felt disconnected from these, "old white dudes with beards," who were the so-called heroes of Southwestern archaeology. He pondered whether there was a connection at all between this field of study and himself, a Hopi man. He said that he became very critical of archaeology and ethnology, fields that all too often write about Indigenous people in the past tense: "It divides you from having an active role in the present. We are real people with an active connection to the past." Through his wariness of what some in the Hopi community call "The Tyranny of the Ethnographic Past," Balenquah gained renewed purpose: "I want to help make this field familiar and accessible to the Hopi people."

Balenquah has worked as an archaeologist for the park service, and then for the Hopi Tribe. He now works as an independent cultural resource contractor and hiking/river guide. Through his effort to reinvent his role in this field of study, Balenquah said, "I had to relearn a lot about myself, the science of archaeology, not only to learn about the past but also the preservation of cultural landscapes." He stresses the value of getting younger generations involved. This year he worked with a team from the Zuni Ancestral Lands Conservation Corps to restore the well-known "River House" near the San Juan River:

> It's important that younger folks are able to help preserve their cultural history in the field. To learn more—about who they are, where they come from, and why it's important to be a part of the preservation process. The projects that we did at River House involved Indigenous descendant communities of the people who once lived and occupied these ancestral sites; to strengthen and reconnect them to the cultural values and traditions that Indigenous people have with their ancestral landscapes to this day.

Balenquah does feel that twentieth-century explorers like Morris and Wetherill contributed to the field of modern archaeology and helped piece together an understanding of the earlier periods of the Hopi culture. But, he says unflinchingly, "Those guys are not heroes to me; they don't serve a hero role." The word *hero*, like *explorer* and *discoverer*, is emblematic of the false narratives of colonizer history that celebrate when white guys plunder, map, conquer, claim, or learn about places already inhabited by Indigenous peoples for millennia.

An example of how far we have to go happened in 2021 at White Sands National Monument in New Mexico. There, a series of footprints were observed and dated as 23,000 years old. Nick Martin, Indigenous Affairs editor for the *High Country News*, titled the news story "The White Sands Discovery Only Confirms What Indigenous People Have Said All Along"—that many of their ancestors have lived on this continent since time immemorial. The *New York Times* failed to interview or consult a single Indigenous person for their story. This was typical one hundred years ago, when only a few people like Bernheimer were able to bridge the gap between the Southwest and the East

Coast media, but the standard needs to be much higher today.

The *New York Times* article about White Sands exemplifies how these racist biases continue in science, archaeology, and journalism. Every person involved in these fields, past and present, exists somewhere within the spectrum of racism. Today, the field of archaeology is expanding to be more inclusive of Indigenous people, both through tribal involvement and as research, which cannot be limited to Western scientific methods. Balenquah stresses the need to "let Indigenous people share their perspectives," which includes relying on "information from oral history, traditions, songs—this has validity too, not just research."

The work Balenquah is doing sits at this nexus: "We are figuring out how it's a beneficial field for our own communities, using multiple ways of knowing." Balenquah explains that this includes working with Indigenous communities, talking with elders and facilitating intergenerational learning, encouraging Indigenous people to visit cultural sites, fighting for environmental justice, and protecting places used for healing and ceremony.

Bears Ears National Monument is now leading the way for integrating Indigenous values and leadership into federal land management and the protection of cultural sites. This was the topic of a Western Watersheds Book Club discussion between Balenquah, archaeologist R. E. Burrillo, and Regina Lopez-Whiteskunk, former Ute Mountain Ute councilwoman and Bears Ears Inter-Tribal Coalition co-chair. During the conversation, Lopez-Whiteskunk expressed gratitude and optimism for the shortcomings of archaeology in the past:

> One of the things that I pray and hope for future archaeologists is that they learn from the past into today. If we didn't have all of these difficult areas that we've had to grow from then we wouldn't be experiencing that evolution in

this field. I pray that the archaeologists of tomorrow will look back on some of the hardships and disagreements that we've had along the way, and that they'll look back at this time and say, and see, that there was a change and a shift that occurred.

Indigenous leadership is pushing non-Indigenous archaeologists to rethink their approach. In a 2006 interview, Bill Lipe explained:

It's essential for archaeologists to keep working on trying to find common ground with Native American groups. I think it's important morally and ethically because of the history that we all understand—both the larger history of oppression of Native Americans, and the marginalization of living peoples in the way archaeology was conducted for so many years....It's politically important because the tribes, in fact, can have a large effect on what does or doesn't get done in archaeology, and, of course, the tribes employ lots of archaeologists and are part of the system in that sense. Intellectually, I think it's been of great value to archaeologists to have to examine implicit premises about what's important, and how to present the history of traditions and history of a people who are not in the same historical tradition that we come out of.

Ralph Burrillo is unabashedly critical of his own field of work, which entails "describing non-Western cultures, beliefs, and histories...almost entirely in Western terms." Throughout his career, there have been Indigenous-led changes in the field, but more is still needed. When I interviewed him for a *Sierra* magazine article in 2021, he stated:

I'm happy to report that there seems to be more Indigenous employees in the realm of cultural resource management (CRM) every year.... The anthropology program at Northern Arizona University (has) a number of tribal scholars and professors on staff, and their emphasis on applied paradigms and multivocality in the field is probably at the very top of the heap.

As for how the shift can occur, a lot of it comes down to funding. My good friend and colleague Lyle Balenquah has gotten grants for his work, and he's spun much of that effort back out toward "spreading the knowledge," as he likes to put it. What I'd like to see is at least 40 percent of National Science Foundation dissertation grants for archaeological projects going to Indigenous scholars. That would be a good point to reach.

Among this next generation of Indigenous scholars is Ashleigh Thompson, whom I know through the trail running community. She is a member of the Red Lake Ojibwe Nation, an anthropology PhD candidate at the University of Arizona, and an employee of Archaeology Southwest in Tucson. She is focusing her work on advocating for tribes by addressing issues of the past that harm Indigenous communities, destroy sacred cultural sites, and desecrate burials. She often shares her work and perspectives with a broader audience on social media.

- - - - -

There is more ground to cover on this topic than the miles that wind through Grand Gulch. The "Marlboro man" lifts the cigarette from his lips: "Well, I'll be darned. That's pretty good."

The conversation shifts to water sources and hiking plans among the various groups, and when I finally depart, he calls out to me, "I'll talk your ear off if you stay!" I almost oblige. I hike up the trail and ponder the details that were too complex to dig into during a backcountry conversation with strangers. I am grateful that conversations like this are being had right here where they are most relevant. The injustices we acknowledge, the laws we shape, the impacts we mitigate, the language we change, the history we teach, the ethics we value, and the solutions we seek will be our story.

I am not inclined to call Wetherill or Morris heroes. It's doubtful they would want to be called that either. Both men were far from perfect but did show growth and adaptation to improved archaeological ethics throughout their careers. I wonder, if Wetherill and Morris were alive now, what their archaeological work would look like. We are nowhere near a finish line for these changes, if one ever could exist. To pull the compass needle closer to center we do not need heroes nor champions, we need teammates and comrades.

- - - - -

I step beneath an alcove into an antiquated cowboy line camp. Although the camp has not been used in decades, it looks like the cowboys never left—there are old rusty tin cans, empty booze bottles, lassos, saddles, and even the remnants of a pair of canvas chaps. The site looks like it was used heavily until Grand Gulch was designated a Wilderness Study Area and cattle grazing got the boot. The well-preserved scene remains a part of the story, embedded within the landscape. I can't help but imagine what the Indigenous cultural sites in Grand Gulch would look like if those artifacts had been left in place, both by looters and researchers. Their absence tells this canyon's history too.

I haul my backpack up the final steep section of a stock trail. Atop the rim, I am exposed, surrounded by open space instead of sandstone walls for the first time in days. The ears of Mother Bear and the round silhouette of Navajo Mountain, both dear friends, greet me on opposite sides of the horizon. Down in Grand Gulch, the evening shadows will soon be falling, but up here there will be an extra hour of daylight. I throw down my pack, hang my hat on a juniper tree, and set up my home on the sand once again.

CHAPTER EIGHTEEN

Lost Cowboy Country

Once the people, my people, plugged into the shortages of water buried in the earth or fuels buried in the earth or metals buried in the earth, all these worlds exploded and the old ways and old customs and old fears became historical footnotes and historical junk. We called this explosion progress.

—Charles Bowden

A distant plume of dust rises in the distance, closes in on the Grand Gulch trailhead. Brent is almost here. He parks the truck in front of me and steps out. I hug him, still wearing my pack, and laugh about how filthy I am. He says, "You smell like you." He hands me a fresh bag of salad to eat.

I hop in his truck, and he drives me back to my rig for one of three planned shuttles to avoid my highway walking nightmares. The windows are rolled down, enhancing the foreign pace of driving speed. Birdsong and my own thoughts are displaced with Rush blaring through the stereo.

On the drive Brent fills me in about the last three weeks of work, skiing, and dinner parties with his friends. My updates are about perpetually howling wind, the mountain lion encounter, and projectile points.

That night I am relieved from my space food diet with a feast of carne asada tacos and fajitas on the campfire. I lose count of how many I devour. We stay up late and drink margaritas while sorting food for the next ten days.

For breakfast I gobble down half of a family-sized chicken pot pie, without a tinge of fullness afterward. The food in my pack is heavy, but I never seem to be able to carry enough to satiate my appetite.

I throw on my pack, as I have done every day these last few weeks, and lock up my vehicle. Brent is instantly appalled by how heavy his pack is. We start hiking up a steep slickrock ramp, guided by faint wagon tracks that abruptly end at a cliff. The slickrock slope on the other side is so steep that we sidestep down. In the bottom of the canyon, cottonwoods shade a spring that gushes through willows and tamarisk. I curse the twenty-five pounds of water in each of our packs for a moment, but on the other side of this canyon it is exceptionally dry. Water is heavy—the price of being without it is your life.

On the other side, banks of sediment tower over us. Lake Canyon is named for a natural lake that was fifty feet deep, a half-mile long, and a quarter-mile wide. The Paiutes called the lake *Pagahrit*, meaning "standing water." Local lore includes an account by cattleman Phil Lyman, who was warned by the Paiutes about the lake's monster. Then in 1915, Lyman watched a massive flash flood roll through that caused the natural sediment dam to breach, emptying the lake into the Colorado River.

We claw our way up the steep embankment, as high as the water in Pagahrit once stood, sliding back two steps for every step forward. Mini-avalanches of sand slough off behind us. I dig my hands into the ground for stability, inadvertently grasping the thorny goat's head burs lurking just beneath the surface. Near the top of the slippery slope, we climb a crumbly segment of rock that disintegrates with even a delicate touch. Brent goes first, and I pass up my backpack to avoid having it pull me backward into the abyss. Safely atop the rim, relief is temporary. The ninety-five-degree air adds weight to what lies ahead.

From here, Bernheimer, Morris, Johnson, and Wetherill traveled along the Colorado River, toward the confluence of the Colorado and San Juan Rivers. The rest of the cowboys stayed behind at Lake Canyon, where there was plenty of feed and water for the pack animals.

This dry and desolate area was notoriously hard on the cowboys, as explained by old-time local Erwin Oliver:

> A new man is not very good to you in red rock country. They get lost so many times. We called that country from Halls Crossing to Lake Canyon 'Lost Cowboy' because they got lost out there so much.

To navigate the deliriously orange landscape, we check the map obsessively every few minutes, lest the rumors about this desert Bermuda Triangle prove true. With no trails or major landmarks, the subtle ridgeline of Lake Canyon is our primary guide. A trio of black cows are the only other contrast to the sandy terrain in front of us. They must be lost...or maybe they are where the water is. The cows disperse as we approach, and we are relieved to find three potholes filled with clean water they could not reach. Ten days is enough time to die out here if we don't get this lucky again. And again.

The monotonous horizon line is punctuated by cairns, rusty metal scraps, and mining equipment strewn intermittently along the slickrock. This isn't trash—it's the Gretchen Bar Trail, once a mining thoroughfare during the Glen Canyon gold rush. The trail's destination, a gravel beach, once offered a welcome respite for prospectors, complete with a stone house, fruit trees, and a piped spring. Today the only traffic is a gray-colored curlew strutting around on lithe stilts and using its long thin beak like chopsticks to pick snacks up off the ground.

Here, the lake has done a brilliant job of cleaning up the old mine. Although I recognize that this is a piece of history lost, more importantly, the land remains. A dynamite-blasted ramp with cut steps descends to a small bone-white beach before fading into the translucent turquoise water of Lake Powell. The red walls surrounding us are coated with a thick streak of white minerals. These deposits, known as the "bathtub ring," emerge as the water vanishes from Lake Powell. I'm glad Bernheimer didn't have to look at this eerie scene.

The Colorado River and its reservoirs are currently the most overallocated in the world, supplying water to forty million people and 4.5 million acres of agriculture. Storing water is only the secondary purpose of Lake Powell; its primary purpose is to generate five billion kilowatts of power for much of the West. Five million people from seven states and fifty tribal energy suppliers, including the Navajo Nation, purchase electricity generated by Lake Powell.

Lake Powell's other role is to retain massive quantities of sediment to prevent the clogging of Lake Mead. Because of sedimentation, the Bureau of Land Management reports that Powell's storage capacity is 6 percent less than in 1986. These sediments are highest in the farthest reaches of Lake Powell, where we are hiking now, but over time they will work their way toward the dam, compounding low water levels. Scientists have thoughtfully named this lake sediment the "Dominy Formation," after Floyd Dominy, the Bureau of Reclamation commissioner who approved this dam.

Overuse and evaporation combined with climate change–induced aridification is gulping the lake down to its lowest levels since it began filling in the 1960s. If the water drops below 3,490 feet, the minimum power pool elevation, the reservoir will not have enough water to propel the power turbines that generate electricity. Another drop to 3,370 feet, and the lake will hit "dead pool," meaning the water is too low to flow out of the dam into the Colorado River. A buffer elevation of 3,525 has been set to sound an alarm of sorts. It would require a decade of persistent high-precipitation winters to limp Lake Powell along and stabilize the situation. Experts predict that the reservoir could dip to minimum power pool as soon as 2023.

Glen Canyon Institute (GCI), a Salt Lake City–based nonprofit dedicated to the restoration and protection of Glen Canyon, asserts the real and imminent possibility of Glen Canyon Dam becoming defunct and obsolete, making Lake Powell ground zero for the climate change and water issues facing the entire Western United States. This is the reckoning of the drying American dream in the not so Wild West.

What happens next is murky. Lower basin states are making meager water cuts, and emergency upper basin water releases continue to prop up Lake Powell to buffer its demise. At one point, the Utah governor simply called for people of all faiths to pray for rain. Under the 1922 Colorado River Compact, these water management decisions were left to the states to decide, but, given the unprecedented situation, the federal government is threatening to intervene if the states do not act quickly enough. A comprehensive federal plan, however, does not exist in this moment either; there is only the acknowledgment that the future of water in the West will never look the same, and that it will require actions that have never been taken before.

In describing this lack of urgency to adapt and make changes, water and climate scientist Brad Udall put it bluntly in an article for *The Los Angeles Times*: "If I've learned anything recently, it's that humans are really reluctant to give things up to prevent a catastrophe. They're willing to hang on to the very end and risk a calamity." Comfort and denial are a hell of a drug combination.

Here, the contrasts between the massive body of water and the near-total desolation surrounding it are striking. By stepping even a hundred feet away from the lake, it's obvious how dire the water situation is. Right now, somebody in an air-conditioned house hundreds of miles away is turning on their faucet and drinking this water without comprehension of the harsh arid land it flows from. I didn't while I was growing up in Southern California, where the water I drank was piped into a reservoir that is the Colorado River's westernmost terminus.

I assess the dryness of my mouth to decide if I need another sip of water. Sometimes I count them, *one, two, three*, to avoid recklessly gulping down too much. The ravens circling overhead are ready for me, if I fail to hydrate. The average American uses upwards of eighty-two gallons of water a day. To stay safe out here, we need to find at least one gallon each per day. The scenario does not make me want to run for the safety of the suburbs, where everyone pretends that water flows freely. The southwestern United States is not far removed from these conditions. While it's doubtful that the metropolises of Utah and Arizona will vanish in our lifetimes, the water and our hydro-electric-powered illusions might.

In 1922 the Colorado River Compact divvied up the water in the Colorado River among its surrounding states, to support agriculture and their growing cities. It segmented the Colorado River watershed into Upper Basin states: Colorado, New Mexico, Utah, Wyoming; and Lower Basin states: Arizona, Nevada, California. The original compact only promised water to Lower Basin states, neglecting the Upper Basin states, Indigenous tribes, and Mexico, which all relied on Colorado River water. Mexico finally received water rights in 1944, followed by Upper Basin states in 1948. In 1963 water rights were granted to some tribal nations whose reservations were adjacent to the river and its reservoirs in California, Arizona, and Nevada.

Most of the water data back then was based upon Colorado River stream gauge readings, which are now considered inadequate because they fail to reflect that the last century was wetter on average than the previous five. The Bureau of Reclamation ignored newly available data, based upon Professor A. E. Douglass's tree-ring research, that documented consistent drought cycles in the Southwest. Today this data is finally being used for climate predictions and has shown that the period between 2000 and 2021 ranks as the driest period in the last 1,200 years. At least 19 percent of these present-day drought conditions can be attributed to anthropogenic causes, including the burning of fossil fuels which have dangerously increased global temperatures. That does not offer much comfort when considering that the Ancestral Pueblo migrated away from the Colorado River basin during the drought period in the 1200s.

Dams were necessary to meet the Colorado River Compact's water distribution quota to lower basin states, which surpassed the actual quantity of water in the river. Upper basin states, Mexico, and Tribal Nations were still not a factor. In 1921 Eugene Clyde (E. C.) La Rue, chief hydrologist for the USGS, proposed a 780-foot dam in Glen Canyon. By 1946 several proposals for dams on the Colorado River were creeping toward reality. The Bureau of Reclamation's reports described the Colorado River as a "natural menace," lamenting how much water was "wasted" into the sea. Fear not, they assured the public, they had grandiose plans to turn water into wealth and transform the desert into an oasis. Looking out at this massive body of water makes it clear what happened next. In 1963 the floodgates closed.

I despise the lake and all that it stands for, but reaching the body of water is still a joyous occasion. I peel off my clothes and submerge. Refreshed after my first bath in weeks, I lay my bare skin against the warm slickrock to dry off. Bernheimer loved his pothole baths, but learned from his Diné guide Bill Halliday, or "Tohahay," that water was not necessary for cleansing. Halliday instead built a small hogan out of branches and mud, and started a fire inside of it to cleanse himself with a good sweat. If only a reduction in bathing water were enough to relieve some of the West's water woes.

A powerboat blasts by us, its waves lapping at the barren white shore. This very scene may soon become a relic in the archives. The National Park Service (NPS) has posted warnings to boaters about low-water hazards, and closed some marinas to motorized watercraft. Meanwhile NPS is spending millions of dollars to extend the boat ramps.

The park service is hell-bent on maintaining recreation at the dying pool. News articles encourage four million annual visitors, including me, to flock to the re-emerging natural bridges, grottoes, and side canyons. The articles are quick to point out what cool new things you can see sticking out of the water, but do little to educate the public about respectful visitation.

The low water is exposing cultural sites that were previously underwater. Bernheimer and Morris's 1929 expedition field notes were recently used by archaeologist Amy Horn and a team from the Museum of Northern Arizona and Glen Canyon National Recreation Area (GCNRA) to help document site impacts and determine management recommendations. Among their findings is a direct correlation between a cultural site's proximity to Lake Powell's shoreline and vandalism, looting, and damage at that site.

Researchers are finding that the reservoir did not fully destroy submerged cultural sites as initially predicted. A 2019 paper by Horn and Brian C. Harmon reports the findings from a recent survey of exposed sites: of 120 locations that were recorded by the Glen Canyon Project before the dam, 25 percent are in good, fair, or poor condition. Not surprisingly, the longer a site is underwater, the greater the impacts it suffers. But that is not always the case. Erik Stanfield, the former compliance archaeologist at GCNRA, told me that a few years ago a group of boaters found an exposed and intact pot, which they handed over to the park service.

Stanfield, who is now employed by the Navajo Nation Heritage and Historic Preservation Department, says that, to date, the park service has not implemented a new management plan or strategy to protect exposed sites below the original high-water elevation. Legally, this process would involve the eleven tribes directly affiliated with Glen Canyon: Havasupai Tribe, Hopi Tribe, Hualapai Tribe, Kaibab Band of Paiute Indians, Las Vegas Band of Paiute Indians, Moapa Band of Paiute Indians, Navajo Nation, Paiute Indian Tribe of Utah, San Juan Southern Paiute Tribe, Yavapai-Apache Nation, and Pueblo of Zuni. A lag in, or lack of, compliance will be increasingly problematic as waters recede because these sites, especially burials, remain significant to local tribes. Laws to protect cultural sites and codify tribal involvement are only effective if they are actually used.

Soon new relics will be exposed—sunken houseboats, old motors, shoes, sunglasses, dead bodies, and beer cans. So will the layer of sludge and sediment. Glen Canyon is a time capsule of how poorly humans treated the earth in the twentieth century. As finger pointing continues between land managers and water stakeholders, solutions evade the places that need them most. Meanwhile, the federal government continues to crawl along, under the illusion that we have a few decades to figure this out.

As the boat passes us, I stand up from the stone slab, exposing myself. Brent calls out, "Are you going to put on your clothes, Mo?"

My naked bliss strips me of self-consciousness or regard for anyone's judgements: "Nah, they're moving too fast to notice. Maybe we should flag the boat down and hitch a ride to the confluence!"

Maybe one day we will be able to walk along the Colorado River just as Bernheimer did. Since that is still not possible without a boat, we will stay on the cliffs high above the water, traversing the rim instead. Hundreds of feet below, we can see canyons flushed free of sediment, lush with hanging gardens on the north-facing walls, and perennial streams flowing into the declining lake. Swaths of plants have recovered their habitat on each side of the streambed. Rushes, willows, and cottonwoods are evolutionarily adapted to regenerate from disturbances like natural flash flooding, which also helps them rebound quickly from unnatural flood events. Nature is giving the Bureau of Reclamation its middle finger.

Travel along the former river was not an easy stroll. Bernheimer's men fought their way through the vegetation, hacking away at thickets, and pulling horses and mules out of bogs. One canyon proved particularly rough, and everyone started referring to it by a name Bernheimer dared not to repeat, so he translated it into Latin, *filius canis*—son of a bitch—canyon. Bernheimer's journals describe the main river channel:

> Soon cottonwoods, willows and reeds had appeared. The bottom lands were quicksandy and muggy. The thicket at times was difficult to penetrate. On the ground, higher up the going was very rocky. The cattails were just shedding, and stripping past them made the air full of minute pollen feathers which made things look like they were on fire, and filled the air with what looked like smoke and the eyes and nose with a fluffy coating.

Overgrazing had already altered the river corridor before Bernheimer described it. Prior to the 1890s, reports and photos depict a muddy river with an unruly course that shifted with each flash flood, and intermittently whisked away native plants. At the turn of the century, grazing increased, along with the introduction of exotic tamarisk and Russian olive. Their dominance reduced the natural scouring of annual flood events, holding the sand bars of the Colorado River and its tributaries in place.

Efforts are being made to eradicate the tamarisk and Russian olive, especially on the Escalante River. Though the plants are tenacious, it isn't fruitless work, and in many exposed canyons the regeneration of native plants far exceeds the invasives. Spindly green rushes and reeds are essential early colonizers in bare streambeds, and they allow plants like cottonwoods and willows to take root. Without excessive overgrazing, the riparian ecosystem can begin to recover.

The sun is relentless as we hike through the blackbrush flats between slickrock domes. We occasionally rest on the ground to unweight our loads, dump sand from our shoes, and pull cheatgrass from our socks. After toiling on our feet all day, we are less than a mile, as the raven flies, from where we were yesterday. It seems like we are going nowhere the long way. We measure the days not in miles, but in water holes. There have been none since this morning.

I stop and lean against a slickrock slab to relive the pressure on my shoulders. Carrying this much water and food is not just tiring, it's painful. My pack weighs forty percent of my body weight. It digs into my shoulders, sending nerve pain down my arms. It never seems to get easier, even after weeks of repetition. My feet ache constantly. Upon waking I am often unsure if I will be able to stand up.

My head pounds from dehydration, and I am starting to lose my appetite in the heat. I tell Brent we need to stop and make camp early. We can ration our remaining water. There is no guarantee we will find more before dark, but the effects of powering through might risk our chances tomorrow.

I crawl into my sleeping bag before dark and let my bones rest against the ground. Even though I feel like a piece of dried-up cow shit, there is nowhere else that I want to be. The days and nights drift like the wind, and the cadence of living this way suits my spirit and fills my soul. Tucked away in the comfort of my chosen home, sleep comes swiftly.

- - - - -

Well rested and rehydrated, I see the world through orange-colored lenses in the morning. We pull out the map and prepare for a shift in terrain. The natural contours of Glen Canyon's edges have guided us through the dizzying waves of skin-colored stone, but today we will hike across a flat, desolate mesa. A faint cattle trail molded into the sand leads us into a shallow valley. The path seems to disappear when we reach a stretch of slickrock, but it only takes a moment for our eyes to adjust and see a white line beaten by hooves across the rolling pink stone.

The trail passes by a cave used as a cowboy line camp, its interior decorated with wire-frame cots, empty syrup bottles, and a name carved on the wall, dated 2000. The trail fades away, so we pull the map out again. I am not sure why we even bother to put it away. A small slip off course costs us an hour and more unreplenished water. We tease each other not to spill a single drop when we drink. Just existing here requires immense self-reliance. It is a primal reminder of what is required to stay alive.

The days and nights roll into one another in a rhythmic continuum, like this landscape. Time and distance are not marked by calendars and calculators, but by light and changes in the earth's geometry. Beyond the hidden valley, a castle made of petrified sand crowns the horizon. Beneath the fortress is a mile-wide abandoned meander, a dry, horseshoe-shaped bend created when the Colorado River slowly shifted its course. Across the abyss is a rock island that Bernheimer compared to decaying molars.

Forceful gales blow up from the lake onto the mesa, an atmospheric change that stirs up the first scuffle of this expedition. Brent wants to spend the evening admiring and photographing the sunset from atop a slickrock ridgeline. I remind him that the point of hiking this section was to locate the stock trail that Bernheimer used. He suggests we each just do our own thing, and walks away. The hot wind vaporizes the tears on my cheeks, as if to assure me that my sadness here is ephemeral.

To settle disputes, Bernheimer put his experience and skills as a labor mediator to work, maintaining that "friendships forged in hazardous joint ventures usually endure." Wetherill and Johnson were not always well-suited to teamwork in challenging moments. Bernheimer noted that their disagreements added an element of tension to the trips:

> If only Wetherill and Johnson were able to get over a kink they have in their make-up and would consult before we start as to the best way. Comparing and blending their very extensive knowledge and desert craft, they would be ideal; and often hardship would be saved those whom they guide. But, perfection does not exist even out here.

The sun sets and so do my hopes of finding the trail. I try my best to enjoy the beams of vermilion light reflecting on the water below, but all I can see is a damn reservoir and the sand blowing in my eyes. The confluence, and the truck, are both several days of walking away. There is no escape or hiding place from the wind or our woes. Our relationship is stuck in the middle too—far from where we started and unclear about where we are headed. We set up camp on the rim, savoring our dehydrated dinners silently in the dark.

My eyelids rise with the pink sunrise, to a view of Navajo Mountain. It reminds me of that first backpacking trip to Rainbow Bridge with Brent and Phil. The differences between us were already apparent then. Opposites attract, right? Although I was hopeful that this hiking trip would eliminate the tensions that have been plaguing us, I now fear we just don't get along; or worse, we don't belong in the same habitat.

Our pace is lethargic in the morning. We avoid the discussion of what to do next, while sipping second cups of coffee. A nearby pothole the size of a spaghetti pot provides luxuriously easy access to water. When the caffeine finally kicks in, we compromise. The new plan is to take a layover day and descend Bernheimer's horse path, hoof it up the nearby dirt road, and then traverse the dramatic ridgeline back to camp.

We walk to the rim, unburdened by our full packs, carrying only the essentials: water, snacks, camera, and maps. It is tough to imagine Bernheimer riding his horse up this precariously loose cliff band from the river. We pace back and forth along the rim until we find a way down it, one step at a time. Here, Wetherill and Johnson led the horses turn-by-turn on foot. They stacked rocks to build makeshift ramps, making the existing trail more comfortable for Bernheimer, who lamented how hard it was for the poor animals and his poor feet. Old hoof scratches on the rocks confirm that pack animals passed this way. Navigating the descent, we often reverse or return to a higher level to find another way down to the next layer of the crumbly Kayenta Formation. Once at the bottom, we pause to look up at the cliff, even more amazed that Bernheimer rode up it.

Nearer to the lake, we untangle the web of thin, tangled tamarisk branches in front of us. The suction of sludgy lake sediment pulls at our feet as we hop over fresh cow patties. On the other side of the thicket, zebra mussels—foreign invaders from the Caspian Sea—cover the shoreline, some rusty beer cans, and a capsized lawn chair that is half-submerged in sediment. I refrain from swimming to avoid slicing my feet on their shells.

Rather than sitting upon the desert seashells, we eat our lunch standing up, and then head back without filling up our bottles. Best to avoid the lake water laced with motor oil, gasoline, human feces, pesticide runoff, radioactive waste, and who knows what else. Bernheimer was not a fan of the Colorado River water, claiming the "cesspool" made him sick, even when boiled. He praised his guides each time they found a clean water hole. The heat radiates as we distance ourselves from the lake, and I regret not taking a dip.

The road back is steep, winding, and rutted. A distant rumbling noise catches us off guard. Moments later a dirt bike comes ripping around a curve in the road, blasting us with dirt as it passes us. Not far behind, a Jeep creeps around one of the tightest turns. The family rolls down their windows as they near us and asks, "Are y'all okay? Where did y'all come from?" They are not impressed, so much as confused, about why we would do this to ourselves. Looking at the condition of the road, I want to ask them the same thing.

A parade of ten ATVs makes its way down next. It makes me wonder, if permits are often required for river trips and backcountry camping, why an endless parade of ORVs is always permissible. Permit systems limit group size and trip duration, while enforcing special equipment requirements for things like firepans and groovers, to help reduce impacts. Such rules seem reasonable, considering how many people can fit into a vehicle. The Glen Canyon National Recreation Area website does mention that a permit system for ORVs in designated zones is currently being developed.

We scramble off the road to avoid the traffic. The surrounding sea of slickrock domes muffles the rumbling motor noises, but gets my wheels turning. I have been grappling with my relationship with fossil fuels and the harsh truth it exposes about my lifestyle: that I burn gasoline to reach the same places I hope to help protect. It is a paradox that all environmentalists, all people, must face. These few weeks of walking do nothing to curtail my lifetime of reliance on this system. A change must come from the top down.

A steep mound of sandstone distracts me from the noise. The arches of my feet flex in my flimsy running shoes as I tiptoe up the ramp. Swirling shades of burnt citrus, cocoa, salmon, and iron oxide hypnotize me. Brent takes in the scene through the square lens of his camera as I prance around with glee. He calls out, asking me to slow down for a photo. Glen Canyon is a cacophony of sandstone that cannot be captured in a narrow view, and neither can I. On top of the steepest dome, I run down in full stride, unbridled, letting gravity handle my brakes. I stop to catch my breath, and lie belly-down on the tiger-striped slickrock, grinning ear to ear, melting into the stone, becoming part of the landscape.

- - - - -

We wind through another maze of slickrock to reach the confluence of the San Juan and Colorado Rivers. Ever concerned with how little water we are finding, we must speed up somehow. So, we accept our fate to walk on the road as far as we can. In the midday sun, the monotonous ribbon of dirt drones on interminably. On the ground we spot a park service sign directing vehicles to stay on designated roads. The tire tracks across it keep going, off-road through the desert's delicate soils.

The road passes Bernheimer's Shoot the Chute camp, which he found to be a depressing spot. We are overjoyed when we see water, until we see a dead lizard floating belly-up in it, like a happy, drunk fool unabashedly willing to risk dying for its liquid of choice. The water Bernheimer found was light green, and he mentioned that it had a funny taste, almost like champagne, English breakfast tea, and varnish. He drank it with his eyes closed. Unwilling to find out whether it still tastes like champagne, we press on without a sip.

The dynamite-blasted chute is incredibly steep, with a steady stream of fresh transmission fluid streaked down the middle. At the top, a caravan of three Jeeps is scouting the risky descent. They roll down their windows and holler, "Where did you hike here from?" followed by, "You're crazy!" An older gentleman with silver hair sticking out from under a Lake Powell cap asks, "Do you have enough water? Want an ice-cold Powerade?" Peering into the Jeep, I can see that there is no shortage of supplies and oblige. The trail angels gift us chilled drinks and an extra gallon of water, almost assuring us safe passage.

The road abruptly ends in sand, signaling our entrance into the rough and jumbled terrain leading to the confluence. The same billows of orange sandstone before us once looked impossibly remote from the other side of the river near Navajo Mountain. No Name Mesa now appears so close, it looks as though I could walk across the water to it. I am stitching my understanding of the landscape together with my feet.

Upon Bernheimer's arrival at the confluence, he wrote, "On earlier jaunts, I had seen from the southeast shore of the Colorado, the stupendous rock walls on the opposite side and the scenically magnificent constellations near where the two rivers enter into wedlock." Later, in a *New York Times* article, Bernheimer explained that he "always looked across the river barrier and planned to invade that blank triangle on the map."

It is certainly a challenge to get here, but the word *invade* lurches out at me. To invade is to arrive without permission, to attempt to take control, and to occupy. Invade is a bold statement—the desert is in charge here, and it will not hesitate to humble or kill you. The word choice is especially problematic in the homeland and hunting grounds of the Diné, Hopi, Ute, Pueblo, and Paiute people. Bernheimer's hyperbole seems odd because he, along with pacifist John Wetherill, was very much anti-war. His first published book was *The Gentleman's Plan to Ending World War I.*

And yet, maybe Bernheimer was on to something. My friend Jonathan Bailey, a conservation photographer and author, considers all recreation in wilderness invasive, at least to a degree:

> It's the accumulation of thousands of little decisions that add up to something much harder to ignore, like slow erosion from our boot prints. We want to belong in nature, but that belonging must be calibrated by reciprocity. When we take, we must give back. We can only belong so long as our participation is greater than our little destructions.

Bernheimer did his best to match his invasive visits with ongoing reciprocity.

I pull the brim of my hat down to cover my eyes and protect them from blowing sand. My eyes are fixed on my feet, to avoid tripping. I don't notice our progress until we are standing on the edge of a cliff. This is the confluence. The water hundreds of feet below us follows a winding course around a horseshoe-shaped bend in the San Juan River. Despite the drought conditions, the water is still deep enough to conceal what Bernheimer described:

> The scenery was majestic and almost defied description as it spread out before us in solemn magnificent splendor, the ageless results of its patient struggle against the elements and time. The rock formed perpendicular walls down to the river level. The scavenging currents swept the banks clean of debris and talus. There was no vegetation. Mesa-like square buttes loomed above us. Wherever the sun reached, illuminated geometrical spaces on the rock walls were sharply defined. Beyond these, shadows were a deep blue-slate gloom.

A large weathering pit in the sandstone slows our momentum as we investigate its fifteen-foot-deep abyss. There is no water. At the bottom, an ochre and rust colored projectile point sits where it landed after being launched, perhaps one thousand years ago. The point is an indicator that the confluence and lower San Juan River was an important location for hunting as far back as the Archaic period.

The dam has inundated far more than material markers of significance. The federal government and the US Bureau of Reclamation should be charged with the crime of invading and destroying this sacred landscape tethered to Indigenous understanding of and reverence for water.

The San Juan Southern Paiute refer to the Colorado River as *Páa-xa*, and it is the western boundary of their traditional territory. In a conversation with Lavern Owl, she recalled a story about the confluence told by her mother, Mary Ann Owl, and grandmother, Bessie Owl. The women described the San Juan River as the grandmother and the Colorado River as the grandfather—at the confluence the two unite. To the Paiute, all sources of water are sacred.

The confluence is called *Tokonavi* by the Hopi Tribe. This is the location where a young boy named Tiyo began his journey down the Colorado River to the Gulf of California. When he returned home from his journey, he brought back the secret of rainmaking. The story continues to be told orally by the Hopi people to explain their history and values, and to describe their lineages, which trace back to people in Mesoamerica and South America, as far away as Peru.

Former Navajo Nation water commissioner Leo Manheimer learned from Diné medicine men like Buck Navajo that this confluence is the origin of rain and snow. He explained that, because the lake is receding, the confluence is teaching us all a lesson through the extreme drought. Leo's outlook about the reservoir is distinctly shaped by his work in water management and traditional knowledge. He believes, "As for the lake, there is no middle. It should be full and thriving, or it should be no more."

The intersection of traditional knowledge and science may hold the key to improved water management and adaptation to climate change. Navajo Nation hydrologist Crystal Tulley-Cordova grew up in Blue Gap, Arizona, where her grandmother taught her that water is connected to the land we live on. When she attended university and began studying climate change and hydrology, she saw the connections to traditional knowledge; but in school scientific proof was required to validate this. So, she began studying stable isotopes, which revealed that water in each of the varied regions of the Navajo Nation has its own signature. She uses her samples and precipitation studies to better understand how climate change affects the microclimates on the Navajo Nation in different ways.

Tulley-Cordova's research and work is motivated by the fact that the majority of Diné people do not have access to running water, despite the reservoirs like Lake Powell that occupy their homelands but are for use by other people. The Colorado River Compact now honors senior water rights for twenty-two out of thirty federally recognized tribes in the Colorado River basin, but many lack the infrastructure and funding to utilize it. The San Juan Southern Paiute and Hopi Tribes are among those with unresolved water rights. Tulley-Cordova views the water challenges facing tribal communities as opportunities, and seeks to share her research and knowledge with Colorado River policymakers and stakeholders.

The Colorado River Compact is up for renegotiation in 2026, for the first time since 1922. In those 104 years, the water and climate have both been mismanaged, while the rights, needs, and knowledge of Indigenous people have been neglected. A coalition of twenty tribes are urging US Secretary of the Interior Deb Haaland to include their perspectives in the upcoming revisions of the compact, and she has confirmed their involvement.

Below us, the San Juan River appears stagnant and consumed by the reservoir, but there is a ribbon of current threading across its center; flowing downstream as it always has. But in this liminal state, the barely functioning reservoir is not yet a wild river, either. Glen Canyon is not simply reemerging; it is becoming something new and not yet discernable.

My relationship with Brent exists in this same nebulous position. Did our currents ever flow together naturally or were they forced in place by the dam of our circumstances? I ache for the simpler time when the desert and this man were both a mystery to me. Now I see history written on every inch of stone. Though it is all laid bare, I resist accepting what I see. In this stasis of denial, humans, like the land, accumulate scars.

As I walk atop the rim of Glen Canyon, the surface beneath my feet transitions between soft sand and stone. With the interface of deep geological time underfoot, I comprehend that I, like all humans, am here for a blink in this story. High winds swirl grains of sand in the dry air. I turn back and my footprints in the sand are already swept away. I am relieved to not leave a trail. I do not need to go back the way I came. The desert is instead continuing to shape me, the way wind, water, and time carve passageways through stone.

The wind is an irritable companion I am willing to put up with. I want to stay and absorb the view, but the sand permeating my eyeballs will not relent. My vision of laying my sleeping bag out on the slickrock right here is blown away. We need to search for a sheltered camp. A bowl in the sandstone looks promising, but once inside, the wind swirls around us, continuing to shape the cross-bedded layers of petrified sand dunes. Doubtful there is any escape, we surrender and zip into our mummy sleeping bags for protection, even though it's way too hot. Sleeping in the wind is not an acquired taste. The only remedy is deep exhaustion and having no other choice.

The cessation of the gusts is announced by the sound of bighorn sheep stomping around camp in the morning. It reminds me of a baby bighorn I once saw on a cliff above the San Juan River. Although it was the size of a puppy, its legs were bulging with muscle. Upon seeing me, it boldly leapt off the cliff into the abyss for safety. The hoofprints around our sleeping bags confirm that the big horn sheep were checking us out, while carrying on with their normal activities—scaling the cliffs to and from water.

Walking away from the confluence stings. The difficulty of reaching this spot increases the value of being here. A return trip cannot simply be done on a whim. Digging through my food bag, I calculate that there's enough for an extra day. In civilization I am always itching to leave, but in nature my only desire is to stay. I look up, and Brent is already hiking down the road, so I pack up and continue.

Bernheimer's return to Lake Canyon followed the current two-track road. The relatively flat, even surface speeds up our hiking pace. Rather than dragging my feet, I remind myself there are delicious treats like fresh vegetables and tequila awaiting us at the truck. That's still two days away though. History warns us that this is still plenty of time for our shortcut to go awry.

In 1879, two hundred fifty Mormon pioneers set off from Cedar City on a 205-mile journey, directed by Brigham Young, hoping to create a new settlement on the San Juan River. The year before, a small scouting party traveled through northeastern Arizona and the Navajo Nation, but the distance and interactions with Indigenous people did not appeal to them, so they decided to take a shortcut. Since no one in the party had ever taken the new way before, and maps of the region did not exist yet, they leaned upon the true meaning of faith.

Once past the town of Escalante, Utah, called Potato Valley back then, they reached a dead-end cliff overlooking the Colorado River. Turning back was the only alternative, but a major snowfall made this choice undesirable. So, they opted to spend over a month blasting a 200-foot ramp down a cleft in the cliffs for their covered wagons. From there, they used ropes to lower eighty-three wagons through the Hole-in-the-Rock. They then descended another thousand vertical feet of steep, rocky slopes spread over a quarter mile before getting across the Colorado River.

The party, mostly comprised of families, presumed that was the hardest part of their journey. Instead, the terrain only got rougher, especially in lost cowboy country. They used explosives to break the trail, and the ruts they cut for the wagon wheels are still visible today. The party traversed Grey Mesa through a foot of snow and headed toward Lake Canyon, where the women and children enjoyed a welcome break by the water while the men scouted ahead. From there they traveled over the Clay Hills, paralleled Grand Gulch, and crossed Cedar Mesa. Finally, they found a way up and over Comb Ridge near the San Juan River, where they settled the town of Bluff. Astonishingly, nobody died during the pilgrimage, and three babies were even born.

The Hole-in-the-Rock road is a modern pilgrimage many Latter-day Saints families take by Jeep or ORV, making it the most frequently traveled historical route around here. For some reason, it's way more popular than retracing the Bernheimer Expedition.

This historic shortcut is supposed to be helping our pace, but Brent is slowing down due to a dehydration-induced queasy stomach. He's fixated on the countdown to returning home to take a shower and resume his life after the ten-day trip. As for me, it is impossible to get homesick when you are already there. The very forces that brought Brent and I together are now keeping us apart. His words express to me how much he misses me, but his actions are incomplete. Content to stay at home, he knows he can wait for me to crawl back to him in the mountains.

Souls eroded down to bedrock reveal each other's deepest layers. We are splintered by geography. To unite our worlds, I migrate between the desert and the mountains. The three-to-six-hour commute defines how vast the distance between us is. My feral spirit cannot be contained at his house, and attempts to escape through the cracks in the ceiling. A crooked picture hanging on the wall captures my image near Rainbow Bridge—its location next to the front door is symbolic. He encourages me to go fill myself up in the desert for as long as I need to before returning home. It's never enough. I frequently return to the red rocks alone, more deflated and confused than liberated. Deciphering a way forward is more convoluted than my dogged pursuit to unravel Bernheimer's expeditions. My heart resides in two places, but not always together. Freedom is displaced by restlessness, an unquenchable longing. When I am in the desert, I think I miss Brent. When I am in the mountains, I know I miss the desert. I miss myself.

Maybe if we walk far enough, Brent will understand my commitment to the desert, and with it my desire to spend time with him here, in *my* home. Perhaps that's geological time taking over, converting ten days into a blink, a few years, a dream, and my hope eternal. Heartbeat thumping, I ask if he can finish the expedition with me. His forehead tenses and he balls his fists. I step back and cower at his sudden outburst. The answer is an obvious no. "You know I have a lot to do, and I've already been out here long enough." Tears stream down my face as he continues, "You are too extreme. No one can live like this. Find another dirtbag to galivant around the desert with you." Then, he unleashes, "It's not like you could have done this without me."

I throw my backpack off, sit on the ground, and sob. His weaponized words build walls between us that are more impenetrable for me to navigate than the blank triangle. I am lost.

I lay back in the warm sand and look up at the cloudless blue sky. Deep breaths soothe me, and I let the desert hold me until I am ready to pull myself back up. I retrieve my pack, and give in to the sudden urge to start running down the road. I quickly catch up with Brent, but run past him to the edge of the blackbrush flats. I stop and look out at the great bend in the San Juan River. This stretch almost mirrors a picture that Earl Morris took in 1929. Today the river meanders through banks of silt remaining from when Lake Powell backed up this far. These will someday be flushed away in higher water-runoff years and flash floods, if they return. Climate and hydrology forecasts warn that below average precipitation, decreasing snow runoff, and resulting low river flows in the Southwest are the new normal. Thirsty air and soil take their share of moisture first, naturally.

I pull out a copy of Morris's black-and-white photo and attempt to recreate it with my iPhone. Bernheimer and Morris often skipped taking photos because of poor lighting and their limited rolls of film. Of the thousands of photos I have taken on this trip, I contemplate which shots would be worthy of precious film. The shift to digital cameras and smartphones has incalculably increased the number of photos I take. I hold my iPhone up to snap a photo and then scroll to Morris's to compare. Besides the high-water mark and sediment, it's a near-perfect match. Brent takes a look and says, "You can't erase the past, but there is always tomorrow." We look up from the camera into each other's eyes and continue walking. I want to believe him, but his promises are perpetually beyond reach.

I know this relationship is unhealthy. Why then, if I am capable of walking hundreds of miles through parched desert, is it so damn hard for me to walk away from Brent? Suffering and denial are a hell of a drug combination.

At our final camp together, Brent falls asleep without finishing his dinner, so I devour the extra serving of beef stroganoff. I lie awake under the stars and suspend my hurt feelings. Many aspects of this trip would not be the same without the support and company shared by all of my expedition mates—Stevo's generous help with planning, Joel's kind encouragement during my tent mishap, and Harvey's stoic wisdom. Brent's presence always leaves me with a feeling that something is still missing.

Living in the desert, or any wilderness, requires accepting the circumstances of the environment and following through with what is necessary to survive. Negligence, like drought, leads to empty potholes. I cannot find what I need to nourish my soul in another human. The desert calls me to look for what I desire within, occasionally forcing me to my knees in the sand, so that I must pick myself up. Here I surrender to the reality that my most reliable partnerships are with myself and the earth that holds me. The steps ahead are mine alone.

CHAPTER NINETEEN

Call of the Canyon

B ack at the truck, after one more full day of backpacking, I rushed to the cooler to prepare a feast of burgers and margaritas without ice. But the shift from dehydrated meals to two-week-old ground beef did not sit well with my stomach. To recover, I took an extra day to rest. This also allowed me to gather the energy to take on the remaining hundred miles, resuming at another tributary of Glen Canyon before climbing and traversing Mancos Mesa.

My feet slide into the feathery orange dune. Finely grained particles infiltrate every crevice of my shoes. The warm tickle against my toes incites déjà vu. In 2017, my first spring in the Four Corners, I went on an adventure date in this canyon. The man had appeared as suddenly in my life as my connection to Bears Ears. "You belong in the desert…Utah," he beckoned to me. The serendipity of our relationship awakened my curiosity to peel back the layers of its mysterious alchemy. This was something deeper than infatuation; it was something calling to both of us.

So we disappeared into the canyon underworld to run away from our problems. We ran thirty miles through a slot canyon, splashing in the mud, and laughing incessantly. Our smiles lasted until our cheeks cramped. I kept sliding in the mud, falling head over heels as I gawked at the smooth rust-colored walls high above me instead of my footing.

After our run, we hopped in our rigs and headed a few hours north to meet up with some of his friends. Driving through the night, I followed his truck in my Jeep. Enraptured in the naivety of new romance, I never bothered to ask the guy where we were going, enhancing the sense of reckless adventure and magic. We drove up a precipitous three-mile-long dugway overlooking desert towers and the snaking meanders of the San Juan River. In the dark I could not see much more than the dust illuminated by the taillights in front of me, until the full moon rose above the Bears Ears.

The drive droned on until we abruptly turned onto an unmarked dirt road. We parked at its terminus and spread our sleeping bags out on the ocean of slickrock, blissfully adrift. The next morning, the guy's friends arrived wearing packs loaded with rock-climbing gear. Since I'm not much of a climber, I laced up my shoes and set off on a run down the sand dune and into the canyon. At the bottom, I stopped to empty the sand from my shoes before resuming my pace down the dusty wash. Around a bend in the curving creekbed, I spotted a high cave. My run slowed to a crawl when I veered up the rocky scree slope. Beneath the shaded alcove, crumbling walls of hand-stacked stone lined the walkway before me.

Despite my limited knowledge of what I gazed upon, I felt an insatiable desire to explore the desert's stories like this one. Who lived here? Why did they leave certain things behind? I asked the same question when the lover faded away, until I realized I was falling in love with the Utah desert and that I did not have to leave. I redirected my affection to canyon country's heart of stone, and it welcomed me home. After that, I was here to stay.

Bernheimer's 1929 expedition journals renewed my interest in this Glen Canyon tributary. The team spent three days here as

Earl Morris studied lavish Basketmaker sites, with findings that included square-toed sandals, bark blankets, strings of yucca, strings wound with rabbit skin, feathers, rubbing stones, a bag made of mountain sheepskin, and a long bone awl. Bernheimer was convinced that they found a thirty-one-inch boomerang that might be proof of a link to the Aboriginal peoples of Australia. I asked perishable artifacts expert Laurie Webster about the head-scratching claim. She said it was likely a Basketmaker II fending stick used for hunting and defense, such as deflecting atlatl darts. Bernheimer also found a "boll of cotton." A *New York Post* article about the trip humorously stated, "Charles L. Bernheimer, cotton merchant, has discovered that the Basketmakers of the Colorado River used cotton, but he has discovered this at least 3,000 years too late to do any business with them."

In 1961 this canyon was surveyed by the Glen Canyon Project (GCP) before Lake Powell filled. Bill Lipe was a member of that team while working on his PhD dissertation at Yale University, and he fondly recalled in an email, "That was my favorite of the four summers I spent in the Glen Canyon. One of the reasons is because I wasn't a crew chief as I had been in previous seasons."

Lipe explained to me that these canyons drain toward the Colorado River, in the sandstone wilderness known as the Red Rock Plateau, and were a marginal habitation zone for the Basketmaker II and Ancestral Pueblo people. Sparse occupation and maize farming were intermittently possible here because of the sand dunes that helped accumulate moisture. The dunes helped form these springs and seeps, keeping the water table high beneath the alluvial deposits. Lipe and his team determined that the ancient farming was limited by an intense period of alluvial erosion. This likely pushed the few inhabitants of this area to migrate elsewhere. Today some of the high cut alluvial banks tower overhead like small buildings.

During their surveys, Lipe and the GCP crew encountered

a rock slab with Bernheimer's name carved on it, so they named the site the "Bernheimer Alcove." This site sparked Lipe's interest in making sense of the cultural history of the Red Rock Plateau. To do this, he took his later research to the highlands of Cedar Mesa, where larger populations of the Ancestral Pueblo people gathered. Lipe's research here helped forge the acclaimed Cedar Mesa Project that began in the late 1960s and continued into the 2000s.

Eager to sleuth for Bernheimer's inscription, I returned to the canyon on a solo backpacking trip as soon as COVID-19 shelter-in-place restrictions lifted in the spring of 2020. Locating the road to the canyon proved challenging several years after my nearly blindfolded trip. I spent the night in my Jeep on the wrong dirt road pull-off. I felt a little bit better about my confusion because both Johnson and Wetherill struggled to find the access point of this canyon in 1929. Wetherill said this was because he had only been there twice, compared to thirty-four times for Johnson, which Bernheimer thought was an exaggeration. Johnson took the lead. I was able to get back on track the next morning after looking at a historic map—the road was not marked on my modern road atlas.

Bernheimer recalled the team's swift but ungraceful descent down the 600-foot-high sand dune on horseback. Now the dune is tracked with an ORV track, which continues down canyon in the middle of the wash. The correlation between looting and access to sites by ORV and motorized boat has been documented by Jerry Spangler, Executive Director of the Colorado Plateau Archaeological Alliance. A different study, focused on the archaeologically dense Perry Mesa in central Arizona, determined that looting and pothunting not only increased but could be expected when sites are more accessible and visible to roads. Spangler's proposed solution to this dilemma is improving and expanding public education, which includes signage, ranger patrol, and interestingly, an increase in visitation by people who would disapprove of and report these types of illegal activities.

Travel by ORV, and even on foot, is frequently slowed in this canyon by high cut banks, some as high as two-story homes, and a succession of deep beaver ponds dammed intricately with tamarisk and cottonwood branches. These industrious critters have been rebuilding their lives as the lake levels continue to drop. Several times the pools force me to either swim across or bushwhack around them.

The water in this canyon is spring fed, and runs year-round. Orange rocket flower blooms burst in spring, and delicate purple stream orchids sprout along seeps. These flowers are rare, in that desert springs like this are relatively rare. Riparian areas like these may be faster to regenerate than others, but the constant impacts from cattle and humans take their toll on these finite oases.

Bill Lipe encouraged me to seek out the Bernheimer Alcove. He also sent me a series of photos he took during his work in Glen Canyon and requested that I take photos of the same spots so he can see how they have changed. To save time, I skipped the cave I went to on my first run here. I stopped frequently to look at rock art and even found an inscription dated 1894, but nothing that said Bernheimer.

I continued hiking with no clue how far down canyon the lake reached, until I saw a Jet Ski speeding toward me. Only a few hundred feet away, the distinction between terra firma and aquatic space blurred. Was I walking on water, or was this guy skiing on land? A few steps later I reached the calf-high water line marking the end of my hike.

For camping, my options were all atop a thick layer of semi-wet lake sediment covered with some dispersed tumbleweeds and cow pies. Not exactly paradise. I sat on the shoreline with my feet in the water, debating whether or not to stay. Around the corner, I heard a group of partiers, presumably on a houseboat, yelling, "LAAAAKE POWELLL!!!"

I turned around to head back the way I came. Despite its cultural significance, this canyon was removed from the boundaries of Bears Ears National Monument by President Trump. The lower portion has been inundated by the reservoir since 1963. Here, I walk through colliding legacies of Glen Canyon.

- - - - -

The next day, there was only one site left—the cave I had encountered on my first run through this canyon years ago. Could it be the one? I dropped my pack and climbed up the steep slope of boulders. Gazing at the walls revealed many more details than my previously unattuned eyes could grasp. Life-sized human figures adorned with feathers and masks appeared as ghosts before me. The delicate white outlines were nearly imperceptible in the bright midday sun. I looked up toward the ceiling, where two blood-red human figures loomed—one holding another tiny human by its head. This matched one of Lipe's photos so I pulled out my camera.

The ancient art was hypnotic, but I resisted its allure in order to remain focused on looking for Bernheimer's name on the rocks. The ground was scattered with so many fragments of dried corn and gourds that it seemed like its inhabitants had just finished dinner. I reminded myself to slow down; it was not a race to find them, it was a puzzle. I studied each wall intently, playing "Where's Bernheimer?" for longer than might seem sane. Surveying all sides of every boulder and slab, I walked the perimeter of the cave and every line in between, again and again. Maybe this was not the right spot after all? The site did seem to match one of Bernheimer's lengthier journal entries in this canyon. Baffled, I even began to wonder if a looter had walked off with the inscribed rock. I considered that the intense heat might be scrambling my brain, and accepted defeat while I hiked away from the alcove. I resolved to try again, and to return with an extra set of eyes.

A week later I talked Ralph Burrillo into joining me. Because it was still the early days of COVID-19, we greeted each other from a distance, near our rigs, with smiles of weary relief on each of our faces. Unlike our twelve-degree escapades at Camp Snowball in 2019, we faced hundred-degree temps and swarms of biting cedar gnats. Bernheimer was so melodramatic about mosquitoes and insects that he brought netting to wear over his head each night, and once an infected bite sent him into a full-blown panic. Ralph hates the goddamn cedar gnats, as he lovingly refers to them, but I just sort of ignore them. I swear that the act of not swatting them causes me and the bugs to lose interest in one another. The red bites all over my body tell otherwise.

Near the start of our trip, a massive thunderstorm rolled through. Ralph was at the grocery store in Blanding getting supplies and I was back at Zeke's Shirt Tail Gas Station filling up my Jeep. In a blink the sky turned from bluebird to doomsday black. With it came wind so violent it shook my Jeep, which by then was also being pelted with golf ball–sized hail. With limited visibility, I could make out only one scene—the wind pulling the gas station roof off and straight up into the air! I was prepared for the winds to pick the Jeep up and take me somewhere over the rainbow. The storm lasted no more than ten minutes, and was quickly replaced by an eerie sunshine. Ralph and I reunited at our camp, where my tent was torn to shreds and filled up like a child's swimming pool with water and ice.

Still on edge, we drove to the sand dune to begin our quest for Bernheimer. Heading down in the heat of midday, Ralph did not mince words, "This is not going to be fun to come back up!" Ralph used to work as an archaeologist at Glen Canyon National Recreation Area, which manages the lower canyon, but he'd never been to the upper reaches. I enjoyed getting to play tour guide and show Ralph some sites for a change. Before climbing up to the site, we cooled off in the shade to drink some water and snack on squeaky cheese. Everything in the world shifted because of the pandemic, but this felt like solid ground.

Under the alcove, we walked in different directions to launch our search. Ralph stopped to pick something up off the ground. Holding it out in his hand, he said, "I bet you can guess what this is!" From a distance, the tubular yellow object just looked like a stick. I walked toward him, scanning the surrounding pictographs, life-sized white human figures, for clues. Looking at it more closely I noticed that the ends were intentionally frayed.

"Is it a brush? Like a *paintbrush*?"

Ralph gently set the two-inch brush made of corn husk in my palm. The bristles painted an intimate scene in my imagination of ancient artists using their hands to craft this brush to color the sandstone walls with stories. Afterward, I gingerly placed the paintbrush back on the ground, but this time behind a rock to prevent it from blowing away.

The brush was amazing, but even more so is that it remains in situ. A lot can go missing in plain sight unless people come to understand that these objects belong where they are found. It is common in Utah to hear stories from people who picked up small artifacts like this brush, or potsherds and arrowheads, as kids. They likely learned to do this from watching their parents do so, or from looking at their grandparent's small and seemingly innocent collections of mementos. The education required to change this is not just about rules, it's about shifting a culture.

Bernheimer admitted to pocketing artifacts from sites as keepsakes. Even with Morris's archaeological permit, taking items home instead of sending them to the museum blatantly violated the Antiquities Act. Interestingly, Bernheimer did not hide his actions and made a note of the objects he took home, and he offered their return to the American Museum of Natural History, which finally occurred after his death. The archivist at the museum told me that they do not have records of what he may have additionally returned prior to his passing.

Ralph and I refocused on our search for the Bernheimer and Wetherill inscriptions. Pacing in the opposite direction, Ralph stopped, looked down at his feet, and called out, "Oh Morgan …" I turned around and walked over to Ralph. In front of us were the letters "JW" carved on a slab with two dates, "10-26-23" and "6-11-29," next to Bernheimer's thinly scratched name, dated 1929. Ralph laughed, "I was just about to ask you how you missed this, but in this harsh light, I can see why." I walked right over this spot on both of my previous trips here.

I dropped down to my knees in the sand, and lowered my face just inches above the faint letters inscribed in stone. Like the humans painted on the wall behind me and the corn husk paintbrush on the ground, this made me feel even more connected to the stories marked upon the pages of the desert itself.

- - - - -

Even the wind is quieter on this lonely afternoon. My only conversations now are with the sound of my footsteps. Past the sand dune, I am tempted to stop and visit my friends whose images and names adorn the rocks. But I need to head in a new direction. I walk past the cave and hike up a steep stock trail out of the canyon, the same that Bernheimer's forty horses ascended. From the edge of the rim I can see the site below me. I smile knowing that Bernheimer has been with me all along.

CHAPTER TWENTY

The Hermitage

These were men who believed that to let oneself drift along, passively accepting the tenets and values of what they knew as society, was purely and simply a disaster.

—Thomas Merton

Existential loneliness and the thought that one's life is inconsequential, both of which are hallmarks of modern civilizations, seemed to me to be derived in part from our abandoning a belief in the therapeutic dimensions of a relationship with place. A continually refreshed sense of the unplumbable complexity of patterns in the natural world, patterns that are ever present and discernable, and which incorporate the observer, undermine the feeling that one is alone in the world, or meaningless in it. The effort to know a place deeply is, ultimately, an expression of the human desire to belong, to fit somewhere.

—Barry Lopez

Red dust swirls and dances through the purple-streaked Chinle Formation crowned by pinnacles of rust-hued Wingate Sandstone. The only footprints through here are my own and a those of few hundred head of cattle. Perpetually howling wind reminds me that solitude is a state of mind, even in this desolate canyon. The gusts briefly pause. Silence sits heavy on my chest, amplifying the rhythm of my thumping heartbeat. I turn back to look up at the top of Mancos Mesa, where I stood just an hour ago.

Bernheimer's route to the Colorado River is no longer possible, because the lower portion is under the water of Lake Powell. So I crossed the mesa in the opposite direction, aiming for a steep 1,800-foot descent through a rock chimney known as The Squeeze into Red Canyon. There is no way Bernheimer and his horses could have traveled this precarious way. The forty-mile-an-hour gusts ripping around me did nothing to soothe my nerves as I stepped down the steep slope on loose rocks. After sliding down the first fifty feet on my rear end, I stood up and took a deep breath.

Within the passage, I used a rope to lower my pack off several drops before down-climbing them. The thought of doing this alone rattled my nerves for weeks. Safely past a difficult section, I yelped, letting my joyful relief echo back to me, only to trip and grab a cactus with my hand. I did my best to pull out the spines. They usually work their way out on their own time.

At the bottom of The Squeeze an intoxicating geological rainbow engulfed me—purples, pinks, teals, and yellows. Walking through thin eroded passageways of hardened mud mounds, the beauty is a devilish reminder that this is uranium country, and that radioactive minerals abound in these soils.

- - - - -

It's dry. There are only six liters of water in my backpack. To ration, I plan to drink only three liters as the midday sun heats up. The other three are for cooking. If necessary, I will eat granola bars and beef jerky for dinner—those dehydrated backpacker meals requiring a cup or two of water to reconstitute aren't designed for scenarios like this. Bernheimer warned me that the water in Red Canyon was undrinkable. This offers minimal comfort considering I have not found any water at all.

This landscape is both scarred by humans, and largely

ignored by them. It is a place most people and animals only pass through. Unless, of course, you are seeking to be alone. In which case, it's an excellent choice. Old tire tracks fading into the sand guide my retreat from the civilized world deeper into the desert. The word desert, both noun and verb, is derived from the Latin *desertum*, which means "to abandon, to leave, forsake, give up, leave in the lurch."

Acts of desertion arrive in sudden eruption. The void of connection, physical and emotional, haunts me with a knot in my stomach that does not go away, until I accept that there may never be an explanation, closure, or repair. Away from the desert, I temporarily become the abandoner, and I exist in a trance where my body is present, but my vision is sandstoned. Only a return to where I belong can remedy the schism.

But why here? How can a desolate radioactive canyon possibly reside along the path to self-discovery? This is no Walden Pond. I can smell the loneliness that lingers here. Perhaps I am drawn to the sense of anonymity nearly guaranteed in places perceived as damaged. Finding beauty in the chaotic refuse brings me hope in a world that often appears doomed.

I cannot help but contemplate abandonment here. Almost everyone with a reason to spend time in Red Canyon eventually left. The earliest inhabitants of Glen Canyon were present over ten thousand years ago. Nomadic people foraged, hunted, gathered, and left minimal traces of their presence. When the Ancestral Pueblo inhabited the river corridor and its tributaries, they developed more sedentary residences and the use of pottery, tools, and jewelry, and they painted images on sandstone walls. During this period, a hardy soul, or family, built a solitary two-story dwelling near the mouth of the canyon, perhaps to get away from the "crowds" of more populated habitation zones.

By AD 1280, almost everyone, including the residents of Red Canyon, migrated from what is now Bears Ears, due to climate change and other associated factors. This was not an abandonment; the Ancestral Pueblo still dwelled here. Sparse human presence in Glen Canyon continued with the Paiute, Ute, and Diné—who continue to utilize this area, but not as a major habitation zone. Leo Manheimer has told me stories about crossing the San Juan River to this canyon annually to hunt deer with medicine man Buck Navajo. In Red Canyon, I spot a sweat hogan tucked away in a wash. Outside the door of the hogan is a magazine dated 2021; a mark of how past and present reside together.

River explorer John Wesley Powell briefly stopped at Red Canyon during his 1869 and 1871 expeditions. There Powell and his team documented an Ancestral Pueblo site and hypothesized that the structure was a ceremonial kiva. Bill Lipe explained to me that Powell was familiar with Hopi kivas and was able to make the connection between this site and the construction of sites in the Tusayan, Arizona, area, where he had visited the Hopi Tribe. Powell did not linger at Red Canyon and continued boating down the Colorado River from Glen Canyon into the Grand Canyon.

In 1884 Lemuel Redd, an original member of the Hole-in-the-Rock Expedition, started running cattle on the flanks of Mancos Mesa. This canyon was named for Redd, but was erroneously labeled as "Red Canyon" by map makers. By the time Bernheimer arrived, he assumed it was named for its color, as did I. Redd's legacy may not be on the map, but the impacts of overgrazing will last a lifetime. Most of the sagebrush and even cacti have been nibbled down into nubs. Looking around, it's hard to believe that, prior to Redd's arrival, perennial grasses and shrubs would have blanketed the red earth.

That same year, the Glen Canyon gold rush ushered in foolhardy prospectors. Mining activity picked up in the 1890s, and the dream of striking it rich hung on to its muddy shores into the next century. Glen Canyon's gold came in the form of fine flakes deposited in sand and silt on the riverbanks and bars surrounding the main channel. Because the gold was so hard to collect, nobody exactly hit the jackpot. The most industrious enterprise was Robert Brewster Stanton's Hoskanini Company, which built a large gold dredge in the river in 1897. The dredging failed to harness much of the Colorado River's gold powder, and he only made $66.95 back on his $100,000 investment. The dredge was left to rust until Lake Powell covered it.

Prospectors later learned that uranium was much more plentiful and profitable. In 1898 John Wetherill claimed the first documented discovery of uranium in Red Canyon—explorers do not limit themselves to one genre. Wetherill did submit a mining notice, but never extracted any ore. Wetherill's claim site later became the Blue Lizard Mine, operated by Cal Black, whom author Edward Abbey modeled the character Bishop Love in *The Monkey Wrench Gang*.

Uranium boomed midcentury, bolstered by the Cold War arms race with the Soviet Union after World War II ended. The industry was heavily subsidized by the Atomic Energy Commission between 1940 and 1960, which generated jobs for people on the Navajo Nation and in San Juan County.

This very dirt road I am walking on is the result of the uranium industry, where roads were created to access mining operations and claims. It is not even noon, and the red dirt and dark Wingate walls around me are already radiating heat. Author Tom McCourt described this road as

a long stark, bleak, and depressing scratch on the earth's surface even today....It is a rough and rocky moonscape— the backside of the red planet Mars....The road teetered on the edge of a deep, ugly desert gulch for most of the way.

It's quite the destination. I contemplate a conversation with the cows, suggesting that they revolt and follow in the footsteps of the Ancestral Pueblo, hermits, and miners and get the hell out of here.

Uranium profitability barely hung on in the later twentieth century, until another resurgence occurred in the 1980s. Today uranium prices are down, and the mines in the Four Corners have largely been abandoned without cleanup, but some are ready for action if the price of yellow cake ore increases again.

Red Canyon and the area surrounding it were strategically left out of the 2016 Bears Ears National Monument designation. However, including it would not have stopped mining, because preexisting claims are grandfathered into new national monuments anyway. This zone encompasses the Daneros Mine, the region's largest and most recently active uranium mine. It is owned by Canada-based Energy Fuels Inc., the largest producer of uranium in the United States. Although it has been sitting idle since 2012, the mine remains on standby, ready to resume operations as soon as extracting uranium becomes economically viable again.

Uranium mining poses extensive threats to people, wildlife, and water sources long after the underground work is done. Defunct mines that are not cleaned up continue to pollute groundwater, and they release radioactive dust into the air on windy days. Both forms of exposure are known to cause cancer and reproductive organ damage in surrounding communities.

Indigenous homelands are among the most affected. There are over five hundred abandoned uranium mines on the Navajo Nation. After decades of uranium-related health issues, the Navajo Tribal government now opposes permitting these activities on or near tribal lands. The most recent data from the Pulitzer Center estimates that 85 percent of Navajo homes are currently contaminated by uranium.

Adjacent to the Ute Mountain Ute reservation and the boundaries of Bears Ears, White Mesa Mill, constructed in 1980, is the last of its kind in the United States. The mill, also owned and operated by Energy Fuels Inc., processes and stores 700 million pounds of radioactive waste. White Mesa Mill's uncovered radioactive waste storage system emits ten times more radon, a carcinogenic gas, than if it was covered as it should be, in adherence to EPA requirements. The mill is authorized to accept radioactive wastes from across the United States and as far away as Estonia and Japan.

The Ute Mountain Ute community, home to three hundred people, reports a distinct taste to their water, and many refuse to drink it at all. Contamination affects tribal hunting grounds and the collection of traditional plants. The mill sits precariously on top of the Navajo Aquifer, which provides water to much of southeastern Utah.

Walking through the arid badlands, it's clear why this is not a tourism hot spot. Who wants to peruse the relics of defunct mines and walk among the cattle subsisting on this waterless hellscape? The very things that are scarring the desert are unintentionally protecting it from recreation impacts. It plays nicely into the hands of the extraction industry, as it is silently getting away with environmental murder—realizing this is what first drew my interest out here.

In February 2018, I filed the first mining claim in the area that was newly excluded from Bears Ears National Monument boundaries. Joined by my boyfriend at the time, we had no interest in mining the earth for minerals. We wanted to extract experience and knowledge. The monkey-wrenching scenario we dreamt up was to race big corporations staking mining claims, hoping to block them out of sections removed from Bears Ears. If successful, we hypothesized that larger conservation groups and eco-conscious outdoor brands could use the same method to collectively protect these sensitive zones that are susceptible to future mining.

Staking a mining claim is legal so long as all of the procedures, protocols, and payments are followed—most of which were drafted up in the General Mining Act of 1872. The archaic laws governing this process raise important questions of efficacy and relevance in the twenty-first century. Given the 150-year-old law, we both thought it would be fun to go to the BLM offices dressed up like 1800s prospectors, in old leather boots, dirty work pants, straw hats, flannel shirts, and a coating of dirt on our faces. Sitting in the BLM office, the Department Head of Energy and Minerals looked me straight in the eye with a smile on his face and said, "Look, I know you're not uranium miners," and then handed us the paperwork, and a pamphlet the BLM gives to anyone interested in staking a mining claim—from hobbyists to megacorporations.

It took us a week to file the twenty-acre mining claim on the edge of a mesa overlooking a Cedar Mesa sandstone canyon. We chose the spot for its location in a zone at high risk for new mining claims. Using ice axes, climbing ropes, and a PVC pipe as our monument post, staking the claim itself turned out to be the easiest part. The modern BLM SR-2000 software used to locate available claim sites was not as user friendly as the 1872 mining act. To finalize the claim, we paid the fees and had our paperwork notarized with the county clerk in Monticello.

A few months later, the BLM deemed our mine too large and mailed us a tiny paper ruler to remeasure it—a real "fuck you, nice try," considering the maximum size for a placer mine is twenty acres. Then the BLM declared the mine obsolete by sending ten copies of the same letter. If we wanted to keep our mine we would have to start over.

I also learned that any increase in mining helps the BLM determine how the land is managed and what uses are prioritized. So, we abandoned the prospect. This is not to say everyone else did. Fourteen new mining claims have been staked within the excluded Bears Ears boundaries since 2018, six of these in 2021. None of these mines are active and there has not been a revived uranium boom in the United States. A part of me will always be proud that the first of these new mining claims was staked by two environmental activists, although I may never grow accustomed to that label.

Afterward, I wrote an article about the experience, "Staking a Claim for Public Lands," for REI's website. Journalists from *Reuters* and *HuffPost* interviewed us and featured our efforts to bring attention to the mining threats to Bears Ears. We even made a television appearance on *NBC Left Field*. It was not unlike the East Coast reporters looking to Bernheimer for information about the Southwest—we were not exactly mining experts, but through the experience we came to know a bit more than someone sitting in a cubicle on the other side of the country.

Though we walked away from the mine, the media did not. *HuffPost* continued to mention our mining claim in just about every news story about mineral extraction in Utah, complete with a link to our former mailing address. Other toxic side effects included more online harassment, some claiming that our efforts were merely a publicity stunt, which excavated any common ground on which a productive conversation between all sides could be held.

Those messages cannot reach me out here, which is part of the reason I keep coming back. Historically speaking, I am not alone. Several hermits in the last century have called Red Canyon home. This road was once the driveway for Albert "Bert" Loper. A roaming hobo since his teens, Loper supported himself working odd jobs like ditch digging, milking cows, making bricks, hauling freight, and mining coal across the West, from the San Juan Mountains of Colorado to southern Utah and even Mexico.

In the fall of 1893, he began a fifty-year love affair with the Colorado River, leading him to take jobs on and off the waterway. The river instilled in him a passion for boating, and Loper began to build a watercraft with the ambition to row down the mighty Colorado, through the Grand Canyon.

On Loper's first attempt, a 1907 prospecting trip, he had to stop to repair his boat and was separated from his party. When Loper finally arrived at Lee's Ferry, the expedition had left without him. So, he turned around. That winter, he traveled up Glen Canyon solo, hauling his boat upriver by pulling on willows along the riverbanks, which he called "willerin."

Loper decided to stay in Glen Canyon, prospect for gold, and deliver the mail on horseback to Hanksville, Utah. There, he befriended legendary miner Cass Hite, who was guided along the Colorado River by Hoskinnini, the Diné Fearing Times hero. Hite was searching for the elusive lost Merrick-Mitchell mine, and Hoskinnini likely wanted to distract him away from it. Hite was more notorious for his mining scams than for the minerals he extracted, and the publicity he generated about it sparked the Glen Canyon gold rush. In 1883 Hite established a ranch at Dandy Crossing near the mouth of Trachyte Creek, before moving downriver to Ticaboo Creek. He later established a post office in Hite City to serve the local mining community.

Red Canyon is where Loper decided to settle, living in a small cabin he called The Hermitage. Old photographs depict a shanty with a thatched roof, small windows, two entrances, and a diminutive chimney. The plot was surrounded by large cottonwoods, and Loper built a reservoir, using one of the lower springs, to grow peaches, grapes, apples, and hay on seven to nine acres. Ancestral Pueblo inhabitants used this same delta to farm cotton. Loper spent his time either on the river or mining for gold. "I lived with that river so much, it pretty near became a part of me; I would sit on the banks and watch it; I would boat it; I would do everything; about the only companion I had."

At age forty-seven, Loper began to grow weary of the hermit life and married eighteen-year-old Rachel Jameson. She spent one winter with Loper at the ranch before insisting that they move because she could not stand the isolation—imagine that. He moved on to become a guide on the Colorado and Green

Rivers, a job that he had for the rest of his life. Loper turned seventy in 1939 and finally fulfilled his lifelong dream of continuing down the Colorado River to boat the Grand Canyon. A decade later, at age eighty, he had a heart attack while rowing his boat at the river's mile 24.5 rapid, went overboard, and perished.

On June 14, 1929, Bernheimer's team stayed at Loper's Hermitage, with its new caretaker and resident, Mr. William A. Carpenter. Bernheimer called him "Scarf" and was astounded by his mysterious desert hermit lifestyle—shabby, torn khaki clothing, dirty skin, uncombed hair, rough talking, and untidy home.

I am certain Bernheimer would have written some interesting descriptions of me if we crossed paths. My skin is darkened by a mixture of dirt and sweat, my hair is matted, and the clothes I have been wearing for a month are tattered. Bernheimer wrote that Scarf seemingly did nothing except keep his soul together. And that reinforces why I am here with a sturdy nail; self-reliance reclaims my soul.

As mining fizzled, recreation ignited, especially among Colorado River runners who enjoyed a brief heyday before the dam construction. Boaters who made Red Canyon home for a night visited both the Loper cabin and the Loper Ruin, before continuing downriver. Folk singer and author Katie Lee, known as the Goddess of Glen Canyon, was among the frequent floaters. Her passion and intimate connection with this river corridor ignited her lifelong devotion to it. "Best lover I ever had was that river." When they drowned *her* river, as she called it, she mourned the loss deeply: "With pounding heart I walked to where the cliff dropped to the river…and fell to my knees." After that, Lee refused to run any rivers between 1963 and 1974. She grieved the loss of Glen Canyon for the rest of her ninety-eight-year life, channeling her rage into a compact with the Colorado River to fight the dam and defend the desert.

Archaeologists roamed Glen Canyon contemporaneously with the river rats during this period. In 1958–59 the Glen Canyon Project was the final group to study the mouth of Red Canyon before Lake Powell filled. Bill Lipe recalls excavating a site they named "the Loper Ruin," due to its proximity to Loper's home. Lipe dated the site to the 1200s (AD), during the Pueblo III period, and recalls that the remnants of cotton plants were found during the survey. Not far downriver, the GCP encountered a site called "Creeping Dune," which included a spring-fed irrigation system. The site, which displayed a sustainable approach to desert water use, now lies beneath a failing reservoir.

Lipe noted that his field crew did little survey and no excavation in Red Canyon proper because it did not seem like it would have very many good farming locations, making it an unlikely spot for significant Ancestral Pueblo sites. To counter the colonially informed archaeological perspective, the lack of human traces on the ground does not necessarily mean that nobody was there. Ute Mountain Ute Tribal member Regina Lopez-Whiteskunk explained to me that the Ute tradition is always to leave a camp as if you were never there. Non-Indigenous minds don't often credit Indigenous people as the first stewards of the land and as the originators of the "leave no trace" ethics advocated today.

The last resident of The Hermitage was uranium prospector Bud Vinger. One time, Lipe and his friends followed Vinger home from the Fry Canyon Store, as he tossed his empty beer cans out the window. At the cabin, Lipe recalls a distinct sign: "The Vingers, Bud, Sally, and Dewey," which was odd because they never saw anyone else around. During the few brief encounters with the young archaeologists, Bud was cordial.

Vinger's obituary described him as an adventurous spirit, on his own from an early age:

His laws of survival were sometimes at odds with the laws of man which gained Bud an early reputation as a "Maverick."...Bud always had unusual projects going, such as searching for a lost Spanish gold mine in the Henry Mountains of Utah, placer mining and homesteading in the seclusion of Red Canyon on the Colorado River below Hite, Utah, and undertaking many business ventures. Bud's typical approach to life was one of optimism and confidence. He was undaunted by problems and never considered the possibility of failure, no matter what he attempted.

Lipe's sendoff email before this hike prodded me to drink a beer for Bud in Red Canyon. I don't have any beer, but today I stumbled upon a rusty barrel containing old beer bottles filled with sand. I picked one up and lifted it toward the rising moon to salute Bud Vinger and Red Canyon's hermits, mavericks, and other folks working on "unusual projects," myself included. Out here, I am not drinking alone.

- - - - -

The lonesome road I walk now ends in Lake Powell, a monument to the way humans are abandoning their relationship with the natural world; abuse slips through the cracks of this disconnection. Is the cycle of human belief in their right to control nature any different?

Every thirty minutes or so, sand fills my shoes, so I stop walking to dump the excess out. It's as if the grains of sand are begging me to carry them away from here, to journey with me to Natural Bridges by clinging to my soles. Most will be left where they belong, right here. Though the accumulation of sand never ceases, ignoring it is unsustainable. I must repeatedly pour it out of my shoes, only for the process to begin all over again. Like everything else in my life that adds weight without purpose, I leave only sand and footprints as I walk away. We could all stand to desert the things that do not serve the land, wildlife, other humans, and even ourselves.

Fear and Loathing in White Canyon

True courage is in facing danger when you are afraid.
—*The Wizard of Oz*

Somewhere in White Canyon I realize that I might not make it. It's a startling realization after covering more than three hundred miles on foot, and with only twenty to go. The towering walls attempt to swallow the first words I have uttered in days. My expletives are useless here, and the stone corridor mocks me with an echo. Staring up at the jumble of ten-foot-tall boulders with thick cottonwood logs wedged between them, I dread my options.

Walking in the desert is never just walking.

Most folks travel through canyons downstream. The downward-sloping terrain makes hiking through obstacles created by rockfall and flash flood debris easier. For instance, if I were to descend these boulders, I would use my rope to lower my pack. Then, free of the extra weight on my back, I would down-climb the big rock until I felt comfortable letting go, and jump down the last few feet, gingerly, onto the ground.

Hiking up canyon goes against the flow of water and gravity that formed these Cedar Mesa sandstone narrows. My legs are shaky with exhaustion from climbing up and over rock fall and logjams, so I rely on my upper extremities to do the work. This is not only poor technique, it's just silly, considering my noodle arms. As the fatigue mounts, so do my fears, knowing that being sore and tired increases the chances of an accident.

It's not a question of whether I can do this on my own, I can, but that doesn't mean it is wise. A fall of six feet could be a disaster in this remote canyon. It's the reason that when I head out solo, people smirk and tell me not to end up like Everett Ruess or Aaron Ralston, lest I end up trapped in a canyon with no other option than to saw off my arm with a pocketknife. Disappearance, death, and disaster have become synonymous with desert travel. In biblical tales, Satan usually appeared on the fortieth day of a journey. I have lost count of what day this is, but I suspect I may be near forty.

Backcountry travel comes with inherent risks. I have made plenty of naive and careless mistakes in the past. In the last decade, rangers on Cedar Mesa started noticing an uptick in visitors with minimal backcountry experience. Recent rescues in the Grand Canyon are the highest they have been in twenty-one years. While the Grand Canyon is on a different scale of danger and remoteness than Cedar Mesa, the perils lurking here are similar for the unknowing or unprepared.

"Stay focused!" I remind myself to be confident, that I am prepared and experienced for this exact scenario. Besides, there have been far scarier days for folks in White Canyon, like the 1884 Soldier Crossing battle. The situation ignited when US soldiers and cowboys clashed with a band of Utes led by Mancos Jim, due to a dispute over a stolen horse. The Utes took off on horseback and made camp at White Canyon. The arrival of soldiers and cowboys quickly escalated into a gunfight. The Utes, joined by the renegade Narraguinnep band of Utes, Paiutes, and Diné men, taunted the soldiers and cowboys, shooting and killing two of them. The white men retreated, and the Utes took all possessions of value from the dead men. Afterward, they retreated over Mancos Mesa, and returned to their reservation. Having just come from Mancos Mesa, I can envision what their escape route was like.

History cannot distract me from my fear of heights. My legs quake like Elvis, my palms sweat, and guttural squeals exit my mouth. Looking for alternatives to scrambling upward brings me down to the ground. I slither through holes between boulders and murky crevices slimed with mud. Some of the passageways are too narrow for me to fit through while wearing my backpack, so I take it off and push or pull it through. Picking my pack up and swinging it back on has become so tiresome that I lie down on top of it, pull my arms through, and then swing my legs in the air to rock myself onto my feet. I finally catch my balance and press up to a standing position, and let out a victorious, "Woohoo!" like a toddler in the canyon jungle gym.

Bernheimer roped up a few times, but more often he left the climbing to the rest of his team while he stood by and observed. I want to pull a Bernheimer right now, but I can't. Turning around and quitting is not an option. Neither is asking for help. The only way out of White Canyon is through. I grab a caffeinated energy gel out of my pocket and remind myself not to be "such a Berny," and to cowgirl up for the moves ahead. Too soon, I face another boulder jam, more significant than the ones before. *You've got to be fucking kidding me! Again?*

It occurs to me that if I had forty horses and mules, maybe I would not even be able to get myself into trouble like this. The mules could not travel in the canyon and traversed along the rim instead. Bernheimer entrusted his life to his pack animals, who seemed simultaneously wise and stupid, or on the verge of committing suicide. Today, I am my own stubborn and stupid mule.

- - - - -

This section that I am hiking solo comprises almost a third of the total expedition mileage. With a few weeks of hiking under my belt, my body is strong. I had worried that the most significant challenges might be loneliness and boredom, but every single day brings new elements to overwhelm my adrenal glands.

One night hiking alone in Red Canyon, a herd of black bovines surrounded my camp. At first, I assumed they would lose interest. The swarm of cows stayed for an hour and rattled me, so I tried to chat them up, "C'mon, don't you all have somewhere else to be? It sure looks nice over there!" Nobody budged.

I once read that more people are killed annually by cows than by shark attacks. What was meant as a silly fact to assure nervous swimmers that it's safe to splash in ocean waves has the opposite effect on me. Hiking through the open range of Utah is like diving without a shark cage. Hoping not to get trampled in the middle of the night, I scoured my brain for the right words to say to the cows: "Go on now, GIT! G'ON GIT! YAAAAAAH!"

The cows immediately turned around and ran away. It's hard to say where those words came from, having never uttered them before in my life.

I slept peacefully until I heard a loud clomping nearby in the middle of the night, so I unzipped the tent and pulled out my headlamp. Ten feet away, two glowing eyes stared at me. In my sleepiness, I gasped—is it a massive coyote? A mountain lion? I pointed my light on the motionless little beast—a calf. The *Jaws* theme song played in my mind as I howled, "Go'on now, GIT!" into the darkness, and the baby darted away.

Overconfident that the next stretch would fly by, I carried a minimal amount of water to hike down the old mining road. I sensed trouble might be upon me when my planned exit from the canyon turned out to be a sheer ten-foot-high wall. It took three attempts to find an exit. My relief lasted only a few minutes. The rim of the next canyon was rougher than the first. This game of climbing in and out of small, steep side gullies persisted all day. I trusted my light grip on crumbly purple layers of Chinle Formation to pull myself and my pack up and out of them. If

I got knocked out, no one was coming for me, not right away. Only Steve Allen would have any clue where to find me, but he would be somewhere unreachable too. I pushed away defeating thoughts: *Mummified remains of a woman were found three feet below the rim of an unnamed canyon.*

The distance from my previous water source grew with each committing step, so I kept scrambling up and over the next chossy ledge of loose stone. Quitting would be more dangerous than spurring myself on. With a mere two liters of water left in my pack and not a drop to be found, inching my way forward remained the safest course. A rush of relief pulsed through my veins when I intersected with an old mining route, leading to water I had cached.

- - - - -

The smooth boulders grow taller as I proceed up White Canyon, and the spaces to crawl through them are more tangled with debris. It's hard for me to assess whether the obstacles are getting more difficult or if I am losing momentum. As fatigue mounts, negative thoughts creep in: *You're too anxious, sensitive, and scared. Use your brain.* I pause and tell the voice in my head to shut up. No one else helped me bypass the last series of obstacles. It was all me. *You've got this, Mo. One step at a time.*

I scramble over the awkwardly angled rocks, and keep my eyes up in search of a campsite above the narrows—well aware that there are only a few hours of remaining daylight. Although there are no clouds in sight, sleeping in a flash flood zone still does not appeal to me. Finally, I find a spot I am willing to settle for. The sandstone slab is as big as an office desk, tilted slightly downward into the abyss and surrounded by thorny shrubs that claw at my calves. On second thought, I would prefer to meet my end riding down a raging torrent of muddy water than falling off this ledge while trying to pee. I gingerly return through the obstacle course, with blood dripping down my legs.

Exhaustion mounting, I trudge on and consider how long I can keep this up. Another mile later, I notice a decent camp that requires no crawling, climbing, or bushwhacking to access. Without second-guessing it, I commit, and set up my tent and boil a pot of water. I devour a packet of tuna, a chocolate bar, and handfuls of snacks as my dinner cooks. It's not only because I am ravenous; this will help lighten my pack. If tomorrow is anything like today, I will need all the performance-enhancing help I can get. Once the warm sun drops behind the canyon walls, I hop into my sleeping bag, but I fail to sleep as I battle my mental demons. To counter my dread and anxiety of what might be next, I remind myself there is no danger in lying safely in this spot tonight. Then I remember the mountain lion in Grand Gulch.

My stomach is in knots when I wake up. I don't feel like eating, but I fuel up anyway with another round of overfeeding myself to reduce my backpack weight further. I choke down a double oatmeal laced with trail mix and wash it down with two packets of instant coffee. I dump all of the remaining electrolyte powder into my water bottles. I still don't feel full, and my backpack still doesn't feel that much lighter.

The sunlight has yet to reach me, and the air is crisp. I move quickly to warm up, ignoring my chronically sore feet. Around each bend, I cross my fingers and am overjoyed each time I see a flat, sandy wash leading me on. I remain concerned, even as the hours pass with easy walking. Rounding another corner, I dread facing a large boulder or obstacle, until I look up at Kachina Natural Bridge, arching like a thick slab of bacon overhead.

Only three miles remain. My dread shifts to relief and then back to dread. I am not ready for this to be over. I do not want to turn on my phone, take a shower, or go inside. My urgency fades. I look back and consider walking the other way. To slow down, I sit down underneath the bridge and eat some gummy bears, the only snack I have left.

In his later years, Bernheimer reflected that the desert always seemed vast and mysterious compared to the skyscraper island of Manhattan. However, he wrote that the desert men he traveled with never seemed to be satiated. They always wanted to know what lay beyond the horizon, to make it feel bigger still. I am of this ilk. I crave stepping into the perpetual unknown. To feel both at home and forever arriving somewhere new.

A woman hikes past me, and we exchange greetings. She comments on my massive backpack and asks where I came from. I briefly explain.

"All alone? Were you afraid?"

Fear is not usually the deciding factor for me; if what I am doing is worth it, the question is whether I am willing to go anyway. Of course, if something went wrong, I might die. But I am alive. I never went hungry or without water. My cuts, scrapes, and bruises are all minor. My clothes and backpack only have a few holes.

Of the challenges on the 1929 expedition, which included bloodthirsty mosquitoes, countless cold sleepless nights, bushwhacking, and riding his mule up cliffs, Bernheimer concurred:

> I cannot pick out, Zane Grey style, one particular point and make a romance out of it. They were all different, most of them very difficult and some desperately so.

Living outdoors keeps me rooted in the present moment. I am far more terrified of the twenty-four-hour news coverage that makes my brain spiral into existential crisis and persistent anxiety. Concerns about basic survival, from an evolutionary standpoint, tend to make humans more hyper-focused so that we can act on instinct, be it running from a mountain lion or holding on to a rock ledge. Modern technology, on the contrary, has our fears running in a million directions while we sit safely on our sofas. Having experienced both spectrums of fear within the calendar year, I would prefer to attempt surviving in the desert rather than passing time under glorified house arrest, waiting for news updates. Hanging on to a slab of sandstone in the sun like a lizard sometimes is the most important thing to do.

While the human world is seemingly trying to burn itself down, the natural world lives on, and it adapts. The wild is increasingly the only place I feel at home; meaning truly free. The terrain and elements keep me alert to the utterly simple task of staying alive. Doing so requires listening to my inner voice and, above all, to nature. This is one of countless reasons that modern humans need open spaces—to contextualize the dangers we have evolved to respond to in order to keep us alive. Away from nature, we apply these responses to alerts, screens, and trivial stressors. In preserving these habitats of refuge from civilization, complete with their hazards, we also protect our human nature.

- - - - -

Sipapu Natural Bridge stretches across the canyon like a finish line. Craning my neck up at the creamy ribbon of sandstone pressed against the cerulean sky, I lose myself in the landscape once more. I could go on like this forever. Hiking up the steep slickrock trail out of the inner gorge of White Canyon, I slow down. I remind myself that leaving will be only temporary. This is the real world. It is where I will always return.

CHAPTER TWENTY-TWO

Bernheimer's Dream National Park

We don't manage the land. The land manages us.
—Bears Ears Inter-Tribal Coalition

In the months since the expedition, I've spent many weeks out backpacking and camping in the desert. But every few months or so, I force myself to leave the canyons to attend to personal matters I often neglect. You know, things like picking up my mail at a post office box in Arizona. I cram oil changes, visits with friends, and other appointments into these one- or two-week trips, all to get ready to pack up and return to southern Utah again.

Autumn in the desert is a pause between monsoon season and winter storms that asks, will there be water? Late August rainstorms replenished many of the potholes this year, but that supply is now dwindling, along with the springs that seem to run lower and lower each year. Waiting for President Biden to do something about Bears Ears and Grand Staircase–Escalante is beginning to feel the same way.

I take a bite of a bean and cheese burrito and scroll through my phone while I wait for a mechanic to work on my truck. There is a cloud burst of unexpected news:

President Biden set to restore Bears Ears and Grand Stair-case–Escalante National Monuments tomorrow.

Tears stream from my eyes. I collapse to the ground. High mesas, sinuous canyons, petroglyph panels, and mountains painted orange and red by maple leaves dance victoriously in my mind. I am overwhelmed with the urge to get in my truck and drive north—I need to go to Bears Ears so I can celebrate with the land itself.

But I resist. I still have relevant business to attend to down south. I hop in my truck to meet Harvey Leake at his central Arizona home. He's invited me over to scan documents related to Bernheimer's Rainbow National Park proposal—a serendipitously fitting day to do so. Harvey opens the door and we exchange relief over the good news. I think Bernheimer would have celebrated this too, after devoting his post-expedition efforts to protecting large areas now within the restored monument boundaries.

Inside, the coffee table is piled high with newspaper clippings, interviews, letters, and maps. We sit down, and Harvey unrolls a copy of Bernheimer's proposed park map, drawn up in 1928. The diamond-shaped boundaries are divided into three sections, each representing areas of proposed protection, with the primary focus on Rainbow Bridge which was included in all three plans. Although it was already a national monument, he hoped making Rainbow Bridge a national park would more thoroughly protect it from development.

Bernheimer's entire team rallied behind the idea. Wetherill and Johnson gave tours to park service personnel, and Morris met with prospective supporters. Popular support for the proposal was bolstered by Bernheimer's book *Rainbow Bridge* and a color slideshow presented by Bernheimer, hosted in the Department of the Interior's auditorium in Washington, DC.

In 1929, the Department of the Interior rejected the proposal because it was too similar to other national parks and monuments, like Mesa Verde and Canyon de Chelly, that protected areas of cultural and geological significance. Their primary concern remained the portions of the park's boundaries that fell within the Navajo Nation that would pose significant bureaucratic challenges.

I question whether Bernheimer's vision for a national park was a truly progressive idea or just another version of manifest destiny. Conservation and its figureheads, like John Muir, are currently undergoing a long-overdue reevaluation. In the early twentieth century, Muir blatantly aimed to erase Indigenous people from land to keep it "untouched" and "clean" from human intrusion. The 1964 Wilderness Act hauntingly echoes this tone with its call to protect areas "where the earth and its community of life are untrammeled by man, where man himself is a visitor who does not remain." This is directly at odds with the fact that so-called Wilderness areas are the past and present homelands of Indigenous people.

To his credit, Bernheimer worked and traveled with Diné guides and even spoke out against racism. Prior to the 1929 expedition, Bernheimer stayed the night at a hotel in Blanding, Utah, where the owner, Mr. Adams, asked if he opposed eating dinner with five or six men of color. Bernheimer made clear that he had no objections and proceeded to eat dinner with the other men.

Bernheimer's national park proposal would not displace current residents and the park lands would be co-managed by the Navajo Nation. Furthermore, Bernheimer and his supporters insisted that the park not relocate any Diné or Paiute people living within the boundaries or disrupt their grazing practices.

The Navajo Nation still opposed the idea, fearing it would affect their grazing ranges, which were suffering from reduced feed. The Nation's concerns were exacerbated by the inclusion of the former Paiute Strip in the suggested park boundaries, which had been in the public domain since 1922. By 1928, pressure was increasing to annex the Paiute Strip to the Navajo Nation, a legal discussion that the San Juan Southern Paiute tribe was never a part of, nor were they involved in any matters related to the national park on their homelands.

Bernheimer understood that Diné involvement would be necessary to proceed, so he looked to the Canyon de Chelly National Monument as a model. Designated in 1931, the national monument falls within Navajo Nation jurisdiction, and is co-managed between the Navajo Nation, local Diné families, and the National Park Service.

That does not mean this was a happily-ever-after situation. A report on tribal co-management, written by Dr. Barbara Dugelby of Round River Conservation Studies, explains, "Although on paper, the monument (Canyon de Chelly) may represent the best example of a co-management arrangement between tribes and the NPS, in practice there has been limited participation by Navajo tribal members and periods of strong resistance to NPS staff and their efforts." However, the outcome at Canyon de Chelly National Monument did nudge the National Park Service and Bureau of Indian Affairs to seriously consider the Rainbow National Park proposal.

A new version of Bernheimer's park was drawn up that year to include much of present-day Bears Ears National Monument. *The Salt Lake Telegraph* described the layout: "In the plans, the new national park will extend from Utah into northern Arizona, and will include the following: Rainbow natural bridge, Navajo national monument, the Goosenecks in the San Juan River, Monument valley, the Utah natural bridges [national monument], and Arch canyon." Much of this terrain encompasses Bernheimer's 1920 and 1929 expedition routes.

Harvey picks up a photo, and I set down the stack of documents I am sifting through to look at it. John Wetherill stands on the shoreline of the Colorado River in Glen Canyon, a cigarette resting in his mouth. He is wearing a winter coat and hat, and there is ice in the river. A caption written onto the color photo reads, "A lifetime passes by, yet to win or fail, it's always the great unknown."

The photo was taken in the winter of 1931, when John Wetherill took an adventurous boat trip with Henry Martin "Pat" Flattum up Glen Canyon to rally support for the park. Navigating the ice and risking hypothermia in low temperatures, the duo took photos in hopes they would encourage the park service to give the proposal a second look. Wetherill, the man of few words, even started keeping a journal on this trip. In one entry he wrote, "the hardships only added value to a wonderful experience." This is a necessary outlook if one wishes to doggedly pursue protecting precious endangered places. After that trip, Wetherill guided park service director Horace M. Albright to Rainbow Bridge, and he was impressed. Several members of the NPS Wetherill had taken to the bridge wrote in favor of Rainbow National Park, on the condition that it did not disturb the lives of Indigenous people.

Harvey tells me that, in 1932, residents of San Juan County, Utah, met with the Bureau of Indian Affairs and seemingly settled the national park issue concerning the Paiute Strip. In a written statement, Charles Redd, Benjamin D. Black, J. M. Stewart, and Mark W. Radcliff declared: "It is agreed that the scenic tracts are to be developed by the National Park Service, with the cooperation of the Indian Service." When the Paiute Strip was annexed to the Navajo Nation in 1934, the federal agreement left out the land rights of Hopi and San Juan Southern Paiute Tribes, and it also failed to mention the national park agreement. The entirety of the proposed Rainbow National Park was now fully on the Navajo Nation.

Bernheimer and Wetherill did not relent. In 1932 Wetherill guided Ansel Hall, the first chief naturalist of the national park system, to Rainbow Bridge. Hall, who was immediately smitten with the idea of a National Park, later spearheaded the Rainbow Bridge–Monument Valley Expedition (RBMVE) from 1933 to 1938. The expeditions aimed to gather enough information to solidify the case for the need of a national park, and to contribute discoveries to the fields of biology, geology, paleontology, and archaeology.

During the great depression, the NPS was more inclined to use its funding to maintain its current lineup of parks rather than develop new ones. Hall, a master marketer, looked to corporate support to fund his conservation efforts. He successfully solicited sponsorships from corporations like Ford Motor Company to fund the expeditions. In 2018 outdoor brands like Patagonia similarly stepped in to help fund the lawsuits intended to restore Bears Ears and Grand Staircase–Escalante National Monuments. Patagonia also provided a grant to grassroots conservation group Friends of Cedar Mesa (now the Greater Bears Ears Partnership).

Hall used some of the funds to hire Wetherill as an expedition guide, and Bernheimer even made an appearance in 1936, at the age of seventy-two. To round out the team, Hall created an "Explorers Wanted" ad targeting well-to-do young lads, inviting them to sign up for the summer adventure of a lifetime. The RBMVE was an enriching educational and formative experience for all involved; however, they failed in their quest to secure a national park.

The Navajo Nation's refusal to accept the proposal was a potent stand against the federal government's tendency to use conservation to justify the takeover of Indigenous land. Hall remained optimistic and continued to lobby for the park, even writing a new proposal suggesting that the Navajo Nation continue living traditionally while developing ways to profit from the tourists rather than being pushed aside by them.

Still fixated on protecting Glen Canyon, both NPS Superintendent Roger Wolcott Toll and Secretary of the Interior Harold

Ickes started exploring alternative proposals that would protect the broader region without stepping on the toes of the Navajo Nation. In 1935, Ickes drew up a proposal for a four-million-acre Escalante National Monument. In addition to the expansion of Rainbow Bridge National Monument, this plan would have protected Glen Canyon, Grand Staircase–Escalante, Bears Ears, 280 miles of the Colorado River, 150 miles of the Green River, and 70 miles of the San Juan River.

The state of Utah opposed the idea because the park service intended to phase out grazing from the monument. Ranchers were already angered by the new grazing restrictions implemented by the Taylor Grazing Act of 1934. As a result, the Escalante National Monument proposal boundaries were kicked down to 1.56 million acres. The 1937 designation of nearby Capitol Reef National Monument once again bolstered hope. But the opposition from ranchers and the state of Utah coupled with the eruption of World War II thwarted the designation of the Escalante National Monument.

Postwar federal efforts shifted from land preservation to development and progress. The Bureau of Reclamation began serious discussions about hydroelectric projects throughout the Colorado River. Glen Canyon was mostly off the public radar in 1950 when Floyd Dominy, Bureau of Reclamation Commissioner, proposed two dams in Dinosaur National Monument on the Green River. Thanks to public opposition, spearheaded by the Sierra Club and its president David Brower, the Echo Park and Split Mountain Dams in Dinosaur National Monument were bypassed in what was considered a major win for conservation and the environment.

The dream to protect Glen Canyon finally died when dam construction was authorized in 1956. Many blamed Brower, who agreed not to oppose the Glen Canyon Dam if the Echo Park Dam was canceled. Of course, no one discussed this swap with the Diné, Paiute, Hopi, Ute, and Pueblo people. Rather than protecting the landscape and preserving its history, humans were now reshaping nature and salvaging pieces of its past.

During dam construction, the Glen Canyon Project rapidly surveyed and excavated ancestral sites to be inundated by the reservoir. These items were collected and transferred to museum and university archives, which often meant the canyon walls of dusty basements. Bill Lipe was a crew chief in his twenties when he spent three summers in Glen Canyon watching the Colorado River get dammed:

> I was born in 1935 and grew up at a time when the country was coming out of the Great Depression and then surviving World War II and was devoted to "progress" defined as building bigger buildings, bigger businesses, bigger highways, etc.—and bigger dams on major river systems. Most of us on the Glen Canyon Project thought it was a shame that such amazing places as Glen Canyon would go underwater, but we just accepted that as the way things were supposed to be. If you had a river, you could expect a dam. It wasn't until people began to fight for saving special places that the national consciousness began to change, and mine changed with it. The battles to keep dams from backing water up into the lower Grand Canyon helped turn me and many others into active environmentalists. But those changes took hold with most of us in the early 1960s, after our time in the Glen and after the dam was closed in 1962.

Lipe's efforts have since shifted to conservation archaeology, specifically on Cedar Mesa, and supporting efforts to protect Bears Ears National Monument.

Completed in 1963, the Glen Canyon Dam backed up the Colorado River creating Lake Powell, one of the world's largest artificial reservoirs. In 1972 the Glen Canyon National Recreation Area was established to manage 1.25 million acres of land in and surrounding the reservoir. Other portions of the surrounding landscape were not protected from new human development until the 1996 designation of Grand Staircase–Escalante National Monument by President Clinton, and the 2016 designation of Bears Ears National Monument by President Obama. Then, in 2017, President Trump removed protective status from over 2 million acres of these monuments. Today, President Biden's restoration of both monuments affirms the public lands Merry-Go-Round ride the US has been on for well over a century.

- - - - -

A knock at the door interrupts our conversation. It's Harvey's friend and neighbor, Gus Scott. We walk over to let him in. Gus has the biggest smile on his face. This is our first time meeting in person after three years of email correspondence. Greeting me spryly, he announces that it is his eighty-seventh birthday. I ask him if he has plans to celebrate, and he replies, "I have a bottle of wine at home!"

Gus is within the generation of living people who experienced Glen Canyon before the dam, and he has boated through it on a free-flowing Colorado River not once, but five times. The canyon lives on in memories that only he and a few other people possess. Gus candidly admits that his only regret in life is not taking his wife Sandra down Glen Canyon before the dam was complete. Abruptly switching subjects, he asks me, "So do your friends even know who Bernheimer is?"

His wide eyes and smirk anticipate my response. "Actually, Bernheimer introduced me to some of my friends," I say. Harvey nods.

I tell Gus that floating down Glen Canyon would be at the top of my time-travel list. It's not a totally outlandish dream. The restoration of Glen Canyon is possible in our lifetime if low water levels make the outdated dam obsolete. As I start to ask him, "What was it like?" tears well up in his eyes. He covers his face and manages, "I…can't.…Don't…ask." Through his tears, I hear riffles on the muddy river as it passes between brilliant orange walls adorned with lush hanging gardens and ancestral images. His grief helps me further understand the weight that restoring protections to Bears Ears and Grand Staircase–Escalante carries; his current of emotion reminds me that we must paddle in this direction before it's too late.

- - - - -

On October 8, 2021, President Biden signed a proclamation fully restoring Bears Ears and Grand Staircase–Escalante National Monuments. I sat glued to the livestream on my laptop with tears gushing out of my eyes. Before signing the proclamation, he said, "This may be the easiest thing I've ever done so far as President." The ceremony was held in the presence of the Bears Ears Inter-Tribal Coalition (BEITC) members including Shaun Chapoose, representing the Ute Indian Tribe, who stated:

> President Biden did the right thing restoring the Bears Ears National Monument. For us the Monument never went away. We will always return to these lands to manage and care for our sacred sites, waters, and medicines. The Monument represents a historic opportunity for the federal government to learn and incorporate our tribal land management practices. Practices that we developed over centuries and are needed more now than ever. President Biden was right to reinforce the action taken by President Obama almost five years ago. We battled for this Monument because it matters.

Indigenous-led land management is gaining momentum, bolstered by this year's appointment of Deb Haaland, the first

Indigenous Secretary of the Interior, who is a member of the Pueblo of Laguna. This is one among the many steps required to make more space for Indigenous leaders, stewardship, management, and sovereignty.

Biden's new Bears Ears proclamation states: "The Secretaries shall provide for maximum public involvement in the development of that plan, including consultation with federally recognized Tribes and State and local governments." The proclamation also restored the Bears Ears Commission which will collaboratively manage the monument with the Bureau of Land Management and the Forest Service.

With no determination about the legality of President Trump's efforts to use the Antiquities Act to nullify the monuments, some questions remain unanswered about their future. Utah Governor Spencer Cox stated plans for the state of Utah to use taxpayer dollars to file a new lawsuit against the federal government, opposing Biden's restorations. While no new moves have been made, in the event that Utah does file another lawsuit, the past plaintiffs in the previous case to restore Bears Ears are now preparing to serve as defendants. Without a resolution in the lawsuit, future presidents may turn this into a public lands punting match, reversing and redesignating monument boundaries to suit their platform.

Steve Allen heard the news in between backpacking trips, and rushed home early from Utah to update his contributions for the lawsuit. The miles that Stevo has covered and documented in canyon country have quietly played a role in many environmental efforts over the last three decades. Stevo participated as an affected interest for Great Old Broads for Wilderness in the earlier lawsuits aimed at restoring both monuments. He is now rewriting his declaration, asserting that only "full and final restoration will stop the abuse."

Wasting Utah taxpayer money to fight the monument restorations runs counter to the fact that outdoor recreation contributes $6.4 billion to the state economy, with national parks and public lands as the primary assets accruing this revenue. This is nearly identical to the state's earnings from the extractive industry, including hard-rock mining, and oil and gas leases. One of these industries is sustainable and renewable, and the other is not. And at some point, tourists might lose interest in mountain biking around open pit mines or drinking uranium-laced water on a backpacking trip.

The future of land protections will require our collective devotion and patience. Bernheimer has taught me that conservation is an ongoing journey, and that many improvements to our current system are necessary. We cannot lose momentum simply because our desired outcome appears distant. The steps we take today will carry us into the future.

Lyle Balenquah affirmed this during a recent conversation about the future of tribal input on Bears Ears. He says that there is no finish-line rainbow: "The management plans are the goal, but the process never ends." Balenquah is assisting the Hopi Tribe with their contributions to the Bears Ears collaborative tribal management plan, working alongside the Navajo Nation, Ute Mountain Ute Tribe, Ute Indian Tribe, and Pueblo of Zuni. The unprecedented nature of the task adds to its complexity. Balenquah believes it is important to not rush this process. He remains hopeful for the outcomes but admits, "I don't know if that is for our generation to figure out."

I wonder how anybody in history ever thought they had all the answers, or why that seemed necessary? We cannot undo the past, but the steps to listen, learn, and act from a different perspective can begin right now. These things are best contemplated in their location of origin. My truck is serviced and my mail is retrieved. The next item on my to-do list is to head north to Bears Ears.

CHAPTER TWENTY-THREE

An Unexpected Ray of Light

"Some women come to the desert to erase previous lives, to seek a different way to live in the world. Others choose home not by familiar ties. but by color and light. Something prevented what I thought I wanted to do and pushed me into what I did."
—Ellen Meloy

Windshield wipers move in unison with my hands, clearing raindrops and tears so I can see the narrow two-lane highway. I watch Mother Bear in the distance. She is pulling a blanket of clouds overhead, preparing for a storm. This winter, weather in the Southwest has been especially unstable—solar-heated stretches followed by snow that melts as quickly as it comes. Wearing a swimsuit under Furrnando, my vintage fur coat now tattered with a few more years of wear, I am prepared to hibernate with the ground squirrels, or shed my emotional snakeskin when the sun comes out.

The dry air is accumulating sadness instead of snow. The Omicron surge rolled in and spared almost no one from infection. Thanks to obsessive masking and hiding out in the desert, I avoided the plague, but my loved ones did not. I lost my Uncle Bill, who cheered me on to stay feral and to keep up my vehicle maintenance. My grief is exacerbated by the collective grief—over six million known coronavirus deaths, the escalating Russian invasion of Ukraine, rumors of Roe v. Wade being overturned, and accelerating climate change. Global events increasingly echo the historic moments of the last century, or ripple into uncharted territory.

When Lake Powell dropped below the buffer line of 3,525 feet, it gave me momentary satisfaction that I may get to experience the return of Glen Canyon before the sixth mass extinction sets in. It feels like humans are on the brink of undoing any forward momentum gained toward human rights and environmental protections in the last century. We are unraveling the illusion of that progress. Perhaps modern Western society's flawed trajectory needs to fall apart completely so that we must rebuild in a new direction.

Following Bernheimer has been a Zen meditation—something to sink my focus into without concern for the illusion of success or completion. I needed to walk with the desert and listen to it; to let the land open up to me, and to allow myself to go within. It's time to turn down the volume on society, and return to where I belong. The real world, the one I want to be a part of, exists between sandstone walls and atop sandy mesas. Where I always have a blue roof overhead, an automated UV lighting system, and flesh-colored walls to hold me. It's a world I can always go back to; the one where no one can force me to leave. Physically, I can be almost anywhere, but my soul knows where it needs to be, especially to heal.

Compared to mine, Bernheimer's world sounds like it was so stable. No one's life is uncomplicated though. What was Bernheimer really hiding from, or seeking, in the canyons? After his first few trips, Bernheimer admitted that his annual sojourns generated tension with his wife Clara. When she encouraged him to go to Rainbow Bridge for the first time, it was under the premise that he would not rest until he had done it. Rather than move on, it became his obsession. Bernheimer's journals, initially written as love letters to his sweetheart, evolved into more formal, albeit still romantic, field notes. Did Bernheimer use his research and conservation efforts to justify the challenges his expeditions created in his love life? Were his expeditions a hideaway from the realities of his day-to-day life? Bernheimer may have lived in Manhattan, but his spirit dwelled in the desert. It is excruciatingly hard for one's heart to be split in two.

I may be guilty of letting my present shape my view of the past.

It's been almost a year since I retraced Bernheimer's 1929 expedition. 2021 offered a welcome relief from the difficulties faced in the previous years. After that trip, I did not stay inside very long. I went out and explored rivers, canyons, and mountains that span from the Colorado Plateau to the Eastern Sierra. In all, I spent over a third of the year in the backcountry. Fully vaccinated, I reconnected with friends and family I had not seen since the pandemic began. This quirky Bernheimer quest transitioned into a book deal, and I spent fall in the desert writing among stacks of Bernheimer's journals and my own. The restoration of Bears Ears and Grand Staircase–Escalante National Monuments added to the strong aura of positivity in my inner and outer worlds.

I reclaimed my wild life, but spread myself thin racking up frequent-raven-flier miles between the desert and the mountains. I may have the time and ability to adapt, but that does not mean I can carry the weight. Being pulled in so many directions that are not my own cages my spirit instead of letting it fly its migratory course. The illusion of finding a way through this terrain with Brent is now shattered. Picking up the pieces is futile. Keeping my soul together is an urgent matter. Leaving has been more daunting than weathering an electrical storm on a mesa alone. But every journey begins the same way, taking the first step in a new direction.

In the darkness of the new moon, I drive away from my

problems with worn, dog-eared copies of *Wolfkiller* and *Rainbow Bridge* riding in the passenger seat. The desert welcomes me back into its embrace. My muscles shift intuitively with the familiar turns of this dirt road, past shadowed sandstone spires, heading toward the Bears Ears buttes. I often question whether my life is making any progress if I keep ending up in the same place? I already know the answer. I am no longer the scared girl running away to start her life over. I am a focused woman who wants to go home.

For all of the privilege that Bernheimer's life afforded him, he did not have the option of living here. Years after his expeditions, he reanalyzed his motives. It seems clear that his migration from Germany to the United States illuminated a desire to understand how one comes to belong to a new place, and an interest to learn more about the people who resided there first. In the desert, there is defensible space that helps preserve this history. Bernheimer's life and travels plunged him into the realities between colonial occupation and human migration. It's a spectrum we all reside within. We must live somewhere, and for a myriad of reasons, may not be able to stay where we start.

The thin-aired alchemy of the desert make space for wonder and possibility. Dreams once viewed at a distance are now my life. The photos of sand dunes, rock art, and dinosaur tracks in Bernheimer's book are now all familiar places to me. Hidden passages lead through unimaginable places. Water gives reason to drink up and celebrate every single day. The conditions are such that the things that belong here, truly belong, and those that don't simply cannot. Accepting that has challenged me to the brink more than any heat wave or snowstorm.

My shoulders relax and the knot in my stomach eases upon arrival at the remote camp spot. Stevo is waiting there in his camper van. This year he reluctantly invested in a smart phone and emailed me this morning to see if I was in the neighborhood. It's a relief to be able to meet up with a friend after a difficult day. And I have Bernheimer to thank for introducing me, once a lone coyote, to a pack.

I park my truck and Stevo pops his head out of his van to greet me: "Welcome home!" He has been camped out for over six weeks. We sit inside his van and chat about life and our recent adventures. Stevo assures me that there are other people who thrive in this habitat. He needs the desert, and the desert needs him to defend it. We all need a place to go home to. And a place, in turn, to care for. Strong gusts of wind howl outside the van, and we both laugh about intentionally choosing to be out in these conditions. With a big smile on his face, Stevo shrugs, "You only go around once."

My mind spins back to a moment during a backpacking trip last year. Inside a sun-scorched alcove, a faded white spiral painted on the mauve sandstone wall directed my gaze. With eyes fixed meditatively on the descending rings, I took three steps back to improve my perspective. Kneeling onto the sand to balance myself, I looked down upon the mouth of a small painted pot. Two holes pierced its sides, which were once threaded with twine so that loving hands could transport seeds, beads, and dreams. The link between the spheres swallowed me, pulling me further into a winding trance. That night, sleep evaded me, my thoughts orbiting around the full moon as a star streaked overhead, ascending from the direction where the pot remains in situ.

All of life is connected in cycles. Our bodies and anything we create, one day returns to the earth—the very sand we walk upon is soul dust. We only go around once in our physical bodies, but after that, we always go around.

Decades later, Bernheimer distilled a philosophy from his vivid reflections, illuminated by vivid rays of desert light:

> The desert furnishes another sensation. It conveys a sense of vastness, of timelessness, a fuller realization of man's

place in the universe. He there feels alternately humble and proud, little, and big, reverent always, occupying by grace a point in the center of things.

When matter forms so microscopic a portion of the universe, why do men spend so much time thinking and fighting about it. Man is certainly little in the presence of such dimensions of space.

Coming down to earth, let me remind that the globe's diameter is less than one percent of that of our sun, which in turn is one thousand times smaller than other suns in the firmament. We small things make trouble enough, but things so much smaller, the insects and microbes are making it still more difficult to keep the world in a placid mood. Each unit struggles to elbow its neighbor out of the way, be it little or big. Such are reflections conjured up by the desert.

We humans let trivial problems consume our lives while we collectively destroy our home planet. In the last one hundred years we have done way too good of a job on this. We are not altering our behavior quickly enough. We don't have another century to figure this out. Bernheimer recognized that when we no longer view ourselves and the natural world as separate, we are more invested in protecting these sacred spaces. At times, my efforts to make a difference or help protect a place like Bears Ears feel trivial, but I am learning to show up anyway. I believe the earth can sense it.

- - - - -

I open my eyes to morning light spilling in from the east. Wet sage, the lingering scent after a storm, reminds me that potholes are now full. My life slows down to the pace of the desert. I believe if I sit with the land long enough, I can become a part of it, belong to it. The red dust permeates my skin first, through cactus pricks, and then infuses my soul. My heart beats to rotating pulses of sunlight, moonlight, starlight.

Five years ago, when I first learned about the Bears Ears, which today are dusted in snow, I did not comprehend or anticipate how long I might need them. Am I doomed or a failure for still being here? No. Healing is something we must choose again and again. The forces that continually push me back to where I started might be a signal that I am finally heading in the right direction.

Spring announces itself with warmer temperatures and occasional violent gusts of wind. My mood shifts accordingly—I chart a course with my inner thermals, and soar. For the first time in over a week, I leave camp. The rutted dirt road to The Hermitage is longer than I remember. I bypass the exit route I took last spring and continue toward Lake Powell, where, until recently, much of lower Red Canyon hibernated. A mile later, the red dirt is moistened by a trickling spring, which becomes a flowing creek, joined a mile later by warm water gushing out of a crack in a sandstone wall. The spring, lined by green grasses, smells of sulfur; the sand is painted orange by colorful algae in bloom. I dip my fingers in the water and touch my tongue. Salty.

I find a spot to claw my way up the steep lake sediment banks and through a barricade of tumbleweeds. Atop the Dominy Formation, I meander through the detritus of a dying reservoir: a tennis shoe with grass growing out of it, rusty beer cans, and a pair of sunglasses. I pick the shades up and wear them to protect my eyes from the wind-blasted sand.

There are no bovines to be found here today. Instead, native wildlife abounds. A fat coyote with a lush blonde tail stops and stares at me along the now exposed shoreline. Often, I daydream about being rescued from my loneliness by a coyote in the desert; to peacefully walk alongside another creature who belongs in this habitat. Now I understand that no rescue is necessary. Wild things cannot be pets. And in nature, I am never alone.

My sticky footprints parallel the coyote's until I am halted by bear tracks. Perhaps she is awakening from a winter of hibernation to return home to the desert too. Snakes slither across the canyon, and violet-blue damselflies dance atop a swimming pool–sized beaver dam gilded by sinewy green willows. At dusk my thoughts harmonize with birdsong and the chorus of coyotes as bighorns play percussion on the talus slopes, all chiming in with the water gurgling down Red Canyon.

The wildlife that thrives in the arid aura of abandonment teaches me to care for and defend abused places. Glen Canyon's re-emergence affirms that healing and renewal are always possible. What I seek in the land, I seek within myself. I lean into Wolfkiller's teachings: I must give up something for everything I receive. In exchange for what I have shed this winter, the mud, sand, and sediments stick with me this time around.

Revived from my retreat at The Hermitage, I delve further into my center—the canyon that first opened my heart to love at the pace of geological time. I dash down the familiar orange sand dune. Silky particles hitch a ride in my boots and caress my feet as I squeal with joy. The spark is still there. Dirt bike tracks crawl like spiderwebs, wrinkling the smooth slope. The warm wind soothes the impacts.

Solar-heated Wingate Sandstone walls embrace me as I cruise down the sandy wash, glancing up at familiar caves and cottonwood trees. I cut the turns tight, focused on my destination. Upon arrival I smile, refraining from waving and hollering, "I'm back!" just in case everyone is resting on this warm and peaceful afternoon. I climb the five hundred feet up to the alcove, sweating just enough to cleanse my pores. Before entering, I pause to gently make my presence known.

Rainbow-colored handprints and the human figures painted on the walls greet me. I take a seat with my friends—the 1929 inscriptions left by Bernheimer and Wetherill. They welcome me home and remind me that I did not find my way here alone. The way found me. The three of us are facing two life-size human figures painted in white. Plumes levitate above their heads like thoughts and dreams taking flight. I do not know what they mean, only what they look like, how they make me feel. Between the figures, three yellow handprints reach through time. I press my hand into the sand, to commune with my desert friends, and extend my heart to defend wild spaces on the earth and within— to honor and care for the very land I will one day become. The path of light is an expedition with no end.

CHAPTER TWENTY-FOUR

Beyond the Rainbow

The simple men who lived their lives out to a good old age among the rocks and sands only did so because they had come to the desert to be themselves, their ordinary selves, and to forget a world that divided them from themselves....And thus, leaving the world, is, in fact, to help save it in saving oneself....They knew that they were helpless to do any good for others as long as they floundered about in the wreckage. But once they got a foothold on solid ground, things were different. Then they had not only the power but the obligation to pull the whole world to safety after them.

—Thomas Merton

Bernheimer planned his Southwest expeditions as if they would go on indefinitely. Then the stock market crashed in 1930. That year, he took a major financial hit, downsized his lifestyle, and moved into an apartment. The next year, Clara's health deteriorated and she passed away. The expeditions abruptly ended. Despite this, Bernheimer continued to travel: across the country to California to visit his brother; overseas to Europe, which he considered far more exhausting than roaming the desert; and to Guatemala to observe archaeologist A. V. Kidder at work.

Bernheimer spent his final years writing a second book, *A*

Cliff Dweller from Manhattan, about his 1924–1930 expeditions. The book is more reflective than his first, and he muses on how much those experiences meant to him and his life. He submitted the manuscript to the American Museum of Natural History nine months before he passed away, but it was never published.

What happened to the other members of the team, and their relationships with one another, remained a bit of a mystery to me. This gave me another excuse to explore the CU Boulder Museum of Natural History and American Museum of Natural History archives. For the remainder of his life, Bernheimer exchanged letters with Earl Morris. Like retrieving something lost in the mail, reading letters from their correspondence revealed a deep friendship, mutual respect, and a fire for exploration that never dimmed. The two men even dreamed up ideas for future expeditions that never came to fruition.

Both men rarely corresponded with Wetherill and Johnson. Life happens. Paths diverge. Some friendships persist through these changes, while others fizzle. Wetherill continued guiding clients and running the Kayenta trading post with his family. Johnson moved to Salt Lake City for his wife's medical treatments, but they divorced before she passed away. He remarried three more times and worked as a guard at the Utah State Prison, but continued serving as custodian of Natural Bridges National Monument every spring.

Morris continued to work at cultural sites across the Southwest, but he pulled back on his trips to Mexico because Ann was in poor health. In addition to caring for her and looking after their two daughters, Morris continued to tend to the adventurous spirit he shared with Ann, even taking the family on a trip to Rainbow Bridge in 1939. He wrote to Bernheimer:

> After the field season was over, I took Mrs. Morris and the little girls on a long trip….From Mesa Verde we went via Monticello, Bluff, Mexican Hat and Monument Valley

to Kayenta. I had not seen Hosteen John for several years and it was good to find him in such form. From Kayenta we went by way of Shonto to Rainbow lodge. There we left the little ones and rode into the Bridge. It seemed strange seventeen years later to travel that trail we worked so hard to blaze. It has been rerouted in a few places but is essentially the one we picked. I hunted up our base camp in Cliff Canyon just for sake of old memories and brought back some nice paper weights of the banded chalcedony from the bed of Cliff Canyon.

Our most profound memories influence dreams of the past and actions in the future. This is why falling in love with the land is a vital link to their ongoing and future protections. As explained by Senegalese forestry engineer Baba Dioum, "In the end, we will conserve only what we love; we will love only what we understand; and we will understand only what we have been taught."

- - - - -

Free from the burden of living anyone's life but my own, I can see that the desert is revealing new passageways to guide me onward. I have spent this spring out in the canyons, either writing or exploring. The work I am being called to do insists that I stay out here, including a reporting assignment to document the re-emerging riparian plant life in Glen Canyon. Best of all, my solitude is intermingled with quality time among my community of desert friends. I now understand how my homeostasis is affected as much by the company I choose to keep, as by my habitat.

Bernheimer's legacy lives on through the men I have met along his trail. In May 2021, Jim Knipmeyer, the historic inscription expert who helped me track down Clyde Whiskers, rallied a gathering of what he called "The Filthy Five," for a history hike on the Navajo Nation. It's a decades-old tradition between Harvey Leake, Steve Allen, Joel Arnold, and Leo Manheimer. Each of them has shared many steps of this journey with me, whether hiking, exchanging emails, or fact-checking my stories. And yet, I have never met with all of them at one time. Jim travels furthest, from Missouri, and laments that, at age seventy-five, this will be his last trip to the Southwest. I don't believe him.

- - - - -

At Navajo National Monument the guys are sitting around a picnic table. They wave enthusiastically when my truck pulls into camp. We will stay here tonight and then begin our backpacking adventure the next day. Leo has secured permissions for us to camp at his friend's and family's homesites. Camping in someone's backyard normally would be of little interest to me, but doing this connects us to the present-day Diné lifestyle. We are grateful visitors who have been granted passage by the Navajo Nation and Leo's family through this neighborhood.

An elderly woman next door herds sheep in a velveteen blouse and ankle-length skirt, and is dripping in turquoise jewelry. Leo converses with her in Diné before we carry on to our camp, located near a bright pink home built in the style of a hogan. Above the door is a new address label, provided by the Rural Utah Project to ensure that residents here were able to vote in the 2020 presidential election. There is a picnic table under an old cottonwood tree, which we gather around for supper—cans of soup, bags of salad, and freeze-dried meals. No time is wasted on cooking or cleanup—there are too many stories for this group to tell.

We go over the plan for our backpacking trip while we eat. The objective is to locate two trails within the Piute Canyon system that Wetherill used to guide Bernheimer and his other clients to Rainbow Bridge. Tomorrow we will hike into the canyon through one of its tributaries and head back to where we are now, a marathon distance away, via a stock trail. The exact location of the route is nebulous. "What if we don't find it?" I ask.

Stevo chimes in, "Well then our trip will be twice as long." The real challenge will be finding water. Leo assures us that there will be plenty.

- - - - -

We caravan down the switch-backed road into Piute Canyon and up the other side. The wide canyon is flanked by Wingate sandstone walls, the color of burnt embers. In the distance, a splash of blue contrasts against the red landscape, highlighting where Lake Powell, once the San Juan river, backs up into Piute Canyon.

Bobby Atene, a Navajo Mountain local, stops his truck at the end of the dirt road near the edge of the canyon. He watches us pile out of the truck bed and pull on our backpacks. He laughs, only partially joking, "If you guys can't make it, call me." We locate the stock trail without much effort, but getting down the sun-baked slope takes its toll.

Temperatures are scorching, into the mid-nineties. We are carrying two gallons of water each, realizing that if the springs are dried up, tomorrow we may have to turn around and hike up and out of our canyon. No one is optimistic as we trudge down the sandy wash, until we start to see patches of damp ground, and eventually mud. Everyone swarms the first puddle we see to fill up our bottles. We decide to camp in the sandy wash since there is very little threat of flash flood in these conditions. Leo digs a few holes nearby, so that more water can pool up from the ground in the morning.

After setting up our tents, we sit in a circle for dinner. Everything we encountered today has a story, be it Leo's connections to families who graze nearby, Harvey recalling a trip John Wetherill took, or Stevo noticing different hogan constructions. It's a lot to absorb. Joel and I, who both have plenty of our own stories to tell, contentedly listen. Jim cheerily pops open a can of Beanee Weenee for dinner as he tells stories about his most beloved explorations. Someone teases Jim that they have already heard all of his tales. He confidently asserts, "Well Mo here is new, so I get to tell all of my stories at least one more time for y'all." He then proceeds to rename the group "The Silty Six" to include me. I cannot stop smiling and laughing around these guys.

The persistent dry and windy conditions make a campfire unsuitable, so Leo tells us stories about them instead. His grandmother taught him to make a fire when camping alone, so that your ancestors can see you, watch over you, and can be invited to the fire. This brings me comfort and new understanding of why a fire offers more than warmth on a solitary night.

He smirks and asks: "How can you tell a white man's fire from an Indian's?" I have no guesses. Neither do the other guys. Leo continues, "The Indian leaves the fire poker (stick) at the fire ring for someone else to use. The white man burns it."

- - - - -

In the morning, we fill up our water bottles in the now full puddles. A half mile away, there is even more water, but the relief is temporary. Hiking through the wide, dusty wash within Piute Canyon there is not a drop anywhere.

I hike behind Leo and step into his footprints in the sand. Without turning his head back, he teasingly asks me who the bad guy is going to be in my book. Before I can respond, he says, "I think the villain in your story is progress." Leo grew up herding sheep in these canyons and has seen the springs and creeks change. Some have dried up completely.

The group conversation shifts to the realities of human impacts and climate change. Harvey believes that humans need to choose a simpler way of life, closer to nature, to improve this predicament: "Following the path of light means turning our backs on arguments." Increasingly, even nature has no choice but to fight back. Are we listening?

Humans as a species are in an abusive relationship with Mother Nature. Some exploit her without a care, while others feign concern without intending to ever follow through with a change. Backpacking brings me closer to the earth, reminding me of the work required to love our home. Acknowledging shortcomings and weaknesses is the first step to forgiveness and healing.

I need to cut down on driving.

A mature juniper tree offers shade from the sun, so we stop to eat our lunch. It's hot. I try to stay hydrated without chugging too much of my water all at once. We discuss our options, especially the possibility that we may not find water. Leo points to a high bank above the wash. "My brother says there is a spring up there." It looks like a bleak, dry Chinle bench.

It is unnecessary to send everyone on reconnaissance, so Stevo and I grab our day packs to hike up and look. Atop the layer of red earth, we walk toward a massive cottonwood. The span of its large trunk would require at least four of us to wrap our arms around it. Cottonwoods often draw up ground water to form springs, but it is impossible to tell if there will be any water here until we get closer.

Mud is our first sign of moisture. Cow and burro hoofprints encircle the tree, each one filled with water. Lucky us. We hoot and holler, "YO-YO-YO-YO-YO!" to alert the other guys. We carefully scoop up the brown liquid with our cups and strain it through handkerchiefs before treating it with Katadyn tablets. Twenty minutes later, Leo and Joel join us to top off their bottles. We sit and talk in the shade to wait out the afternoon heat. On a drier patch of grass, I doze off for a bit. Relaxed, safe, totally content. Water and friends are the source of life in the desert.

The temperatures cool by a few degrees once the sun shifts to its evening angle. Everyone in the group feels rejuvenated and rehydrated from the rest stop, so we resume hiking. We don't travel far. A juniper tree shading a wide flat sandy bench invites us to set up camp.

Now that we know where the nearest source of water is, we are at ease about tomorrow's challenge to find a way out of this canyon. The stories roll around the sitting circle while the cooking stoves boil water. Memories of the Vietnam War draft evolve into an exchange of ideas about how to mitigate overgrazing. We begin to hash out ideas for another trip to the Navajo Nation next year.

We all stay up longer than anticipated, but right before we turn in for the night, Joel tells us to look up at the rising blood moon, the beginning of a total lunar eclipse. Everyone tilts their head skyward in reverence. The night is silent. My sleeping bag is spread out on the sand, and I lie back to gaze up at the sliver of red-tinted light curving over us, illuminating the canyon. Surrounded by stars, sandstone, and my friends, there is no inner or outer turmoil. Only peace. Everything I need is right here.

Epilogue

A hummingbird buzzed into the back of my truck, waking me up with a message—I could not wait another moment to get up and greet this day. The bird hovered with wing beats over my bed until I sat up. The sun already high on the horizon, aligned with what modern humans call the summer solstice. A promise that no other day this year would be longer or brighter.

A few days earlier Bears Ears National Monument finally received an official sign, erected in the presence of leaders from the Navajo Nation, Hopi Tribe, Ute Indian Tribe, Ute Mountain Ute Tribe, and Pueblo of Zuni. Included on the sign are the seals of each Tribal Nation, honoring their homelands and signifying the monument's co-management between the Tribes and federal government.

I crawled out of my truck bed and instinctually knew where to go.

My feet scraped red dirt as I followed a family of deer hoofing it through pine trees and mangles of scrub oak. Purple lupines and high grasses brushed my legs as butterflies, birds, and bees danced around me. I kept a steady momentum until I reached the precipice of the Bears Ears buttes, overlooking the sandstone kingdom I am a devoted servant of. I stripped off my clothes and sat on the smooth warm red sandstone, and looked out upon Comb Ridge, Cedar Mesa, the San Juan River, Navajo Mountain, Natural Bridges, and Glen Canyon.

Atop the Bears Ears, I prepared myself to purge my emotional exoskeleton, to face anything I may have been avoiding in my healing process. Instead, I felt overwhelmed by only one thing—love. Present in the air molecules around me, the grains of sand touching my skin, and gushing out from inside me like a spring. This landscape has held me in its embrace for years, offered me a home when I had none, and taught me to love deeper than I previously understood to be possible. A love of nature is a love for all, including the sacred mystery of existence. We are our environment.

After the hike, an unexpected urge took over me. I left Bears Ears. The desert called me towards water, into a storm where I followed the pulse of a flash flood that washed over the highway in Capitol Reef National Park. Ignoring the warnings, I drove through the road blockades and continued southwest over Boulder Mountain and towards the surging muddy green Escalante River.

For years I have devoted myself to exploring the desert at its driest. Each season seems thirstier and hotter than the last, because it is. This summer, the water returned. Healthy monsoons were predicted, but because of the persistent aridification, I did not trust the forecasts unless I was submerged in the downpours. Sight was not enough to awake me from the dehydrated nightmare of the last few years.

Within a tributary of the Escalante River I placed my fingers in the flowing stream of water rushing into the canyon. The water had been heated upon contact with the sun scorched sandstone. Variation in droplet size and cadence orchestrated a symphony echoing off canyon walls. The ethereal alchemy of liquid permeating the desert's surface unlocked the petrichor of wet sand, sage, and ponderosa. Even the black cryptobiotic soils and lime-green lichen suddenly smelled alive. Lightning seared the edges of the mass rehydration event as thunder beckoned desert creatures big and small to feast on the arrival of watery delights.

The desert's relationship to water is built on having faith through times of drought and dropping to your knees in worship when wet. Rain does not bring the desert back from the dead—it's an adrenaline rush taking everything in its path from survival-mode dormancy to full-throttle thriving. One can never anticipate such an experience. Like falling in love, it's best to put it out of your mind, to forget about it most of the time. But when it does arrive, you better be ready to peel off your excess layers, hop in, make a splash, drink it up, and ride the pulse.

- - - - -

My monsoon season romance in a different part of the desert was not a fling. The first sign was when I started to receive mail in town, including an original 1924 copy of Bernheimer's *Rainbow Bridge* sent to me by Bill Lipe. It felt like a homecoming gift. I slept out in the canyons until I encountered a community who welcomed me to stay in town. Although I often slept indoors, each time the sky unleashed I set out into the maelstrom to watch the river rise. At night I joined the desert's nocturnal procession and swam with toads into the flooding potholes under a full moon with lightning cracking overhead.

I completed this book with a view of the Escalante River, an entrance gate to Glen Canyon, surrounded by four walls built in 1910 that knew how to hold me gently alongside the century of lives and stories that have also drifted in and out of them. Open windows, unlocked doors, and cracks in the walls allowed me, and other desert critters, to crawl outside. Most days, my truck remained parked on the roadside, the urge to roam incessantly replaced with a longing for intimacy with the scene in front of me. Embraced by warm desert light shining into the windows, I finally felt safe to stay in.

And I needed to. Not only to revive my weathered spirit, but to put my pen to work writing letters to protect the canyons that have protected me. I spent weeks meticulously writing a public comment letter to the Bureau of Land Management about the proposed Resource Management Plan for Grand Staircase-Escalante National Monument. The tedious task required careful reading of legal documents, specific details about various impacts I have witnessed in the monument, and many hours of revision. When I completed the letter, I knew it was only a warm-up for the comments I will write for Bears Ears National Monument next. My investment in this monument saga only began in 2017 and it already feels like a lifetime. But hope is a kick in the rear to keep doing the work.

On August 24, 2022, the state of Utah, joined by Kane and Garfield Counties, filed a lawsuit against President Biden's restoration of both monuments. San Juan County, once a prominent voice in the anti-monument movement, is not a part of the lawsuit this go around. The San Juan County Commission has shifted from a white Republican majority to a Diné Democratic majority with commissioners Willie Grayeyes and Ken Maryboy at the helm.

Change is on the horizon.

The Bears Ears Inter-Tribal Coalition (BEITC), released their recommended collaborative land management plan for the monument—a historic and important step toward Indigenous people leading the care of their homelands. While each tribe's perspective and suggestions are different, there is a common reverence for the entire environment within Bears Ears, not just the cliff dwellings and rock art that have become associated with this landscape. The Tribal Nations of the Bears Ears Inter-Tribal Coalition explain:

To the Tribal Nations of the BEITC, the landscape is much more than just a natural realm to sustain the material needs of life. It is imbued with spiritual powers, and everything in the natural world—rocks, trees, animals, water, air, light, sound—has meaning and character. Cultural resources and natural resources are not two different categories in Native life. An individual depends on other living plants, animals and surrounding land to survive; thus, the natural resources gathered, hunted and walked on for survival become a cultural resource.

Then in September, Secretary Deb Haaland and the Department of the Interior released guidance for including Indigenous knowledge and perspectives to strengthen the role of tribal governments in federal land management. The document affirms how an Indigenous perspective will benefit how all land and water is managed in the United States. Haaland stated:

From wildfire prevention to managing drought and famine, our ancestors have used nature-based approaches to coexist among our lands, waters, wildlife and their habitats for millennia. As communities continue to face the effects of climate change, Indigenous knowledge will benefit the Department's efforts to bolster resilience and protect all communities....By acknowledging and empowering Tribes as partners in co-stewardship of our country's lands and waters, every American will benefit from strengthened management of our federal land and resources.

- - - - -

Autumn came overnight. I did not believe it until I hiked to a high point on Boulder Mountain surrounded by the change manifesting itself on the leaves of electrified aspens. Marble sized hail, followed by slushy raindrops, fall from a blackened sky. The only clearing in the storm frames the golden embers of Glen Canyon far below the Aquarius Plateau. For a moment my heart sinks, not ready to let go of sun-drenched hikes and skinny dips in the river. The chilled air slows the circulation of blood inside my freezing fingers. As I look out toward the desert, the rain clouds thicken, shrouding the sunlight and view of the desert. I close my eyes and smile. I do not need to see what I feel holding me.

Acknowledgments

Staring at the long list of people I want to thank for helping me with this project reminds me that, no matter how remote my explorations, I am never alone. I've forged many real-life friendships by going down Bernheimer's rabbit hole. This was something almost unfathomable to me during the first winters I spent in Cedar Mesa, so, I suppose I should start at the beginning.

Ralph "R. E." Burrillo, your support and friendship are immeasurable. Thank you for walking and writing with me in canyon country. Camp Snowball was a ray of sunshine during one of the coldest, darkest winters. As much as I want to express my gratitude for you, I thank Bears Ears for aligning our paths. Harvey Leake, this book is only possible because of your generosity in sharing your and your family's philosophies, experience, and history. Thank you for showing me the path of light; it has altered the course of my life for the better. Bill Lipe, thank you for your thoughtful email correspondence, brimming with research suggestions, edits, fun stories, and perspective. Steve Allen, thank you for your guidance, maps, wisdom, laughter, incredible backpacking trips, and for reminding me that some of us truly are meant to live in the desert! Fred Blackburn, your help and encouragement are only second to your humor and storytelling. It is a pleasure to work with you, and I am grateful that you so generously share your research with me. Victoria Atkins, thank you for lending your discerning eye for detail and thoughtful perspective of history. Lavern Owl, I am forever glad that Clyde introduced us to each other. Our conversations are always a delight, and I am grateful for stories, friendship, and teachings passed down by your mother and father, Mary Ann and Jack Owl. Thank you to the San Juan Southern Paiute Tribal Council for trusting me to listen to and share some of your stories. It was an honor to join your holiday party and to work with the Tribal Council during the early portion of the COVID-19 pandemic. Thank you, Leo Manheimer, for your willingness to meet up to walk with me, even in snowstorms; for sharing your stories and wisdom, and your knowledge of Diné traditions and place names; and for reviewing many chapters in this book. Lyle Balenquah and Regina Lopez-Whiteskunk, thank you both for taking the time and making the effort to share your knowledge and perspectives with me, and for reviewing portions of this book for cultural sensitivity and accuracy. Monica Prelle, our friendship makes the writing life less solitary. Thank you for encouraging me to write the messy truth all over the page and worry about editing later. Jonathan Bailey, I am grateful for your encouragement and friendship throughout this project, and your advice for navigating the most daunting emotional terrain. Dave Wilson, it was an honor to travel with you and visit your family's home and Canyon del Muerto. Thank you to Frederick Burns and Bobby Atene for the wild-ride car shuttles and great conversations. Rowan Blaisdell, thank you for your support, guidance, and encouragement throughout this journey.

Kirsten Johanna Allen, when you met me in Bears Ears to discuss this book during the 2021 expedition, there was no doubt in my heart that I wanted to work with Torrey House Press. Thank you for welcoming me into this family of inspiring authors and helping me bring this dream into the wild light. Your encouragement and thoughtful edits flow beyond the margins—they have pushed me to dive deeper into my center, to stand in my truth on the page, but even more so in my life. I am so grateful to you and Mark for welcoming me into your home in Torrey to nest with my words and shelter from the summer monsoons while I worked on the final revisions.

Thank you to everyone who read, fact-checked, edited, or provided feedback for my manuscript drafts: Bill Lipe, Harvey Leake, Fred Blackburn, Victoria Atkins, Jim Knipmeyer, Steve Allen, R. E. Burrillo, Joro Walker, Leo Manheimer, Robyn Interpreter, Logan Hebner, Marc Coles-Ritchie, Seth Arens, Erik Stanfield, Lyle Balenquah, Regina Lopez-Whiteskunk, Wendy Natt, Natalie Cunningham, Jonathan Bailey, Monica Prelle, and David Roberts.

It was an honor for this amateur researcher, as Bernheimer also considered himself, to work with the following archival institutions for this book: American Museum of Natural History, University of Utah Special Collections, Canyon of the Ancients Archives, CU Boulder Museum of Natural History Archives, and the Utah State Historical Society. For additional research suggestions, support, and guidance, thank you Laurie Webster, Rosemary Sucec, Kelley Ann Hays-Gilpin, Marc Coles-Ritchie, Gary Topping, Catherine Fowler, and Martin Stamat.

I am indebted to the inspiration and writing of the other desert explorers who also followed in Bernheimer's footsteps in the last century: anthropologist Clyde Kluckhohn, explorer Carl Wheat, archaeologist Christy Turner, historian Gary Topping, river runner Harry Aleson, Stan Jones ("Mr. Lake Powell"), and Batman cartoonist Dick Sprang, who illustrated Bernheimer's Rainbow Bridge routes in the 1999 edition of *Rainbow Bridge.*

While working on this book, it has been a privilege to contribute to *Arizona Highways*, which has become a primary home for many of my stories, especially about Southwest history. It is a joy to work with their editorial family, including Kelly Anne Vaughn and Robert Stieve.

For two years Coleman USA has provided me with generous funding to fully immerse myself in this project, including a grant to complete several research trips and to digitize some of Earl Morris's archived photos at the CU Boulder Museum of Natural History. Janji running company has supported the physical steps of this project while backing clean water initiatives in the Southwest and worldwide. Food For the Sole, Peak Refuel, Big Agnes, Gu Energy, Sierra Nevada Brewing Co., and Lace Locks all provided me with the gear and provisions necessary to complete the rendition of Bernheimer's 1929 expedition covered in this book. Thank you all for being my Bernheimers!

I pinch myself for friendships with other desert rats I have met because of Bernheimer. In 2021 and 2022, Joel Arnold, Jenny West, and Joro Walker helped bring Bernheimer's 1924 expedition on the Navajo Nation to life. So did Giles Wallace and Julie Marple—thank you for letting me borrow your heated van while I worked on this book during the winter of 2022 at my heart's home. Hikes and stories around the campfire with my fellow Cedar Mesa desert rats—Aaron O'Brien, Connie Massingale, Ed Moss, and Roland—made it feel even more like home. Thank you to my Cedar Mesa "neighbors," Jim Krehbiel and Natalie Cunningham, for the good company, meals, and hot showers.

To my friends who I have missed dearly while I crawl around the desert, you know who you are, I cannot wait to wander your way and visit you soon! Darius Bastani, "Boosef,"—thank you for always having my back and feeding me. It was memorable and so comforting to have you stay with me during four of my writing retreats at the Dirt Barbie trailer, where temperatures ranged from 12 degrees to 120! Fran McKay, thank you for opening up your home to me, surrounded by our shared loved for canyon country and beautiful books. Your spirit brings joy to this community even when you are in Vermont. The Escalante corridor of canyon country has been calling me home for some time— Aaron Crosby, how grateful I am that I met you upon arrival. Our shared laughter, delicious meals, long walks, and monsoon storm-chasing were the best way to end one story and begin a new one. Thank you for holding me gently.

Aunty Kristy, you have given my words and heart a refuge

when they need it most. Uncle Bill, your spirit and support is with me everywhere, in the dirt beneath my feet and the warm desert air.

To my parents, Steven and Cynthia Sjogren, thank you for your unwavering support of my lifelong dream to write, explore, and live outside. Mom, thank you for listening and talking through so many of these stories and life events with me on our phone call walks. The coyotes and ravens in Glen Canyon surely recognize the sound of your voice.

Above all, I am indebted to Glen Canyon, Escalante, and Bears Ears for welcoming me and my words home; for giving me a reason to open my heart to love again.

Wilderness Tithing

To be a #Bernheimer, please consider becoming a member and/or donating to the conservation groups doing the heavy lifting to protect the natural world and Indigenous homelands in the places you hold dear. Here are some suggestions for the terrain Bernheimer and I covered:

Archaeology Southwest
Bears Ears Inter-Tribal Coalition
DigDeep
Glen Canyon Conservancy
Glen Canyon Institute
Grand Canyon Trust
Grand Staircase–Escalante Partners
Greater Bears Ears Partnership
Great Old Broads for Wilderness
Navajo Santa
Southern Utah Wilderness Alliance (SUWA)
Sierra Club
Tó Nizhóní Ání
Utah Diné Bikeyah
Western Resource Advocates
Wilderness Society

Selected Bibliography

A note about sources: Throughout this project I have maintained a full research record of primary source documents, periodicals, and online materials. For the sake of saving some trees, only the books and essential articles have been included in this selected bibliography. So much of the research for this book occurred off typed pages, through interviews and conversations that I have documented, with the exception of more informal hiking conversations. While this may not be of interest to every reader, I hope that by keeping a record of study, these sources can be accessed by future researchers and explorers.

Ahlstrom, Richard V. N. *Pothunting in Central Arizona: The Perry Mesa Archeological Site Vandalism Study*. Cultural Resources Management Report 13. Phoenix: USDA Forest Service Southwestern Region and USDI Bureau of Land Management, 1992.

Allen, Steve. *Canyoneering 3: Loop Hikes in Utah's Escalante*. Salt Lake City: University of Utah Press, 1997.

———. *Utah's Canyon Country Place Names*. Durango: Canyon Country Press, 2012.

The Archaeological Resources Protection Act of 1979. https://www.govinfo.gov/content/pkg/COMPS-1707/pdf/COMPS-1707.pdf

Atkins, Victoria M. *Anasazi Basketmaker: Papers from the 1990 Wetherill–Grand Gulch Symposium*. Cultural Resource Series 24. Salt Lake City: USDI Bureau of Land Management, 1990.

Babbitt, James E. *Rainbow Trails: Adventures in the Rainbow Bridge Country.* Page, AZ: Glen Canyon Natural History Association, 1990.

Balenquah, Lyle. "Beyond Stone and Mortar: Preserving Indigenous Presence within Ancestral Landscapes." *Colorado Plateau Advocate Magazine*, Spring/Summer 2022. https://www.grandcanyontrust.org/advocatemag/spring-summer-22/Bears-Ears-Beyond-Stone-Mortar.

Bradley, Zorro A. *Canyon de Chelly: The Story of Its Ruins and People.* Washington, DC: Office of Publications, National Park Service, US Department of the Interior, 1973.

Bears Ears Partnership, *Visit With Respect* video series. https://bearsearspartnership.org/visit/visitor-info/visit-with-respect-videos.

Bernheimer, Charles L. "Encircling Navajo Mountain with a Pack-Train." *National Geographic Magazine* 43, no. 2 (1923): 197–224.

———. *Rainbow Bridge: Circling Navajo Mountain and Explorations in the "Bad Lands" of Southern Utah and Northern Arizona.* Garden City, NY: Doubleday, Page & Company, 1924.

———. The papers of Charles L. Bernheimer, 1864–1944. American Museum of Natural History, Division of Anthropology Archives, B4764, New York.

———. Charles L. Bernheimer expedition field notes. ACCN 0553, box 1, folders 1–4 and 6. Special Collections, J. Willard Marriott Library, The University of Utah.

Bernardini, Wesley, Stewart B. Koyiyumptewa, Gregson Schachner, and Leigh J. Kuwanwisiwma, eds. *Becoming Hopi: A History.* Tucson: University of Arizona Press, 2021.

Blackburn, Fred M. *The Wetherills: Friends of Mesa Verde.* Durango: Durango Herald Small Press, 2006.

Blackburn, Fred M., and Ray A. Williamson. *Cowboys and Cave Dwellers: Basketmaker Archaeology in Utah's Grand Gulch.* Santa Fe: School of American Research Press, 1997.

Bunte, Pamela A., and Robert J. Franklin. *From the Sands to the Mountain: A Study of Change and Persistence in a Southern Paiute Community.* Lincoln: University of Nebraska Press, 1987.

Burrillo, R. E. *The Backwoods of Everywhere: Words from a Wandering Local.* Salt Lake City: Torrey House Press, 2022.

———. *Behind the Bears Ears: Exploring the Cultural and Natural Histories of a Sacred Landscape.* Salt Lake City: Torrey House Press, 2020.

———. "Coyote Skull and Digging Sticks: Behavioral Models and Preservation Imperatives in the Archaeological Southwest." *The SAA Archaeological Record* 16, no. 4 (2016): 32–37.

———. "Mother Bear's Ears." *Preservation Archaeology Blog, Archaeology Southwest,* June 17, 2017. https://www.archaeologysouthwest.org/2017/06/15/mother-bears-ears/.

Burrillo, R. E., and Benjamin A. Bellorado, eds. "Sacred and Threatened: The Cultural Landscapes of Greater Bears Ears." *Archaeology Southwest Magazine* 32, no. 1 (Winter 2018).

Chapman, Bert. "Colorado River Compact (1922)." In *Encyclopedia of Politics of the American West,* edited by Steven L. Danver, 251–52. Thousand Oaks, CA: CQ Press, 2013.

Chuipka, Jason M. A. "Bears Ears Inter-Tribal Coalition: A Collaborative Land Management Plan for the Bears Ears National Monument." Woods Canyon Archaeological Consultants, Inc., Cortez, CO, July 5, 2022. https://www.bearsearscoalition.org/beitc-land-management-plan/.

Cole, Sally J. *Legacy on Stone.* Boulder, CO: Johnson Books, 1990.

Colorado River Compact, 1922. https://www.usbr.gov/lc/region/

pao/pdfiles/crcompct.pdf.

Crampton, Gregory C. *Ghosts of Glen Canyon: History Beneath Lake Powell*. Salt Lake City: Bonneville Books, 2009.

Deloria, Vine. *Custer Died for your Sins: An Indian Manifesto*. Norman: University of Oklahoma Press, 1988.

Dunlop, Richard. "After Six Centuries of Silence: Life Again in Mummy Cave." *Popular Mechanics* 118, no. 2 (August 1962): 76–81, 200.

Farmer, Jared. *Glen Canyon Dammed: Inventing Lake Powell and the Canyon Country*. Tucson: University of Arizona Press, 1999.

Fowler, Don D. *The Glen Canyon Country*. Salt Lake City: University of Utah Press, 2011.

Gaede, Marc, and Marnie Gaede. *Camera, Spade and Pen: An Inside View of Southwestern Archaeology*. Tucson: University of Arizona Press, 1980.

General Mining Act of 1872. https://www.govinfo.gov/content/pkg/COMPS-5337/pdf/COMPS-5337.pdf.

Gillmor, Frances, and Louisa Wade Wetherill. *Traders to the Navajos: The Story of the Wetherills of Kayenta*. Albuquerque: University of New Mexico Press, 1934.

Gregory, Herbert E. *The Navajo Country: A Geographic and Hydrographic Reconnaissance of Parts of Arizona, New Mexico, and Utah*. USGS Water-Supply Paper 380. Washington, DC: Government Printing Office, 1916.

Gregory, Herbert E., and Malcolm R. Thorpe. *The San Juan Country: A Geographic and Geologic Reconnaissance of Southeastern Utah*. Washington, DC: Government Printing Office, 1938.

Grey, Zane. *The Rainbow Trail*. New York: Grosset & Dunlap

Publishers, 1915.

Hays-Gilpin, Kelley, Ann Cordy Deegan, and Elizabeth Ann Morris. *Prehistoric Sandals from Northeastern Arizona: The Earl H. Morris and Ann Axtell Morris Research*. The Anthropological Papers of University of Arizona Series. Tucson: University of Arizona Press, 1998.

Hebner, Logan. *Southern Paiute: A Portrait*. Logan: Utah State University Press, 2010.

Hopkins, Maren P. "A Storied Land: Tiyo and the Epic Journey Down the Colorado River." PhD diss., University of Arizona, 2012.

Horn, Amy, and Brian C. Harmon, "A New Low in Cultural Resource Management: Insights from Monitoring Archaeological Resources Re-exposed by Low Levels of Lake Powell in Glen Canyon National Recreation Area." Paper presented at the 15th Biennial Conference of Science and Management on the Colorado Plateau and Southwest Region, Flagstaff, AZ, September 2019.

Judd, Neil M. *Men Met Along the Trail: Adventures in Archaeology*. Norman: University of Oklahoma Press, 1968.

Knipmeyer, James H. *Butch Cassidy Was Here*. Salt Lake City: University of Utah Press, 2002.

———. *Cass Hite*. Salt Lake City: University of Utah Press, 2016.

Keeler, Jacqueline. *Edge of Morning: Native Voices Speak for the Bears Ears*. Salt Lake City: Torrey House Press, 2017.

Lacy, Steve, and Pearl Baker. *Posey: The Last Indian War*. Salt Lake City: Gibbs Smith, 2007.

La Rue, Eugene Clyde. *Colorado River and Its Utilization*. USGS Water-Supply Paper 395. Washington, DC: Government Printing Office, 1916.

———. *Water Power and Flood Control of the Colorado River Below Green River, Utah.* USGS Water-Supply Paper 556. Washington, DC: Government Printing Office, 1925.

Leake, Harvey. *Hosteen John.* Prescott, AZ: self-published, 2018.

———. "The Gentleman Explorer: Charles Bernheimer and His Canyon Country Expeditions," "The Path of Light," "The Early Fight for Glen Canyon and the Rainbow Plateau," "Discovery … ," "The Desert is Home," "Through the Camera Lens," and "The Strenuous Life." *The Canyon Country Zephyr* (history blog), 2018–2021. www.canyoncountry-zephyr.com/tag/harvey-leake/.

Leake, Harvey and Gary Topping, "The Bernheimer Expeditions in Forbidding Canyon." *Utah Historical Quarterly*, Volume 55, Number 2, 1987.

Lipe, William D., Mark D. Varien, and Richard H. Wilshusen. *Colorado Prehistory: A Context for Southern Colorado River Basin.* Denver: Colorado Council of Professional Archaeologists, 1999.

Lipe, William D., ed. "Tortuous and Fantastic: Cultural and Natural Wonders of Greater Cedar Mesa." *Archaeology Southwest Magazine* 28, no. 3/4 (Summer/Fall 2014).

Lipe, William D. "Grand Gulch: Three Days on the Road from Bluff." In *Camera, Spade and Pen: An Inside View of Southwestern Archaeology,* edited by Marc and Marnie Gaede, 55–59. Tucson: University of Arizona Press, 1982.

Lister, Florence C. *Prehistory in Peril: The Worst and Best of Durango Archaeology.* Niwot: University Press of Colorado, 1997.

Lister, Florence C., and Robert H. Lister. *Earl Morris and Southwestern Archaeology.* Albuquerque: University of New Mexico Press, 1968.

Luckert, Karl W. *Navajo Mountain and Rainbow Bridge Religion.* Flagstaff: Museum of Northern Arizona, 1977.

Matson, R. G., William D. Lipe, and William R. Haase. "Adaptational Continuities and Occupational Discontinuities: The Cedar Mesa Anasazi." *Journal of Field Archaeology* 15, no. 3 (1988): 245–64. https://www.jstor.org/stable/530307.

Matson, R. G., and Timothy A. Kohler, eds. *Tracking Ancient Footsteps: William D. Lipe's Contributions to Southwestern Prehistory and Public Archaeology.* Pullman: Washington State University Press, 2006.

McPherson, Robert. *Thru Navajo Eyes: Bluff to Monument Valley.* San Juan County, Utah: Four Corners Digital Design, 2014.

McNitt, Frank. *Richard Wetherill: Anasazi: Pioneer Explorer of Southwest Ruins.* Albuquerque: University of New Mexico Press, 1966.

Meko, David M., Connie A. Woodhouse, Christopher A. Baisan, Troy Knight, Jeffrey J. Lukas, Malcolm K. Hughes, Matthew W. Salzer, "Medieval Drought in the Upper Colorado River Basin," *Geophysical Research Letters* 34, no.10 (May 2007). https://agupubs.onlinelibrary.wiley.com/doi/full/10.1029/2007GL029988.

Miller, David E. *Hole-in-the-Rock: An Epic in the Colonization of the Great American West.* Salt Lake City: University of Utah Press, 1959.

Morris, Ann Axtell. *Digging in the Southwest.* Garden City, NY: Doubleday, Doran & Co., 1933.

Morris, Earl H. "An Unexplored Area of the Southwest." *Natural History Magazine* 22, no. 6 (1922), 498–515.

———. "Exploring in the Canyon of Death." *National Geographic Magazine* 48, no. 3 (1925): 263–300.

———. Earl Morris archives. Collection of the University of Colorado Museum of Natural History. Personal Papers, 1897-1984.

National Park Service. "Canyon de Chelly National Park History." NPS History eLibrary. http://npshistory.com/publications/cach/index.htm.

The Native American Graves Protection and Repatriation Act of 1990. https://www.blm.gov/sites/blm.gov/files/Native%20American%20Graves%20Protection%20and%20Repatriation%20Act.pdf.

Pauly, Thomas H. *Zane Grey: His Life, His Adventures, His Women*. Urbana: University of Illinois Press, 2005.

Powell, James Lawrence. *Dead Pool: Lake Powell, Global warming, and the Future of Water in the West*. Berkeley: University of California Press, 2011.

Prudden, Lillian Eliza, ed. *Biographical Sketches and Letters of T. Mitchell Prudden, MD*. New Haven: Yale University Press, 1927.

Roberts, David. *In Search of the Old Ones: Exploring the Anasazi World of the Southwest*. New York: Simon & Schuster, 1996.

San Juan Southern Paiute Tribe (official website). https://www.sanjuanpaiute-nsn.gov.

Schlanger, Sarah, Richard H. Wilshusen, and Heidi Roberts. "From Mining Sites to Mining Data: Archaeology's Future." *Kiva* 81, no. 1–2 (November 2015): 80–99.

Smith, Jordan, Emily Wilkins, and Anna B. Miller. "Bears Ears and Outdoor Recreation in San Juan County." Institute of Outdoor Recreation and Tourism, Utah State University, 2021. https://digitalcommons.usu.edu/extension_curall/2129.

Smithsonian National Museum of the American Indian. Native

Knowledge 360°. "The Long Walk." https://americanindian. si.edu/nk360/navajo/long-walk/long-walk.cshtml.

Smithsonian National Museum of the American Indian. Native Knowledge 360°. "The Navajo Treaty of 1868." https://americanindian.si.edu/nk360/navajo/index.cshtml#sq1.

Sproul, David Kent. *A Bridge Between Cultures: An Administrative History of Rainbow Bridge National Monument.* Cultural Resources Selections No. 18. Denver: Intermountain Region, National Park Service, 2001. https://www.nps.gov/ parkhistory/online_books/rabr/adhi/adhi.htm.

Southern Ute Indian Tribe (official website). "Early History." https://www.southernute-nsn.gov/history/

Wilderness at the Edge: A Citizen Proposal to Protect Utah's Canyons and Deserts. Salt Lake City: Utah Wilderness Coalition, 1990.

The Wilderness Act of 1964. https://www.nps.gov/orgs/1981/ upload/W-Act_508.pdf.

The Taylor Grazing Act of June 28, 1934, with Amendments to September 1, 1955. https://uscode.house.gov/view.xhtml?- path=/prelim@title43/chapter8A&edition=prelim

Topping, Gary. *Glen Canyon and the San Juan Country.* Moscow: University of Idaho Press, 1997.

Towner, Ronald H., ed. *The Archaeology of Navajo Origins.* Salt Lake City: University of Utah Press, 1996.

Tulley-Cordova, Crystal. "Navajo Nation, USA, Precipitation Variability from 2002 to 2015." *Journal of Contemporary Water Research and Education* 163, no. 1 (2018): 109–23.

Turner, Allen C., and Robert C. Euler. "A Brief History of the San Juan Paiute Indians of Northern Arizona." *Journal of California and Great Basin Anthropology* 5, no. 1–2 (1983): 199–207.

United States Department of the Interior. *The Colorado River: A Natural Menace Becomes a Natural Resource*. Bureau of Reclamation Project Planning Report 34-8-1 (1946): 211.

United States Geological Survey. *Colorado River Basin Studies, Utah Water Science Center* (webpage). https://www.usgs.gov/centers/utah-water-science-center/science/colorado-river-basin-studies.

Ward, Albert E. "Charles L. Bernheimer: The Tenderfoot and Cliff Dweller from Manhattan." In *Rainbow Bridge: Circling Navajo Mountain and Explorations in the "Bad Lands" of Southern Utah and Northern Arizona*, by Charles L. Bernheimer. Albuquerque: Center for Anthropological Studies Gift Shoppe, 1999.

Wolfkiller. *Wolfkiller: Wisdom from a Nineteenth-Century Navajo Shepherd*. Recorded and translated by Louisa Wade Wetherill, compiled by Harvey Leake. Salt Lake City: Gibbs Smith, 2007.

Wuerthner, George, and Mollie Yoneko Matteson. *Welfare Ranching: The Subsidized Destruction of the American West*. United Kingdom: Island Press, 2002.

Notes

All "field notes" sources refer to the Charles L. Bernheimer expedition field notes, listed in the Selected Bibliography. "Cliff Dweller from Manhattan" refers to Bernheimer's "Cliff Dweller from Manhattan" manuscript, 1943. B4764_b5_f3. The papers of Charles L. Bernheimer, 1864–1944 refer to the American Museum of Natural History, Division of Anthropology Archives.

PALIMPSEST

"Man can do almost anything if": Bernheimer, *Rainbow Bridge*, 95.

"Discoveries either happen or are": Luckert, *Navajo Mountain and Rainbow Bridge Religion*, 11.

"She had learned": Abbey, Edward, *The Monkey Wrench Gang*, 45.

"To instill a love for nature": Bernheimer, *Rainbow Bridge*, vii.

"to do in a small way": Bernheimer, *Rainbow Bridge* 1.

"I do not recommend that others follow in our footsteps": Bernheimer, *Rainbow Bridge*, 179–80.

"The path of light is always": Wolfkiller, *Wolfkiller*, 3–4.

CAMP SNOWBALL

"The lure of the desert is so intense": Bernheimer, *Rainbow Bridge*, 145.

"mystery to be penetrated only": Bernheimer, *Rainbow Bridge*, 1.

He performed a myriad of jobs until he: "CL Bernheimer, Merchant, 79, Dies," *New York Times*, July 2, 1944, https://timesmachine.nytimes.com/timesmachine/1944/07/02/85184655.html?pageNumber=19.

"to something more substantial": Bernheimer, *Rainbow Bridge*, 1.

"I believed him to be a safe pilot": Bernheimer, *Rainbow Bridge*, 2.

"My Mormon guide": 1919 field notes, box 1, folder 1.

"that ain't no way to treat this country": Lundberg, Ann, "'Mile-and-a-Half' Johnson's beloved Natural Bridges," *The San Juan County Recorder*, August 19, 1993.

"I am taking chances & going over": 1919 field notes, box 1, folder 1.

"My lunch is usually beans": 1919 field notes, box 1, folder 1.

The silhouette of the two: Office of the Press Secretary, "Presidential Proclamation—Establishment of the Bears Ears National Monument," December 28, 2016, https://obamawhitehouse.archives.gov/the-press-office/2016/12/28/proclamation-establishment-bears-ears-national-monument.

The Diné associate this area: Burrillo, "Mother Bear's Ears."

Known habitation of Cedar Mesa: Lipe, William D. "Change Through Time in the Northern Southwest," *Archaeology Southwest* 28 (2014): 6–7.

The advances in this period: Lipe, "Change Through Time," 6–7. Matson, R. G., William D. Lipe, and William R. Haase. "Adaptational Continuities and Occupational Discontinuities: The Cedar Mesa Anasazi." *Journal of Field Archaeology* 15, no. 3 (1988): 250-251.

A widespread period of drought: Lipe, "Change Through Time," 6–7.

"I do not even pretend to be even an amateur naturalist": Bernheimer, *Rainbow Bridge*, vii.

Now *Ancestral Pueblo* is more commonly: Childs, Craig, "Anasazi: What's in a name?," *High Country News*, October 3, 2005, https://www.hcn.org/issues/307/15815.

The Hopi Tribe uses: The Hopi Foundation, Lomasumi'nangwtukwsiwmani, "Hopisinom," n.d., https://www.hopifoundation.org/about-hopi.

the Zuni call themselves *A:shiwi*: Zuni Pueblo Main Street, Halona: Idiwan'a, "About Zuni Pueblo," n.d., https://zunipueblomainstreet.org/about-us/about-zuni-pueblo/.

The Navajo prefer to be called *Diné*: Reuters, "Navajos weigh return to old name: Dine," *The New York Times*, December 17, 1993, https://www.nytimes.com/1993/12/17/us/navajosweigh-return-to-old-name-dine.html.

"You have no idea how cut off from": 1919 field notes, box 1, folder 1.

THE DESERT IS HOME

"The desert will take care of you": Topping, *Glen Canyon*, 112.

"It snowed all day, but we did not mind": Wolfkiller, *Wolfkiller*, 64.

"In the inevitable course of human history, the individual races will probably fade out": Hinsley, Curtis M., *The Smithsonian and the American Indian: Making a Moral Anthropology in Victorian America* (Washington, DC: Smithsonian Institution Press, 1981), 113.

"The complete absorption or blotting": Holmes, W. H., "Some Problems of the American Race," *American Anthropologist* 12, no. 2 (April–June 1910): 149–82, https://www.jstor.org/stable/659948?seq=1.

The items that Nordenskiöld took: Romeo, Jonathan, "Artifacts taken from Mesa Verde are coming home," *The Journal*, October 8, 2019, https://www.the-journal.com/articles/artifacts-taken-from-mesa-verde-are-coming-home/.

"I'd have studied the customs": Topping, *Glen Canyon*, 109.

"When I was a young boy, about six years old"; "There have been times in our past when people have"; "We must give up something for everything we receive"; "A good thought will bring all of our people good": Wolfkiller, *Wolfkiller*, 1–5.

"The snow will be with us": Wolfkiller, *Wolfkiller*, 64.

RAINBOW CHASING

"As all roads lead to Rome": Bernheimer, *Rainbow Bridge*, 4–5.

"We have plenty of trouble": 1920 field notes, box 1, folder 2.

I have with me the best man south: 1920 field notes, box 1, folder 2.

"Mr. Wetherill is, of course": 1921 field notes, box 1, folder 3.

"Johnson, our quick, brilliant": Bernheimer, *Rainbow Bridge*, 15.

"Fortunately on all of our journeys": Bernheimer, *Rainbow Bridge*, 11–12.

In 1904 Morris's father was murdered: Leake, Harvey, and Gary Topping, "The Bernheimer Expeditions in Forbidding Canyon," *Utah Historical Quarterly*, Volume 55, Number 2, 1987, 152, issuu.com/utah10/docs/uhq_volume55_1987_number2.

"Irrepressible Johnson kept us singing": 1920 field notes, box 1, folder 2.

"cowpuncher, cook, athlete, and a general": Ward, "Charles L. Bernheimer: The Tenderfoot," 33.

"There were gathered Jew and Gentile": Bernheimer, *Rainbow Bridge,* 30.

"a cheering warmth over the entire body if tightened": Bernheimer, *Rainbow Bridge*, 101.

"The entire nine or ten miles from Surprise": 1920 field notes, box 1, folder 2.

"Imagine a structure so massive": Bernheimer, *Rainbow Bridge*, 78.

Manheimer says that Rainbow Bridge is one of the cornerstones: From an interview with Leo Manheimer conducted after this backpacking trip, in December 2020. Out of caution for COVID-19, we sat outside on the rim of Lake Powell while it snowed.

"Nasja-begay—the Pahutes—led us to Rainbow Bridge": Stewart McClary, "Trail Blazer to Rainbow Bridge," *Desert Magazine* Vol. 1, No. 8, June 1938, 34.

"The real discoverer was some unknown": Judd, Neil, "Return to Rainbow Bridge," *Arizona Highways*, August 1967.

The National Park Service reports: National Park Service, "Rainbow Bridge," March 31, 2012, https://www.nps.gov/ rabr/faqs.htm.

"[When] you go by boat, you miss all of the scenery": From an interview with Leo Manheimer, December 2020, Page, AZ; Sjogren, Morgan, "The Other Side of the Rainbow," *Arizona Highways*, July 2021, https://www.arizonahighways.com/ article/other-side-rainbow

THE OTHER SIDE OF THE MOUNTAIN

"The month of June 1922, saw us once more on the trail": Bernheimer, *Rainbow Bridge*, 97.

"In a few places we found stones": Bernheimer, *Rainbow Bridge*,

105.

Leo Manheimer thinks these trails: Leo Manheimer interview, December 2020, Page, AZ.

"Yours may be the great adventure but for a": Farmer, *Glen Canyon Dammed*, 80. This is also my source for other Rainbow Lodge information in this section.

Tsegiizh At'iin, **meaning "trail through a rock crevice":** This information was passed along to Leo Manheimer via Buck Navajo, Ashley Atene, and Eddie Yazzie.

"In this, I was perhaps a bit selfish": Bernheimer, *Rainbow Bridge*, 114.

"We climbed on one baldhead after another": 1922 field notes, box 1, folder 4.

"There were countless awkward": Bernheimer, *Rainbow Bridge*, 123.

"Matt (Hale), Vaughn (Hadenfeldt), and I spent an exhausting": Email to me from David Roberts, March 29, 2019.

TORN UP PANTS MESA

To turn back was impossible: Bernheimer, *Rainbow Bridge*, 106.

WRITING ON THE WALL

It was the desert we grew to love so well: Kluckhohn, Clyde, *To the Foot of the Rainbow* (New York: The Century Co., 1927), 109.

In Clyde's defense, the: Sprinkle, John H, "'Of Exceptional Importance': The Origins of the 'Fifty-Year Rule' in Historic Preservation." *The Public Historian* 29, no. 2 (2007): 81–103, https://doi.org/10.1525/tph.2007.29.2.81.

"so they could make a history": Jim Mike, interviewed by Gary Shumway, 1968, reel 388, Doris Duke American Indian oral history project audio recordings, American West Center,

University of Utah, Salt Lake City.

"for the benefit of the Navajo and such other Indians": Inter Tribal Council of Arizona, "San Juan Southern Paiute," n.d., https://itcaonline.com/member-tribes/san-juan-southern-paiute/.

"I don't like to refer to the Paiutes as reservation-less": Phone call with Robyn Interpreter, 2020.

"It really bothers me sometimes": Hebner, *Southern Paiute: A Portrait,* 33.

"beguiled by a defiant 1986 inscription": Roberts, *In Search of the Old Ones,* 200.

"Had a young Angel Whiskers": Roberts, 204.

A SAN JUAN SOUTHERN PAIUTE HOLIDAY PARTY

"I shall dance tonight": Excerpted with permission from Hebner, *Southern Paiute: A Portrait,* 21.

"Lavern's mother remembers Paiute": Phone call with Lavern Owl, January 10, 2021.

"Jack: The land now, it's different": Hebner, *Southern Paiute: A Portrait,* 28.

BETTER LIVING THROUGH HISTORY

"We'll go on": Gillmor and Wetherill, *Traders to the Navajos,* 238.

"Nasja-Begay, the Paiute who had led": Gillmor and Wetherill, *Traders to the Navajos,* 227.

"When the Wetherills themselves recovered": Gillmor and Wetherill, *Traders to the Navajos,* 226.

In early April 2020, the Navajo Nation ranked among the highest: Silverman, Hollie, et al., "Navajo Nation surpasses New York state for the highest Covid-19 infection rate in the US." *CNN,* May 18, 2020, https://www.cnn.com/2020/05/18/

us/navajo-nation-infection-rate-trnd/index.html; Moore, Gerald R., Jeannie Benally, and Sabrina Tuttle, "The Navajo Nation Quick Facts," University of Arizona College of Agriculture and Life Sciences, 2008, https://extension.arizona. edu/sites/extension.arizona.edu/files/pubs/az1471.pdf; Morales, Laurel, "As Coronavirus Cases Rise, Navajo Nation Tries to Get Ahead of Pandemic," *NPR*, April 4, 2020, https:// www.npr.org/2020/04/04/826780041/as-coronavirus-cases-rise-navajo-nation-tries-to-get-ahead-of-pandemic; Lakhani, Nina, "Tribes without clean water demand an end to decades of US Government neglect." *The Guardian*, April 28, 2021, https://www.theguardian.com/us-news/2021/ apr/28/indigenous-americans-drinking-water-navajo-nation; Reinhart, Katelyn, "Food insecurity amid COVID-19 prompts Native Americans to return to their roots," *Navajo-Hopi Observer*, August 11, 2020, https://www.nhonews. com/news/2020/aug/11/food-insecurity-amid-covid-19-prompts-native-ameri/.

ROAD TO AZTEC

The north wall, comprised: National Park Service, "Archaeoastronomy," *Aztec Ruins National Monument*, 2022, https:// www.nps.gov/azru/learn/nature/archeoastronomy.htm.

A DRIVE IN THE CANYON OF DEATH

"Throughout the ensuing months": Morris, "Exploring in the Canyon of Death," 291.

"Actual observation teaches one much more": Letter from Earl H. Morris to Charles L. Bernheimer, 14 December 1921, EHM01_007_037, Earl Morris archives, Collection of the University of Colorado Museum of Natural History.

"countless ages have caressed": Morris, "Exploring in the Canyon of Death," 263.

"to dig for buried treasure, and explore": Morris, *Digging in* *the Southwest,* 12.

"The superstition of the": 1929 field notes, box 1, folder 6.

In 2010, the Government Accountability Office: Young, Chuck, "Native American Graves Protection and Repatriation Act: After Almost 20 Years, Key Federal Agencies Still Have Not Fully Complied with the Act," U.S. Government Accountability Office, July 28, 2010, https://www.gao.gov/products/gao-10-768.

"this method was first used in airport construction": Dunlop, "After Six Centuries of Silence: Life Again in Mummy Cave." *Popular Mechanics,* 200.

The use of foreign materials in reconstruction has negative: Balenquah, Lyle. "Perspectives from a Hopi Archaeologist," *Science Moab,* Sept 24, 2021, https://sciencemoab.org/perspectives-from-a-hopi-archaeologist/., https://moabsunnews.com/2021/10/01/a-hopi-archaeologist-reflects-on-the-discipline-science-moab-speaks-with-lyle-balenquah-about-indigenous-perspectives-on-archaeology/.

IN THE SHADOW OF THE BEAR

"With a vision of the long, long road traveled": Morris, *Digging in the Southwest,* xviii.

Since the 1960s, oil and gas: Jackson, Robyn, "Protecting Sacred Chuska Mountains from Oil and Gas Industry," *Censored News,* January 26, 2018, https://bsnorrell.blogspot.com/2018/01/protecting-sacred-chuska-mountains-from.html.

Jackson helped reduce: Gabriel, Trip, "A Death in Navajo Country," *Outside,* May 1994, https://www.outsideonline.com/outdoor-adventure/death-navajo-country/.

The pinnacle is called *Tsé Bit' A'í:* New Mexico Bureau of Geology & Mining Resources, "The Ship Rock Landform," 2022, https://geoinfo.nmt.edu/tour/landmarks/shiprock/home. html; Nelson, Kate, "Ship Rock, Icon of Indian Country," *New Mexico Magazine*, 25 Jan 2019, https://www.newmexicomagazine.org/blog/post/ship-rock/.

EXPEDITION PLANNING

"The Urge of the Subconscious Wish": Bernheimer, *Rainbow Bridge*, 1.

"A year passed before I could start my journey": Fletcher, Colin, *The Man Who Walked Through Time: The Story of the First Trip Afoot Through the Grand Canyon* (New York: Alfred A. Knopf, 1967), 9–10.

WATER IN THE DESERT

"Our zeal and a throbbing vein for adventure": 1929 field notes, box 1, folder 6.

OVERVIEW: Climate change stats: Lindsey, Rebecca, and Luann Dahlman, "Climate Change: Global Temperature," *Climate.gov*, June 28, 2022, https://www.climate.gov/news-features/understanding-climate/climate-change-global-temperature; Udall, Brad, "1. Here's the latest version…," *Twitter*, October 17, 2021, https://twitter.com/bradudall/status/1449828004230664195?s=27.

Then in 1934, The Taylor Grazing Act: Bureau of Land Management, "About Livestock Grazing on Public Lands," n.d., https://www.blm.gov/programs/natural-resources/rangelands-and-grazing/livestock-grazing/about.

"Harrison (Oliver) was kind of": Allen, *Place Names*, 391.

"Someone asked me about Janes Tank": Allen, *Place Names*, 7.

"The heat was intense": "'Basket Makers' Home Discloses Old Culture," *The New York Times*, August 11, 1929.

"A trail here means where some": 1929 field notes, box 1, folder 6.

#BERNHEIMER

Over 40 percent of Americans: Vogels, Emily A., "The State of Online Harassment," *Pew Research Center*, January 13, 2021, https://www.pewresearch.org/internet/2021/01/13/the-state-of-online-harassment/; Duggan, Maeve, "Online Harassment," *Pew Research Center*, October 22, 2014, https://www.pewresearch.org/internet/2014/10/22/online-harassment/.

The United Nations considers this a form of violence against: UN Women, "The shadow pandemic: Online and ICT-facilitated violence against women and girls during COVID-19," 2020, https://www.unwomen.org/sites/default/files/Headquarters/Attachments/Sections/Library/Publications/2020/Brief-Online-and-ICT-facilitated-violence-against-women-and-girls-during-COVID-19-Infographic-en.pdf; Mwende Maundu, Cecilia, "Take five: Why we should take online violence against women and girls seriously during and beyond COVID-19," *UN Women*, July 21, 2020, https://www.unwomen.org/en/news/stories/2020/7/take-five-cecilia-mwende-maundu-online-violence.

Leave No Trace's new "anti-shaming" clause: Sjogren, Morgan, "Outdoor Shaming Needs to Stop," *Backpacker*, January 8, 2020, https://www.backpacker.com/stories/online-shaming-needs-to-stop-in-the-outdoors/; Alkaitis, Susy, "Stay Out of the Woods: Shaming in the Name of Leave No Trace," *Leave No Trace*, September 16, 2019, https://lnt.org/shaming-in-the-name-of-leave-no-trace/.

"Glen Canyon died in 1963": Elliot Porter, *The Place No One Knew: Glen Canyon on the Colorado* (San Francisco: Sierra Club, 1963), 7.

In 1921 the US population: United States Census Bureau, "U.S. and World Population Clock," n.d., https://www.census.gov/popclock/; "World Population by Year," *worldomete*r, n.d., https://www.worldometers.info/world-population/world-population-by-year/.

In response, the LNT created guidelines: Leave No Trace Center of Outdoor Ethics, "Leave No Trace and Social Media," 2018, https://lnt.org/sites/default/files/Leave%20No%20Trace%20and%20Social%20Media.pdf.

"Posting a photo that specifies your": Leave No Trace, "Social Media Guidance," September 8, 2020, https://lnt.org/social-media-guidance/.

"Please do not reveal a site's location, GPS coordinates": Bears Ears Inter-tribal Coalition, "Respectful Visitation: Honoring Bears Ears Starts With You," February 9, 2021, https://www.bearsearscoalition.org/respectful-visitation-honoring-bears-ears-starts-with-you/.

Ralph explains misperceptions about visitation: Burrillo, *Backwoods of Everywhere,* 248. Burillo, "Coyote Skull," http://onlinedigeditions.com/publication/?i=339887&article_id=2590109&view=articleBrowser&ver=html5.

A 2021 study, "Bears Ears and Outdoor Recreation: Smith, Wilkins, and Miller, "Bears Ears," https://digitalcommons.usu.edu/extension_curall/2129.

Horseshoe Bend: Lake, Zoe, and Maggie Rulli, "National parks officials grappling with high volume as Instagram tourism booms," *ABC News,* July 29, 2019, https://abcncws.go.com/Lifestyle/instagram-tourism-booms-horseshoe-bend-national-parks-officials/story?id=64638198.

The Wave: Meinch, Tree, "The Paradox of Internet Famous Wilderness," *Discover,* April 9, 2021, https://www.discovermagazine.com/environment/the-paradox-of-internet-famous-wilderness.

a new timed entrance system: National Park Service, "Make Your Reservation," *Arches National Park*, February 23, 2022, https://www.nps.gov/arch/planyourvisit/timed-entry-reservation.htm.

The COVID-19 pandemic does play a role: Office of Communications, "National Parks Hosted 237 Million Visitors in 2020," National Park Service, February 25, 2021, https://www.nps.gov/orgs/1207/02-25-21-national-parks-hosted-237-million-visitors-in-2020.htm; National Parks Conservation Association, "Position on the impacts of COVID-19 and visitation to the National Park System," May 25, 2021, https://www.npca.org/articles/2919-position-on-the-impacts-of-covid-19-and-visitation-to-the-national-park; McGivney, Annette, "'Everyone came at once': America's national parks reckon with record-smashing year," *The Guardian*, January 1, 2022, https://www.theguardian.com/environment/2022/jan/01/national-parks-us-tourism-crowds-busy.

"The desire to escape the crowds": Burrillo, "Coyote Skull."

NEAR TO NATURE

"[T]he important point is that a world": Watts, Alan, *Nature, Man and Woman* (United Kingdom: Knopf Doubleday Publishing Group, 2012), 4.

"Ten miles of Grand Gulch": 1929 field notes, box 1, folder 6.

"I embarked on a personal quest": Leake, Harvey, "The Desert is Home: Rediscovering a Frontier Heritage," *The Canyon Country Zephyr*, February 3, 2019, https://www.canyoncountryzephyr.com/2019/02/03/the-desert-is-home-rediscovering-a-frontier-heritage-by-harvey-leake/.

"The desire to do this as an old man": Bernheimer, *Rainbow*

Bridge, 3.

"I began to understand why John Wetherill": Leake, "The Desert is Home."

"My ancestors, the Greasewood Clan": Interview with Lyle Balenquah excerpted from Sjogren, Morgan, "Bears Ears is a Desert Paradise. It's up to All of Us to Keep it That Way," *Backpacker*, January 27, 2021, https://www.backpacker.com/trips/trips-by-state/utah-trails/bears-ears-is-a-desert-paradise-its-up-to-all-of-us-to-keep-it-that-way/.

R. G. Matson, who worked alongside Bill Lipe: Matson and Koehler, *Tracking Ancient Footsteps*, 53.

Between 2014 and 2019, there has been a 49 percent: Bureau of Land Management, *Business Plan for Cedar Mesa: Fiscal Year 2019*, September 2019, page 10, https://www.blm.gov/sites/blm.gov/files/Utah_Cedar_Mesa_Business_Plan.pdf.

"Approach the land with a respectful mindset": bearsearscoalition, "Tip #2," *Instagram*, September 18, 2021, https://www.instagram.com/p/CT99eeMLSJ9/?utm_medium=share_sheet.

Near the alcove ceiling, abstract polychrome pictographs: "The Cedar Mesa Project: A Brief History of the Archeology of Cedar Mesa," 2001, http://bcn.boulder.co.us/environment/cacv/cacvarch.htm.

"As much as I curse the graffiti left": Lipe, "Grand Gulch: Three Days," 54.

"Where fox, bear, wolf, and puma": "'Basket Makers' Home Discloses Old Culture," *The New York Times*, August 11, 1929.

the arrival of white colonizers in the United States: Bruegger, Samantha, "USDA's Wildlife Services continued its reckless slaughter of coyotes, bears, and wolves in 2020," *WildEarth*

Guardians, March 18, 2021, https://wildearthguardians.org/press-releases/usdas-wildlife-services-continued-its-reckless-slaughter-of-coyotes-bears-and-wolves-in-2020/.

Coyote populations can handle the loss: Project Coyote, *The Coyote News*, vol. 1, http://www.projectcoyote.org/Project-Coyote_FactSheet_CoyoteNews.pdf.

"The scenery is majestic, the quicksands": 1929 field notes, box 1, folder 6.

NO HERO

"We shouldn't be looking": Cogswell, David, "Interview with Noam Chomsky," September 14, 1993, www.davidcogswell.com/Political/Chomsky_Interview_93.htm.

The Tyranny of the Ethnographic Past: Lyle Balenquah referenced this phrase in conversation and attributed it to Bernardini, et al, *Becoming Hopi*.

"I want to help make this field familiar": Balenquah, Lyle, "Weaving Environmental Justice Efforts into our Lessons: Moving toward Balance and Healing," University of Arizona, *Indigenizing Pedagogies Speaker Series*, October 21, 2021, https://itep.coe.arizona.edu/file/441.

"It's important that younger folks": Goodman, Javonne, "Foundations of the Past, Present, and Future: River House Stabilization Project," *Bureau of Land Management*, November 19, 2021, https://www.blm.gov/blog/2021-11-19/foundations-past-present-and-future-river-house-stabilization-project.

Balenquah does feel that: Conversation with Lyle Balenquah, fall 2021.

White Sands National Monument: Bennett, Matthew R., et al, "Evidence of Humans in North America During the Last Glacial Maximum," *Science*, September 23, 2021, https://www.

science.org/doi/10.1126/science.abg7586; Martin, Nick, "The White Sands discovery only confirms what Indigenous people have said all along," *High Country News*, September 24, 2021, https://www.hcn.org/issues/53.11/indigenous-affairs-archaeology-the-white-sands-discovery-only-confirms-what-indigenous-people-have-said-all-along; Zimmer, Carl, "Ancient Footprints Push Back Date of Human Arriva in the Americas," *The New York Times*, September 23, 2021, https://www.nytimes.com/2021/09/23/science/ancient-footprints-ice-age.html.

Balenquah explains that this includes working: Balenquah, "Weaving Environmental Justice Efforts.".

"One of the things that I pray and hope": Torrey House Press, "Western Watersheds Projects Book Club: Behind the Bears Ears," *Facebook*, May 25, 2021, https://www.facebook.com/watch/live/?ref=watch_permalink&v=797906741099545.

"It's essential for archaeologists to keep": Matson and Kohler, *Tracking Ancient Footsteps*, 146.

"I'm happy to report": Sjogren, Morgan, "Paying Bears Ears Its Karmic Debt," *Sierra*, May 29, 2021, https://www.sierraclub.org/sierra/paying-bears-ears-its-karmic-debt.

She is focusing her work: Thompson, Ashleigh, "Run All Day," April 15, 2022, https://janji.com/blogs/travelogue/run-all-day-with-ashleigh.

LOST COWBOY COUNTRY

"Once the people": Charles Bowden, *Blue Desert* (Tucson: University of Arizona Press, 1988), 136.

Then in 1915, Lyman watched a massive flash flood: Allen, *Place Names*, 431.

"A new man is not very good": Allen, *Place Names*, 430.

The Colorado River and: Utah Water Science Center, "Colorado River Basin Studies," *USGS*, n.d., https://www.usgs. gov/centers/utah-water-science-center/science/colorado-river-basin-studies; Bureau of Reclamation, "Colorado River Basin Water Supply and Demand Study: Executive Summary," December 2012, https://www.usbr.gov/watersmart/bsp/docs/finalreport/ColoradoRiver/CRBS_Executive_Summary_FINAL.pdf; Utah Water Science Center, "Baseflow," *USGS*, July 15, 2018, https://www.usgs.gov/centers/utah-water-science-center/science/baseflow; Bureau of Reclamation, "Glen Canyon Unit," April 11, 2022, https://www.usbr.gov/uc/rm/crsp/gc/.

Storing water is only the secondary: Metz, Sam, and Felicia Fonseca, "Lake Powell hits historic low, raising hydropower concerns," *AP News*, March 16, 2022, https://apnews.com/article/lake-powell-drought-hydropower-colorado-river-619790b577eabc81cfa2d9b9b6ca2fe1.

Lake Powell's other role is to: Lassalle, Laurine, "Recent drop in Lake Powell's storage shows how much space sediment is taking up," *Aspen Journalism*, July 8, 2022, https://aspenjournalism.org/recent-drop-in-lake-powells-storage-shows-how-much-space-sediment-is-taking-up/.

If the water drops below 3,490 feet: Hager, Alex, "Lake Powell is critically low and still shrinking. What happens next?," *KUER*, April 22, 2022, https://www.kuer.org/health-science-environment/2022-04-15/lake-powell-is-critically-low-and-still-shrinking-what-happens-next.

Experts predict that the reservoir: Bureau of Reclamation, "5-Year Probabilistic Projections," September 6, 2022, https://www.usbr.gov/lc/region/g4000/riverops/crss-5year-projections.html.

At one point, the Utah Governor: Rodgers, Bethany, "Gov. Spencer Cox seeks heaven's help—beyond the clouds—for drought relief, asks Utahns to pray for rain," *The Salt Lake Tribune*, June 3, 2021, https://www.sltrib.com/news/politics/2021/06/03/gov-spencer-cox-seeks/.

Under the 1922 Colorado River Compact: Sackett, Heather, "Race is on for Colorado River basin states to conserve before feds take action," *Aspen Journalism*, July 5, 2022, https://waterdesk.org/2022/07/race-is-on-for-colorado-river-basin-states-to-conserve-before-feds-take-action/.

"If I've learned anything recently": James, Ian, "They sounded alarms about a coming Colorado River crisis. But warnings went unheeded," *Los Angeles Times*, July 15, 2022, https://www.latimes.com/california/story/2022-07-15/scientists-have-long-warned-of-a-colorado-river-crisis.

The average American uses upwards of eighty-two gallons: WaterSense, "Statistics and Facts," *EPA*, May 11, 2022, https://www.epa.gov/watersense/statistics-and-facts.

Mexico finally received water rights: Sakas, Michael Elizabeth, "Historically left out of Colorado River negotiations, 20 tribes urge Interior Secretary Haaland to include their voices," *CPR News*, November 25, 2021, https://www.cpr.org/2021/11/25/historically-left-out-of-colorado-river-negotiations-20-tribes-urge-interior-secretary-haaland-to-include-their-voices/.

wetter on average than the previous five: University of Arizona, "Historic Colorado River Streamflows Reconstructed Back To 1490," *ScienceDaily*, May 29 2006, www.sciencedaily.com/releases/2006/05/060529082300.htm

Today this data is finally being: Williams, A. P., B. I. Cook, and J. E. Smerdon, "Rapid Intensification of the Emerging Southwestern North American Megadrought in 2020–2021," *Nature Climate Change* 12 (2022): 232–34, https://doi.org/10.1038/s41558-022-01290-z.

A 2019 paper by Amy Horn and Brian C. Harmon: Harmon, B. C., and A. Horn, "A new low in cultural resource management: insights from monitoring archeological resources re-exposed by low levels of Lake Powell in Glen Canyon National Recreation Area," 15th Biennial Conference of Science and Management on the Colorado Plateau and Southwest Region, Flagstaff, Arizona, September 11, 2019.

"Soon cottonwoods, willows and reeds": 1929 field notes, box 1, *folder 6.*

"friendships forged in hazardous": Bernheimer, "Cliff Dweller from Manhattan," 50.

"If only Wetherill and Johnson were able to get over": 1929 field notes, box 1, folder 6.

"On earlier jaunts": Bernheimer, "Cliff Dweller from Manhattan," 52.

"always looked across the river": "'Basket Makers' Home Discloses Old Culture," *The New York Times*, August 11, 1929.

"The scenery was majestic and": Bernheimer, "Cliff Dweller from Manhattan," 60.

The San Juan Southern Paiute refer to: Bunte and Franklin, *From the Sands to the Mountains,* 22, 227.

The confluence is called *Tokonavi* by the Hopi: Hopkins, "A Storied Land," 33.

A coalition of twenty tribes: Letter from Melvin Baker, et al, to Secretary Haaland, November 15, 2021, https://f.hubspotusercontent10.net/hubfs/6000718/Water%20Hub/Letter%20to%20Sec%20Haaland%2011.15.21.pdf.

The San Juan Southern Paiute and Hopi Tribes are among those: Water and Tribes Initiative, "The Status of Tribal Water Rights in the Colorado River Basin," April 9, 2021, https://www.getches-wilkinsoncenter.cu.law/wp-content/

uploads/2021/04/Policy-Brief-1-The-Status-of-Tribal-Water-Rights.pdf.

CALL OF THE CANYON

"Charles L. Bernheimer, cotton merchant": "Old Basket Tribes Used Cotton Fiber," *New York Post*, July 30, 1929, HM01_007_126, Earl Morris archives, Collection of the University of Colorado Museum of Natural History.

"That was my favorite of the": William D. Lipe, *Anasazi Communities of the Red Rock Plateau: Southeastern Utah* (Albuquerque: University of New Mexico Press, 1970), 85.

THE HERMITAGE

"These were men who believed that to let oneself drift along": Merton, Thomas, *The Wisdom of the Desert*, rev. ed., (New York: New Directions, 1970 [1960]), 3.

"Existential loneliness": Lopez, Barry, *Embrace Fearlessly the Burning World: Essays* (New York City: Random House Publishing Group, 2022), 69.

"to abandon, to leave": "Desert," *Online Etymology Dictionary*, December 3, 2019, https://www.etymonline.com/word/desert.

River explorer John Wesley Powell briefly: Fowler, *The Glen Canyon Country*, 271.

In 1884 Lemuel Redd, an original member: Allen, *Place Names*, 625–26.

he only made $66.95 back: Crampton, *Ghosts of Glen Canyon*, 86.

"a long stark, bleak, and depressing": Allen, *Place Names*, 626.

Uranium boomed midcentury: Ringholz, Raye C., "Uranium Mining in Utah," *Utah History Encyclopedia*, n.d., https://www.uen.org/utah_history_encyclopedia/u/URANIUM_

MINING.shtml.

The threats uranium mining poses: Center for Biological Diversity, "Uranium," n.d., https://www.biologicaldiversity. org/programs/public_lands/energy/dirty_energy_development/uranium/index.html; Navajo Nation, "Abandoned Mines Cleanup," *EPA*, June 8, 2022, https://www. epa.gov/navajo-nation-uranium-cleanup/abandoned-mines-cleanup; The Wilderness Society, "Threat to Bears Ears increases with drilling and mining news," September 9, 2021, https://www.wilderness.org/articles/blog/threat-bears-ears-increases-drilling-and-mining-news#. Calvert, Mary F., "Toxic Legacy of Uranium Mines on Navajo Nation Confronts Interior Nominee Deb Haaland," *Pulitzer Center*, February 23, 2021, https://pulitzercenter.org/stories/toxic-legacy-uranium-mines-navajo-nation-confronts-interior-nominee-deb-haaland. The National Institute for Occupational Safety and Health, "Worker Health Study Summaries—Uranium Miners," *CDC*, 2000, https://www. cdc.gov/niosh/pgms/worknotify/uranium.html; Spangler, Jerry D., and Donna Kemp Spangler, "Uranium mining left a legacy of death," *Deseret News*, February 13, 2001, https:// www.deseret.com/2001/2/13/19781194/uranium-mining-left-a-legacy-of-death.

The mill, also owned: Peterson, Tim, "Uranium Mill Near Bears Ears Still Violating Clean Air Act," *Grand Canyon Trust*, April 26, 2022, https://www.grandcanyontrust.org/blog/uranium-mill-near-bears-ears-still-violating-clean-air-act.

Staking a mining claim is legal: "General Mining Act of 1872," https://www.govinfo.gov/content/pkg/COMPS-5337/pdf/COMPS-5337.pdf.

"I lived with that river so much": Allen, *Place Names*, 627.

"Best lover I ever had": Martin, Brett, "Katie Lee, Our Lady of Glen Canyon," *Outside Magazine*, May 24, 2018. https://www.outsideonline.com/outdoor-adventure/exploration-survival/katie-lee/

Bill Lipe recalls excavating: From email with Bill Lipe, and from Lipe, William D., *1958 Excavations, Glen Canyon Area* (Salt Lake City: University of Utah Press,1960), 6.

Lipe noted that his field crew: Lipe, Bill, "Before Lake Powell: Memories of Glen Canyon," *Verde Valley Archaeology Center*, May 10, 2012, https://www.youtube.com/watch?v=0b3xj-4gcLk.

"His laws of survival were sometimes": Selby, Carolyn, and Mary Ann Mellott, "George Spencer 'Bud' Vinger," December 29, 2005, *findagrave.com*, https://www.findagrave.com/memorial/12815603/george-spencer-vinger.

FEAR AND LOATHING IN WHITE CANYON

"True courage is in facing danger": Baum, L. Frank, *The Wonderful Wizard of Oz* (London: Oxford University Press, 2010 [1900]) 190.

In the last decade, rangers on Cedar Mesa: Burrillo, "Coyote Skull."

Annette McGivney, "'Everyone came at once': America's national parks reckon with record-smashing year," *The Guardian*, January 1, 2022, https://www.theguardian.com/environment/2022/jan/01/national-parks-us-tourism-crowds-busy.

the 1884 Soldier Crossing battle: Allen, *Place Names*, 470, 708; Lacy and Baker, *Posey*, 31–34.

I once read that more people: Ingraham, Christopher, "Chart: The Animals that are Most Likely to Kill You this Summer," *The Washington Post*, June 16, 2015, https://www.washingtonpost.com/news/wonk/wp/2015/06/16/chart-the-animals-that-are-most-likely-to-kill-you-this-summer/.

"I cannot pick out, Zane Grey style": 1929 field notes, box 1, folder 6.

BERNHEIMER'S DREAM NATIONAL PARK

In the early twentieth century, Muir: Solnit, Rebecca, "John Muir in Native America," *Sierra*, March 2, 2021, https://www.sierraclub.org/sierra/2021-2-march-april/feature/john-muir-native-america.

The 1964 Wilderness Act: "Complete Text of the Wilderness Act," https://www.nps.gov/orgs/1981/upload/W-Act_508.pdf.

"Although on paper, the monument": Dugelby, Barbara, "Collaborative Management of Protected Areas, with Examples of Collaboration between Native American Tribes and US Federal and State Agencies" (Round River Conservation Studies, 2012), 5.

"In the plans, the new national park": "The Next National Park," *Salt Lake City Telegraph,* March 30, 1931

"The hardships only added value": Leake, Harvey, "The Strenuous Life," *The Canyon Country Zephyr*, August 4, 2017, https://www.canyoncountryzephyr.com/2017/08/04/january-1931-the-strenuous-life-by-harvey-leake/.

on the condition that it did not disturb: Leake, "The Strenuous Life" and "The Early Fight."

"It is agreed that the scenic tracts": Redd, Charles,, Benjamin D. Black, J. M. Stewart, and Mark W. Radcliff, "Memorandum of Agreement Made Between a Committee of Nine Representing the Citizens of Blanding, Utah, and the Commissioner of Indian Affairs, Regarding the Piute Strip," 15 July 1922. Records of the National Park Service, Record Group 79, National Archives at College Park, College Park,

MD.

"I was born in 1935 and grew up at a time": Email from Bill Lipe, April 23, 2020.

"President Biden did the right thing": Bears Ears Inter-tribal Coalition, "Coalition Recognizes President Biden's Decision to Restore Monument as Step Forward," October 7, 2021, https://www.bearsearscoalition.org/bears-ears-national-monument-restored/.

"The Secretaries shall provide for maximum": Biden, Joseph R., Jr., "A Proclamation on Bears Ears National Monument," *The White House Briefing Room*, October 8, 2021, https://www.whitehouse.gov/briefing-room/presidential-actions/2021/10/08/a-proclamation-on-bears-ears-national-monument/.

restored the Bears Ears Commission: Maffly, Brian, "Utah tribes secure co-management role for Bears Ears National Monument," *The Salt Lake Tribune*, June 22, 2022, https://www.sltrib.com/news/environment/2022/06/22/utah-tribes-secure-co/.

Wasting Utah taxpayer money: Governor's Office of Economic Opportunity, "Office of Outdoor Recreation," n.d., https://business.utah.gov/outdoor/; Utah Department of Natural Resources, "Utah One of the Top 10 States for Mining, Production Value up in 2019," n.d., https://naturalresources.utah.gov/dnr-newsfeed/utah-one-of-the-top-10-states-for-mining-production-value-up-in-2019.

Lyle Balenquah affirmed this during a recent conversation: Phone conversation with Lyle Balenquah, March 15, 2022.

AN UNEXPECTED RAY OF LIGHT

"Some women come to the desert": *Meloy, Ellen. The Anthropology of Turquiose* (New York: *Vintage Books*, 2002), 73.

"The desert furnishes another sensation": Bernheimer, "Cliff Dweller from Manhattan," 79.

BEYOND THE RAINBOW

"The simple men who lived their lives out to a good old age": Merton, *Wisdom of the Desert*, 22–23.

"In the end, we will": Quote from Baba Dioum during his speech to the General Assembly of the International Union for Conservation of Nature held in New Delhi in 1968.

EPILOGUE

To the Tribal Nations of the BEITC: Chuipka, Jason, "A Collaborative Land Management Plan for the Bears Ears National Monument," Bears Ears Inter-Tribal Coalition, July 5, 2022, https://www.bearsearscoalition.org/wp-content/uploads/2022/08/FINAL_BENM_LMP_08252022.pdf.

From wildfire prevention to managing: U.S. Department of the Interior, "Interior Department Issues Guidance to Strengthen Tribal Co-Stewardship of Public Lands and Waters," DOI Press Releases, September 13, 2022, https://www.doi.gov/pressreleases/interior-department-issues-guidance-strengthen-tribal-co-stewardship-public-lands-and.

About the Author

Morgan Sjogren is an author, journalist, explorer, and defender of wild places. Her work has been published in *Arizona Highways*, *Archaeology Southwest*, *Backpacker Magazine*, and *Sierra Magazine*. She is the author of three books, including *Outlandish*, *The Best Bears Ears National Monument Hikes*, and *The Best Grand Staircase-Escalante National Monument Hikes*. A nomad by nature, Sjogren lives on the Colorado Plateau and feels most at home in the wild.

Torrey House Press

Voices for the Land

The economy is a wholly owned subsidiary of the environment, not the other way around.
—Senator Gaylord Nelson, founder of Earth Day

Torrey House Press publishes books at the intersection of the literary arts and environmental advocacy. THP authors explore the diversity of human experiences with the environment and engage community in conversations about landscape, literature, and the future of our ever-changing planet, inspiring action toward a more just world. We believe that lively, contemporary literature is at the cutting edge of social change. We seek to inform, expand, and reshape the dialogue on environmental justice and stewardship for the human and more-than-human world by elevating literary excellence from diverse voices.

Visit www.torreyhouse.org for reading group discussion guides, author interviews, and more.

As a 501(c)(3) nonprofit publisher, our work is made possible by generous donations from readers like you.

Torrey House Press is supported by Back of Beyond Books, Country Bookshelf, The King's English Bookshop, Maria's Bookshop, the Ballantine Family Fund, the Barker Foundation, the Jeffrey S. & Helen H. Cardon Foundation, the George S. & Dolores Doré Eccles Foundation, the Literary Arts Emergency Fund supported by the Mellon Foundation, the Sam & Diane Stewart Family Foundation, Camille Bailey Aagard & Robert Aagard, Kif Augustine Adams & Stirling Adams, Diana Allison, Klaus Bielefeldt, Joe Breddan, Rose Chilcoat & Mark Franklin, Lois Cornell & Linc Cornell, Susan Cushman & Charlie Quimby, Lynn de Freitas and Patrick de Freitas, Kirtly Parker Jones, Susan Markley, Mark Meloy, Kathleen Metcalf & Peter Metcalf, Betsy Gaines Quammen & David Quammen, Marion Robinson, Kitty Swenson, Shelby Tisdale, the National Endowment for the Arts, the National Endowment for the Humanities, the Salt Lake City Arts Council, the Utah Division of Arts & Museums, Utah Humanities, and the Zoo, Arts & Parks Program of Salt Lake County. Our thanks to individual donors, members, and the Torrey House Press board of directors for their valued support.

Join the Torrey House Press family and give today at www.torreyhouse.org/give.